S. MICHAEL EDWARDS

AN ATHEIST'S JOURNEY TO THE MOST UNEXPECTED GIFT

A Lifelong Journey from Atheist to Believer

After twenty-one-and-a-half years of being an atheist and turning my back on God, I experienced a modern-day miracle. Over a seven-week period, I had a dialogue with God and tracked the trends, results, and miracles along the way, on my journey to reconnect with God.

Photos courtesy of:

Forrest Corbett, Giraffe Design, LTD http://www.giraffedesign.com/

Giraffe Design, LTD, grants to Customer worldwide, non-exclusive sub-licens-
able (through one or more tiers), assignable, royalty-free, perpetual, irrevo-
cable right to use, reproduce, distribute (through one or more tiers), create
derivative works of, publicly perform, publicly display, digitally perform, make,
have made, sell, offer for sale and import such photographs in any media now
known or hereafter known.

Amanda Sharp, Sharp Designs

Scripture quotations are taken from The Message Solo New Testament © 2007

ISBN-13: 978-1461017592
ISBN-10: 1461017599

Library of Congress Control Number: 2011904830

I dedicate this book to the memory of Brian Klemmer, who's 500 vision created a path where my journey began. May he rest in peace. To my amazing parents, John and Linda Edwards, for their unconditional love; to my hilarious sister for being my guardian; to my buddy Brett Stokes and his wife Carolyn, who taught me that not all Christians are misguided; to Craig Waggenshutz who encouraged me to explore my relationship with God; to Adam Zellmer, who suggested I write a blog, which became this book; to Danielle Venne who stretched me to 365 prayers in seven weeks; to Lisa Darden, who followed her heart and God, and led by example; to Amanda Fillweber (Sharps Designs, Inc.) and Forrest Corbett for the stunning photos; to my amazing Master Mind team (Nelson Brandt, Karen Sizelove, and Lesha Kitts), who allowed me to share their requests to the world; to Janet Henze, Centa Terry, Scott and Kim-Michelle Pullan, Sona Vanderhoof, Brian Miller, Kimberly Zink, and Barbara Salerno who tirelessly change the world one person at a time, with no one left behind, through Klemmer and Associates.

Table of Contents

Chapter 1: In The Beginning

*(Note, some of the names have been changed to protect their identity
in my raw story about my life and journey.)*

I grew up in a small logging and farming community in Tillamook, Oregon, with a population just over 3,000. I never really fit in with the loggers or farmers. I was always different, and the people in my community knew it, and let me know they knew it…in their own way, they made me the man I am today.

You may have even had some Tillamook Cheese. They make the most amazing Tillamook Ice Cream, too. The town thrived on farms that raised cows for milk and logging, not to mention tourism. There wasn't much there. It was an old town, with two fast food joints—Kentucky Fried Chicken and Dairy Queen. Lots of big trucks, flannel, Levis, and guns. We had a lot of churches, sort of like Baskin Robbins, thirty-one flavors, although we probably had ten or so churches of different flavors.

I should say my parents were very young. In fact, they had their first child, my amazing sister, when they were in high school. Then just six weeks later, they were pregnant with me. So, two kids, newlyweds and a journey ahead that they did not expect.

My first memories of my childhood are not pleasant. My father worked at the local lumber mill. My mother stayed at home to take care of the house and her family. My dad worked a lot and had a lot of hostility and anger. My sister and I being less than a year apart would fight a lot.

I was five when I had my first cigarette. My dad smoked, and he would drop his cigarettes and my cousin and I would pick them up to "be like our dads." I am still smoking today, even though my dad quit years ago. I say this because at that early age, I wanted to be like my dad. As I grew older, I realized I wanted to be nothing like my father.

I don't recall what age I was when my mom started to take us to church. My dad didn't go, but my sister, mom, and I would go to church every Sunday. I remember the fire and brimstone preaching, the hymns, and the scripture being used to teach us what was right and what was wrong…in the preacher's mind. He picked passages that he thought would resonate with the congregation, and not every passage of what the Bible said, as some of those might offend. So he would pick passages that were pointed to a particular group that may or may not be present. I don't recall him ever preaching on judgment (although he probably did), I don't recall him preaching on divorce (boy, would that have caused an uproar), but I do remember him preaching on homosexuality. That was an abomination.

I always knew I was different. When I was in third grade, I played with my cousins' dolls, tetherball with the girls, hopscotch, and double-dutch jump rope. The "other" boys played football, and baseball…but I wanted to play with the girls.

This made me different. Different isn't easy growing up. I was called names like "fag," "queer," "faggot," "gay"—and I knew what that meant. I had seen it on television—those parades and "those people," and I was not one of them. This never stopped, and in fact got worse as I grew older and into my own self.

I would not wear the clothing of a farmer or a logger. Instead I chose to go to Portland, Oregon, the nearest big city, and buy my own clothes that were fashionable. My mom reminds me of the day that I asked her to stop buying me clothes, and she reminds me often. I was my own person, totally walking to the beat of a different drummer.

My dad tried to get me to hunt, fish, and be more like the rest of the boys. I'm sure it was frustrating for him that I resisted. I had no interest in those things. We grew apart, and his verbal and physical abuse grew more frequent.

It wasn't until I was thirty-five that I found out that my third-grade teacher and my fourth-grade teacher had told my parents they thought I was gay and needed counseling. They were in denial. I didn't get counseling, and I didn't find out until I had walked through the fire of being tortured as a kid.

I was so scared of my father that I would often hide outside. If I had to go to the bathroom, I would go in my pants, rather than go inside the house. My mother was very strict as well, and often when her form of punishment didn't work, all she had to say was, "Wait 'til your father gets home." I remember one time she broke a wooden spoon on my backside and I laughed, until she said, "Wait 'til your father gets home." Then I cried. He beat me with a belt. I learned my lesson. Don't laugh when getting punished.

My sister and I often got into fights on our way for a "fun family day." This usually resulted in us getting punished in some manner. It took a long time before I could get excited about doing something fun, because I always attached negative punishment with "fun."

When I was in seventh grade, my dad got a call from the local mom-and-pop store. They said, "Your son is buying *Playgirl* magazines." So he ripped my room upside down and found cigarettes and Playgirls hidden in my bunk bed and my trumpet case (behind the padding). When he asked me what these (the magazines) were for, I said, "I was just curious." The fact that I know now is that I knew I was attracted to men, but I couldn't tell him that. I always wondered why the store would sell those magazines to a seventh grader…and then call my parents. Nonetheless, it wasn't a great outcome. I don't recall exactly what he did to me, but I know it was bad. I've blocked those memories out of my mind

I got in my first fight when I was in seventh grade. Steve, an eighth grader, called me a fag and I was at a point where I was so tired of the name calling that I actually punched him in the nose. He started bleeding profusely, and I got scared and ran. I never got in trouble, as I don't think he went to tattle on me. It felt good to stand up for myself, but it was not something I was comfortable doing—fighting.

The constant harassment in seventh and eighth grade was troubling me to the point that one day I decided, "I'll show them!" So I took a pistol to school. It wasn't a real gun, it was a cap gun. Thankfully, we didn't have pistols around the house, or something horrible could have happened. I wanted to scare them and make them leave me alone. I realize now and can understand the frustration and desperation that kids these days go through. When I hear of a shooting at school I think about how that could have been me. I never took the gun out, but having it gave me power and confidence. I only took it one time, but that was enough to allow me to know that should I need it again, my pistol of courage could be in my pocket and I could stand up to those bullies.

My first day of high school was slightly embarrassing, as I showed up with a new perm. That's not the embarrassing part. It was 1984 and perms were in fashion, and I wanted one. So my mom gave me a perm the day before and left the chemicals on a bit too long. I showed up with a new stylish hairdo, and second-degree burns on my forehead with some antibiotic ointment. I can laugh about it now, but it was devastating to have all these upperclassman make fun of me. I was a scrawny kid, with a burn and kinky hair, not to mention an outfit that you wouldn't be milking a cow or falling a tree wearing. It was like I was a magnet for negative attention.

Dad had pretty much given up on me being like the rest of the guys by this point. Mom was rather ambivalent about the whole thing. They allowed me to be my own person, and didn't try to convince me to "blend." They were distant, but I know they loved me…I did my best to make them proud. I joined speech and took second place in state competition. I was in every play and musical. I took tap and jazz. I joined the cross-country team (which was ironic considering I was still smoking). I was in choir. I was involved and got great grades despite the torment I was going through.

We still went to church, but I had distanced myself from God and went out of compliance to make my mom happy. My dad started going to church with us, and so it was a family affair. We would even go to church with my Grandma Myrtle and Grandpa Walt. I remember sitting in the Quaker church, holding my grandma's hands and playing with her rings. Thought I wasn't really interested in what was being said, being with my grandma made me happy.

I decided I wanted to learn to sew in high school, so I was the first guy to ever take sewing. I loved it. I made a prom dress for my friend; I made a satin shirt with sequins for me. I made dance costumes for Angie and I. I didn't let the comments of being gay keep me from doing what I wanted to do…from following my passion and being my own man.

We had a kid join our school who was gay. He stood out more than I did, and I selfishly thought, *Good, they can pick on him. Look at the way he flaunts his flamboyant self.* It was as if I were looking in a mirror, but I couldn't relate to him. Why would he be so "out there?" He was comfortable with who he was, but it wasn't long before he dropped out of high school to become a hair dresser.

I tried to go out with girls. It was awkward. I would get nervous to hold their hands and kissing was just out of the question. So while I tried to date a few times, it was clear that I was not interested in girls…I was interested in their boyfriends.

While in high school I got a job working at the local mink farm. My parent's friends owned it, and they went to our church. They let me drive this huge truck that was a total eyesore, but it got me to work and back home…on about 3MPG. They paid for the fuel, because it would have taken my whole paycheck to just get to and from work.

I would drive these carts down the aisle of mink cages, and at winter time I would have a bin full of sawdust and put it in the nesting boxes. The mink loved it, and sometimes they would come up to your hand as you wiped the sawdust through the holes in their cages.

I didn't wear the big, heavy duty, leather gloves when I was dropping the sawdust in, until the time this mink came up and grabbed a hold of my hand with his teeth. He had a great big chunk of my left hand and I screamed like a girl. The guy that was working with me just laughed. I just screamed. If I ripped my hand away, I'd lose a big chunk of skin. So I screamed and waited for the mink to let go.

Eventually the mink let go, and I looked up at the rating card, which is how the owners could tell if the mink was worth keeping for mating with other good mink. This mink was a 4+, which was the best. So I couldn't kill it. It was worth a lot of money. Frustrated, I kept going.

I also had to shovel the mink manure, which was quite malodorous. Made my eyes burn shoveling it. When the mink would have their babies, we'd put these boards in the cages, so the food could drop down from the top of the cage onto the board and the baby mink could eat the food. When the babies were big enough, we'd go through this ritual of separating them into their own cages.

Every once in a while, a mink would escape. That was money running away, in the owner's mind. So we'd grab a pole with a net and go chase the mink down. Sometimes this lasted an hour, sometimes we'd catch 'em in five minutes. It depended on how tired we or the mink were. We'd also grab the mink one by one and have an assembly line for shots. Usually, we would try to stand aside as we grabbed them, spread their legs and let them spray their nasty spray…think skunk, but very distinctive to mink.

Around the holidays, it was time to "harvest" the mink. The carts had these boxes, with a small spring loaded top, that we'd drop the mink into, filling the box full of live mink. The boxes had a tank of some sort of gas that would eventually be turned on when the box was full. This will kill most of the mink. As I think back on it now, this was like the mink's concentration camp and gas chamber.

The box of mostly dead mink would be taken to the shop where it was spilled open onto a table. If you saw a mink move, you grabbed it and would wring its neck. The rest of the process is a little vague in my memory. I know the guys did some of the skinning but the women who worked upstairs had some role in the process of preparing the pelts, too.

I wrote a play in my English Honors class. My play was about a kid growing up and being tortured as a gay kid. His father took an SOS pad and scrubbed his face to get rid of the acne. The story was a stretch on my childhood…elements that occurred taken to the extreme. The play ended with the lights off, the kid in therapy and a gunshot. Did the kid kill himself? Did he kill the therapist? Nobody knew. I didn't title the play, but turned it in. My teacher wrote, "Blow me away"—that became the title.

The play was so graphic that my teacher had to send a note home to each student to get their parent's permission to watch it. A few students didn't get permission (or didn't want to see it). I got an A on the project. It was a sense of relief to get those thoughts and feelings out in the open.

Shortly after graduation from high school, I went on a road trip with my best friend Shannon. We drove from Oregon to California and went to Disneyland. I got my ear pierced. I told my sister and she turned around and told my parents that I smoked and got my ear pierced. When I got home, all my possessions were packed (sarcasm) in Hefty Garbage bags.

When I went upstairs to my room and saw that everything was packed, I brought the bags down and said, "Thanks for packing for me"—and as I tried to leave, my dad grabbed me by my arm, and twisted it behind my back and asked me for my earring. I think he thought it was a diamond earring…and I owed him $5 for the mirror that I had busted on his 1969 Ford truck. We had a pretty profound moment where I stood up to my dad, gave him my earring, and took my stuff and left.

I stayed with "Steve" (Not his real name), who was dating my friend "Shannon" (Not her real name). His parents took me in, and his mother had an amazing sewing machine. I used it to make silk pajamas and entered them in the state fair. I didn't realize I would have to model my clothing, but I did and won a first place blue ribbon for my garments. I am not sure how long I stayed with Steve and his family. I ended up living with my friend "Charlene" (Not her real name).

I bought my first car and decided to join the Air Force. So in October 1988, I joined the Air Force. I picked a job based on this book of jobs they had. Descriptions of all the jobs was all I had available to make a decision on my new career. So I picked the job where I could "drive an ambulance"—you see, I loved to drive, and that sounded like a fun job to have. I ended up being a medic. They didn't mention bedpans, IVs, blood, etc. I drove an ambulance *once*, in training. That's not to say I didn't enjoy my job, I loved it. I stopped going to church.

I changed my name from Shane Michael to S. Michael when I joined the Air Force. I thought that if I changed my name, it would erase all the painful memories of my childhood. It wasn't until later that I realized that changing my name changed nothing about my past. It would still haunt me.

While in training in Sacramento, I met a friend who was a lesbian. She was the first lesbian I had ever met and we became friends. She had a girlfriend, although that was forbidden in the Air Force. No gays allowed. She introduced me to her friends, and I had my first crush on a "real man." Not a guy from a magazine, but a true man. He was my age, and I was infatuated with him. We started dating, and I remember the excitement I felt. It was nothing like when I had dated a girl in high school. It felt so natural to hold his hand, to kiss him, and we had amazing chemistry.

I called my friend Shannon and said, "Guess who has a new boyfriend?" I felt comfortable telling her, for some reason. I had no idea what she would say. I just knew I had to tell someone and she was the first person that came to mind. I definitely couldn't tell any of my Air Force friends, because I would be sent to a court martial for trial and a dishonorable discharge. She said, "Who?" I told her "Me!" She was so happy for me, and that was my first "coming out" story.

After training, I transferred to Travis Air Force Base and left my boyfriend behind. I worked nights on the surgery ward. I remember one of the doctors was really nice to me. He was a podiatrist. I would see the doctors making rounds first thing in the morning before my night shift would end.

When I started having trouble with my feet, I went to see him because it was so painful to wear shoes. So he examined me, and I remember him doing this procedure where he would place his hands on my hips and rock them. I don't know why, but that's what he did. I remember having butterflies and that same feeling I had when I met my first boyfriend. But I had no idea if this guy was gay. Turns out he was, as he asked me if I wanted to go to dinner with him. I said yes, and went back to the dorms and was so excited. Here was this older guy that was cute and interested in me. He was probably twenty years older than I was. Perhaps I was looking for a father figure, who knows. I just know that one thing led to another and we ended up dating.

I had surgery on my heal to remove a bone spur and was given four weeks off to recover. I was to keep my leg up, so in my infinite wisdom, I decided to drive my Nissan Sentra twelve hours to recover at my parent's house. I put my foot, which was in a cast, up on the dash and drove my stick shift with one good leg from Travis Air Force Base to Tillamook, Oregon. By the time I got to my parent's house, my foot was black. It didn't take long, maybe a few hours, and my foot was normal again.

While I was home, I accidently put pressure on my cast by stepping on the typically wet Oregon earth, and my cast was cracked. I went to the hospital, and they gave me a new cast. I think it was fluorescent orange or pink, I can't remember. I just remember that I chose a fiberglass cast that had some color to it. *Why be normal?* I thought.

I moved in with the doctor after a month. It was so amazing to be living off base. Freedom! I didn't have to share a room with some straight guy and pretend to be straight. It was totally forbidden to not only be gay, but for an officer to date an enlisted member. So we were breaking a few rules. Our relationship started going south when I found out he was also seeing someone else in San Francisco. I started my planning to move out. But I was not moving back on base to the dorms.

I found an ad in the paper for a "room for rent." The ad mentioned "gay friendly" and so I went to the house to check it out. Turns out it was owned by a gay couple. One was living in Portland, Oregon, while the other stayed in Fairfield, California. They had two rooms for rent, but both were currently occupied. One of the guys was supposed to move out, but I couldn't wait, and one of the owners said I could sleep in his bed until the other guy left. So I moved in.

I called my parents to tell them my new address. My mom asked me where I was moving, and I said I am renting a room with these gay guys. She paused, and then said, "But you're not gay, right?" I thought, *Hmmm, here's my opportunity to come out to my parents!* So I told her, "Yes, Mom, I am gay." She told me I was going to burn in hell and hung up on me.

The phone rang, and it was my father. He was very angry and told me that I was going to burn in hell. I hung up on him.

My sister got wind of my coming out from my parents. I talked to her and she thought that I wanted to be a woman. I told her that was not what being gay meant. I was just attracted to men instead of women. She didn't agree, felt it was wrong, and was mad that she stood up for me all those years in high school, when I was, in fact, gay.

I was planning on taking vacation to go back and staff outdoor school. When my dad found out he said he was going to tell the local newspaper that I was gay. He didn't want me to be around those sixth graders, as if all gay people are pedophiles.

We didn't talk for a year or two. It was then that I turned my back on God.

I just couldn't believe in a God that would create me in the way I was created and then banish me to hell. I started reading about how the church had an agenda through the years and interpreted the Bible in ways that would further their own agenda. I got more and more entrenched in this conspiracy of man and the business of religion.

Chapter 2: War, Marriage, and Divorce

I had a relationship with the owner of the house. He and his partner had an open relationship, so it was "okay." I didn't know what that meant at the time, but I do now. They had an agreement that they were not exclusive. This guy took me out to San Francisco to the bars, before I was even old enough to drink. They let me in, and I saw things I had never seen before.

We would laugh at the guys wearing leather chaps and the guys who would stand and model at the bars. I never related to the leather crowd, but there were some handsome preppy guys that I could relate to. We had fun together, and things were great at the house. I eventually got my own room and met another guy who ended up moving in. We had a short relationship before an announcement that we were getting ready to go to war.

Desert Storm is what they called it. Our unit was called up, and we were going to England to set up a hospital for the soldiers that would be sent to us from the battlefield. This was all in preparation before the war started.

I wasn't sure what this was going to look like. Would I die? I decided I should go see my folks before I go off to war. We had a nice visit, but didn't talk about me being gay. It was just a time for us to connect and say our goodbyes, as we had no idea if I'd be coming back.

It was also a time for me to connect with my friends. Turns out my friend Shannon's boyfriend from high school was gay. We hung out and talked, and he wanted more from me. I was not interested in him because he was my friend and I didn't see him that way. The next day his parents drove him to my parent's house, on the way to the hospital in Portland. He had attempted suicide after I rejected him. They were admitting him to a psych unit in Portland, and he just wanted to say goodbye.

I wasn't sure how to take his attempted suicide. I'm sure there was a sense of guilt but part of me wasn't sure how it was my fault that he couldn't handle rejection. I was just grateful that he failed and was getting treatment. I was truly disconnected with my emotions at that time. I was more concerned about going off to war. He died a few years later of AIDS. I didn't go to the funeral. He was the first friend I knew who had died of AIDS.

I had a friend named "Mary" (Not her real name). She was what "we" call my fag hag. She knew I was gay, and we were best friends. She went off to war with me, and we had a great time together. There weren't any patients, and we didn't work very hard. We had very little money, as it was expensive over there.

We lived on the Royal Air Force Base Cranwell in the officer's quarters. I thought, *Sweet, this is why I didn't join the Army or Marines!* There were four or five of us guys to a house. We ate at the cafeteria, and the food was English, not American—a lesson I learned in short order. For breakfast, I took a piece of French toast and poured syrup on it. Turns out it was deep fried toast and not syrup but vinegar! When you are expecting a nice sweet bite of French toast and get deep fried bread with vinegar, you don't need coffee to wake you up! Ick.

While at RAF Cranwell, I met another guy from Florida who I had a crush on. I didn't know if he was gay or not, but I had a connection with him. Turns out my gaydar was pretty good. He was gay and was interested in me. We dated a few times, and it was magical. We were only there for a couple of months as the war was rather short. We saw maybe thirty patients the whole time. I personally only treated one patient. It was a blessing that the war was short and the injuries minor.

So we transferred back to Travis Air Force Base, and I didn't have a place to stay. I had moved out of the house where I was renting a room, as I didn't know how long I'd be gone and couldn't afford to keep paying room rent.

Mary and I decided we'd get a two-bedroom apartment with our friend "Jonathan" (Not his real name) who was also gay. Just to make sure people didn't think I was gay because we were sharing a room, Mary and I decided to share a room.

At work, I asked if I could transfer to work in labor and delivery. They had never had a guy work L&D, but I got the transfer, and it was amazing. I absolutely loved the joy on the mother's faces when I would hand over a freshly wiped down baby, swaddled in blankets with a skull cap to keep them warm. It was those priceless moments that made the labor part of the job worth it.

I have so many stories I could tell about women in labor. From the Navy wife who came in that had more hair on her legs than I did, to the lady that said, "Rub my back, stop touching me, rub my back, stop touching me."

Another memory was when we were working nights and decorating the suite for Christmas. We heard the doors open down the hall, and a shrill voice screaming, "Owie, owie, owie!" Around the corner, the ER techs were wheeling an eighteen-year-old with her head dropped way below her feet to keep the baby from coming out. We lifted the sheet and the baby's head was one-third of the way out, with the bag of water still intact. We rushed her into the delivery room, and they delivered the baby with the bag of water still intact. It's called a veiled delivery and was the first and only one I ever saw. I still laugh about how an eighteen-year-old, who was crying "owie," would turn out as a mother.

My most memorable moment on the labor and delivery floor was Christmas. I was not working, but we had a lady who had been in pre-term labor for a couple of months. She was on mag-sulfate to keep her from having contractions. When I came back from Christmas, I saw she was gone. *It was too soon*, I thought. *Her baby wasn't to term yet.* When I asked where she was, I was informed her baby had died, and she had delivered a stillborn on Christmas day.

I was devastated and felt so sorry for her. It was my first experience with death, and I was glad I wasn't there that day. A few weeks later she came back up to L&D to thank everyone, and I was in the bathroom cleaning up after we discharged a patient. I heard her voice, and how the other nurses were just talking to her like nothing ever happened. "You look so good!" "It's so good to see you." "How are you doing?" It was like they had forgotten her baby died. I knew that wasn't right, yet I had no idea what I was supposed to say to her. So I hid in the bathroom until she left—forty-five minutes in hiding.

I knew I had a problem with death at that point. So I talked to my supervisor, and she sent me to training on peri-natal grieving. Little did I know, I was being trained to be the grief counselor. It was a difficult job, but rewarding to help these families deal with their loss.

Mary and I were having a good time together, and we were such good friends. I started to feel pressure from my family and the Air Force, and thought, *I wonder if I could date Mary. She knows all about me, so if I can be straight, it would be with someone like her.* So we started to date. It was interesting.

She would buy me *Playgirl* magazines, and we'd watch gay porn. I'd think about guys when we'd have sex. But we were happy. We got married seven months later, and my parents came to the wedding in California. They were ecstatic, needless to say! I'm sure they were thinking, "Thank you, God, it was just a phase!"

It was time for Mary and me to move on in our careers, and we really wanted to teach. So we asked to be transferred to the school where we could teach the emergency medical technicians and the equivalent of the LVNs (or LPNs depending on where you live). We got accepted to teach at the Air Force Technical School in Wichita Falls, Texas.

We bought our first house with help from my parents for the down payment. It was a 1,500 sq./ft. house, with three bedrooms and two baths. The kitchen was small, as was the breakfast nook. There wasn't a formal anything. We got to pick all the colors and wallpaper, so we made it very modern. We painted the walls with dove grey paint and trimmed the moldings bright white. Everything was black and white, with some forest green thrown in.

I loved my job teaching. I loved being in front of the students/airmen, and watching them go from zero to hero in twelve weeks. They respected me, because they were taught that they had to. I had no concept of earning respect. I just had it based on my position.

The twelve-week course was broken into segments that each instructor would manage, and you could switch around after you were certified in a segment. The first segment was the fundamentals of nursing. Block 1 was where they learned all the Latin and medical terminology. Block 2, I can't remember. Block 3 was shots and IVs—I remember that because they had to use each other as their test subjects. Block 4 was the emergency medical technician training, which was the longest block and they had to pass their national registry test. Block 5, I can't remember, and Block 6 was unremarkable (if there was a Block 6, I can't recall), the last block (either 5 or 6) was only remarkable in that the students were ready to graduate and move on to another base for two months of practical implementation of their newly gained knowledge.

I met an instructor there who was so well-dressed and had all the jewelry allowed. Three rings, one bracelet. As a guy, that was all you could wear, and this guy wore it all. His clothing was never short of perfect. Neither was his hair. He had dark skin and a great smile. His name was Mario. He was Italian and handsome and the nicest guy. He was also Mary's instructor when she was a student.

He was friends with my boss, "Brandt" (not his real name). Each block of instruction had a senior manager oversee that block, and the instructor that managed it. Brandt, who was taller than I was, had a deep throaty laugh. He was a great boss, with a great sense of humor. Brandt's friend was also in charge of a block, was named "Jake" (not his real name). He was this short guy from Alabama and as feminine as you could imagine. I wondered if all these guys were gay, but Mario had two kids, so I figured not.

I went to school at Wayland Baptist University at night, while working at El Chico to make ends meet. The Air Force didn't pay enough for Mary and me to live on. So I took a second job and worked on my bachelor's degree. One of my favorite classes was a math class. The instructor was so smart and able to teach it in such a way that I got it. His name was "Steven" (not his real name).

Turns out Mario, Brandt, and Jake were wondering if I was gay, too. But being married to Mary threw them off as much as Mario having two kids. I was still gay, I was just married to a woman. The fact I was married didn't turn me straight or make me want to be with a woman anymore than it would for a straight person to be in a relationship with a person of the same sex. Think about it, would that make you want to be gay? It doesn't work that way.

I remember the day that Mario asked me if I were gay. This was against the rules. He had more rank than I did, but I trusted him. Who cares about "Don't Ask, Don't Tell"? So I told him, yes, but that my marriage was real. He then revealed to me that Brandt, Jake, and my math instructor Steven were all gay. Then the bombshell— Steven and Mario were a couple! They had both talked about me one day and realized that they were talking about the same person. We all became great friends.

My marriage was falling apart as I hung out more and more with my gay friends. I didn't want to have sex, but counted down the days to when it had been a month. I had decided I didn't want to have kids, with her or anyone. So I had a vasectomy at the age of twenty-seven. I do remember the doctor asking me why, and I said, "I don't want to be the kind of father that I had. I don't think it's possible to not be that man." A month after I had my vasectomy, I found out my wife had been having an affair.

It was clear that I was not meeting her needs, and it was my opportunity to just be gay again. So I filed for divorce, and we stayed in the same house together. My enlistment was coming up, and I had to decide what we were going to do. Was I going to re-enlist after nine years? If I did any more time, I felt obligated to finish out twenty years and retire and get a paycheck for life. Or did I want to cut my losses and get out and be out of the closet?

I graduated with three associate degrees and a bachelors of science in occupational education with a specialization in education and training. I graduated with a 4.0. That beat my 3.87 in high school. I was ready to make my decision. With just two weeks before my enlistment was up, I told Brandt that I was getting out. He was not happy.

"You don't just "spring" that kind of news on us. We have to find a replacement for you," he said. He gave me the information on where to go to start my out processing—which is the word they use to transition to the civilian world.

The ladies at the out processing office told me I couldn't get out with only two week's notice. I informed them I absolutely could. I had a contract that I could get out with one day's notice. So I told them, "Be happy I am giving you two weeks." I stopped working at the school and spent the next two weeks getting all my physicals and paperwork ready to get out.

I decided I would move to Dallas. My friends Mario and Steven had taken me to Dallas and introduced me to my first "big gay bar" in Texas, and I liked it. It was a fun city. I didn't have a job, but I was confident I could get one. So I moved to Dallas and got an apartment and started looking for a job.

My first job in Dallas was with a company that created distance learning for executives. We flew in professors from Harvard, Berkley, Columbia, and the Center for Creative Leadership, to name a few. My job was the instructional designer, to create compelling instruction that was interactive and instructive. We had television studios, would hire actors to do role plays, and created quizzes. My favorite was a class on marketing. It was a game show, with a full game show set, and we called it "Marketing, the Price is Right." It was fun.

The thing about the military was we took a break each hour of instruction. So I was used to smoking every hour. The thing I realized when I started my first civilian job was they didn't let you take a smoke break every hour. So I quit smoking.

Chapter 3: Toxic Love

Six months later, I met a guy who was dating my good friend back in Wichita Falls. My friend was a doctor and usually would date a guy for two weeks and then move on. I had instant chemistry with his friend "Ed" (not his real name). Turns out Ed had felt the same chemistry. We went to the movies, dinner, riding bikes, etc. One night he asked if he could kiss me. I told him no, because he was dating my friend. He had only gone on three dates, but I didn't feel right about kissing him, even though I really wanted to.

We decided that we would go to Austin to Hippie Hollow. It's the only clothing optional state park in Texas. There is a section of the park that was all gay. Tons of boats would tie up and the people would come out in droves to the lake to swim, and party. Not a lot of people were naked, certainly not the ones you wanted to see naked. We weren't naked either, for the record.

It was an awkward weekend because my friend "Keith" (not his real name) was dating not only Ed, but my friend "Mark" (not his real name). The three of us were going to go down to Austin together, but since Keith was dating both of the guys at the same time, and I had feelings for Ed, we decided it would be best if we just went down and had fun, without sex. We called it "no sex weekend"—to make it less awkward for everyone.

That Saturday night, I asked my friend Keith if he saw his relationship with Ed going anywhere. He said he wasn't sure, and I asked him if I could date him. He said, okay, just wait until we get back to Dallas. Well, I couldn't wait. Ed and I left the bar and went back to the hotel. Let's just say, that no sex weekend was a bust, but Ed & I were the only one that broke the rule.

The drive back to Dallas was titillating. I sat in the front with Ed, and we both had our arms on the console touching. It was our way of connecting without trying to be too obvious. I was giddy. The three-and-a-half hour drive seemed to take forever. Ed and I couldn't wait to get back to Dallas to be together.

Ed and I saw each other every day. We spent every night together after that "no sex" weekend. Two months later, his lease was up on his apartment, so he moved in with me. Shortly after he moved in, his mother, who had been very sick, was having a double lung transplant. We hadn't been apart since we started seeing each other, but he went to be with his mother during her transplant.

His parents didn't know that Ed was gay. He had been married to a woman for four years, and when he got divorced he told his parents that if they asked him why he was leaving their house and going back to Dallas.

When he married "Kristina" (not her real name), she had no idea. Well, she initially thought he was gay. But she shrugged it off, and they got married when they found out she was pregnant. She lost the baby, but they got married anyway. When I met Ed, he was separated from Kristina, and it was bitter as they went through their divorce.

Kristina and I were a lot alike. She eventually became one of my best friends. I used to joke that her and I were the same person, just one of us didn't have a penis. Two peas in a pod, we'd joke. She found forgiveness for Ed, for taking so many years of her life when he knew he was gay.

Ed cheated on Kristina with guys while he was married. I found out about this, and rationalized that it was because he was gay and didn't have the kind of relationship I had with my wife, where she knew and was okay with me looking at *Playgirl* and the like.

My parents thought he was "just my roommate" in the beginning. They said, "You are never allowed to bring a man home with you." I am not sure how long after Ed and I got together that I told them I was seeing him. They were not impressed. Their dreams of me being straight were crushed. They were convinced the reason I got divorced was because I was gay. I don't think they wanted to hear that Mary had cheated on me.

We just didn't talk about Ed and me that much.

About a year after Ed's mom had her transplant, "Angela" and "Buddy" (not their real names), decided they were going to come visit their son. They still didn't know he was gay, but they were coming to Dallas to see his new house (our new house). He was beside himself. I told him I was not moving my stuff into the spare room and pretending to be his roommate. So he wrote them a letter and told them he was gay, the week before they were coming to visit.

They wrote back, "This doesn't come as a surprise to us. We love you, just don't rub it in our face." They came to visit. It was awkward. I could tell that they didn't like me and when they looked at me, they were reminded their son was gay. We had a very uncomfortable visit. I was glad when it was over.

After Ed and I had been together for two years, my mom called and invited us to come home for Thanksgiving. I was blown away. We went home for Thanksgiving, and I asked my mom what had changed for her. She said she had gone to this seminar for parents of gay kids. It was a turning point for her accepting me. All she wanted was for me to go to Heaven. She thought that was her job, to get me into Heaven. At the seminar, she learned that it was not her "job"—it was her job to love me unconditionally.

My dad was still not ready, but he was nice and polite. We had a good visit. My sister and her family came to visit, too. I had long conversations with my mom, as she wanted to learn more about Ed and find out what I was doing in my life. She was genuinely interested in learning more about the son who was so distant for so long.

It turns out, when Mom and Dad moved out of the small town up to another small town near Seattle, Washington, that mom would ride the bus to downtown Seattle. She met a gay man on the bus and realized he was just like everyone else. She also worked with a gay man she adored, and who adored her. She was getting exposed to gay people in real life, as opposed to the vision of what it was like by looking at how the media portrays gay people. She was coming around.

I decided to go to grad school to get my degree in distance learning. It was about an hour drive from our house to the University of North Texas. I took my first class by distance learning. Ironically, I hated it. I got an A, but I wanted to be in the class with the instructor. My second class was on human computer interaction. It was with a professor in a classroom setting. I loved it. Got an A.

I came home from class one night and caught Ed having sex with a guy on the stairs. I was furious. Why did I keep attracting cheaters in my life? What was wrong with me? I had low self-esteem and didn't think I could get along by myself. I decided to stay and work it out. We went to therapy. I quit school.

I had a great time with Ed. We did some things that I'm not proud of, but we did some amazing things, too. We bought a big house, a big yacht, built a business together. We traveled the world, went on a dozen cruises. It was the life I had always dreamed of. But Ed cheated on me on multiple occasions. Every time he'd say he was sorry and it wouldn't happen again.

I remember taking a cruise to Athens for the closing ceremonies of the Olympics. It was a gay cruise, where this company chartered the entire boat. The guys in the cabin next to us were nice guys and were from Austin, Texas. One day, I couldn't find Ed, so I went back to the room. He was having sex with one of the next door neighbors. I was furious. The rest of the cruise was uncomfortable, and I was devastated.

I started smoking again behind his back. I thought I was "getting back at him" because he said he would leave me if I ever started smoking again. I was using it as a way to get back at myself. It was self-sabotage.

We went to therapy each time Ed would cheat. Every time we would talk about how his cheating made me feel and he would talk about how him catching me smoking would make him feel. We would both promise to quit. Neither of us did.

Ed and I started an Internet advertising agency. We built it with one client and then added more and more clients until we were bringing in over a million dollars a year in revenue to the agency. We started the business with three people, and as of December 12, 2010, we had thirteen. I became very good at running paid search. I became certified in Google AdWords, and manage millions of dollars in advertising spend each year, not to mention the team that works for me.

Chapter 4: Klemmer and Associates Journey Begins

My parents were very supportive. They loved Ed, until they found out what he was doing to me. I watched my parents evolve in front of my eyes, as they attended these seminars put on by Klemmer and Associates. My dad in particular became a totally different person. His anger and cynicism were gone, and he was compassionate, insightful, intuitive, and loving.

They bugged me for six years to go to these classes. "At least try the first class, it's just a weekend class. It's called Personal Mastery." Ed went. He liked it, so he went to the next class, which was a weeklong class called Advanced Leadership Seminar. Ed felt like I would get a lot out of it. Ed seemed to be changing. So I went, reluctantly, to the first weekend class.

I remember being in a room filled with about fifty people. My mom was helping to staff the class. Brian Miller, was the facilitator and a formidable man. I was a little intimidated by him. The students were in groups of three. I didn't know anyone, let alone the two people I had just sat with. The facilitator asked, "How many of you believe in God?" All but the three of us in my small group raised our hands. *How ironic,* I thought, *that the three people that don't believe in God are sitting together.*

Brian asked me what I believed in. I said, "Sorry?" He said, "Do you believe in a higher power?" I said, "No, I'm an atheist." My mom started crying. She didn't know. He asked, "Do you believe in something bigger than yourself?" I said, "No." He said, "Do you believe in energy?" I said, "Like what goes through a power line?" We had this back and forth until he finally said, "Let's do this. When I talk about God or a higher power, you think about peanut butter."

I was offended. *For the people who believed in God, that was offensive,* I thought. *So it's either God or peanut butter, you decide.* I decided I was over this class and wanted to leave. My mom asked me if I would stay for one more exercise and then I could go. I didn't know what it was, but I agreed.

That exercise was so powerful, that it made the whole weekend worth it. It was then that I forgave my mom and we reconnected at a deep heart level.

That exercise, called the Love Dyad, allowed my mom and me to go through our life together as if we were reliving it. We relived all the great things and all the bad things, and then just let it all go. It was the most healing exercise for us to do. We reconnected on a level where we had never been. The truth came out, and it was extremely emotional. We felt forgiveness, freedom, love.

I did not sign up for the next class. By that time, my dad had become a facilitator of that class. That's how passionate he was—after seeing how it affected his life, he wanted to teach it! I knew enough about the class to know that I would have to share about my childhood, all the good, the bad, and the ugly. I didn't want to disparage my dad and his new career in front of the class and his peers. I also didn't want to confront my own issues with Ed. It was easier to stay stuck than to step into being vulnerable and potentially get unstuck.

Ed had gone on to the third class, called Heart of the Samurai. He came back energized. He had spent a week in San Diego and came back with this passion about his goals, our company, and moving forward. He was so different than when he left.

So two years after I went to the first class called Personal Mastery, I called the lead facilitator, Kimberly Zink and told her my hesitation on going to Advanced Leadership, for which my dad was a facilitator. She told me to get over myself! She said, "We know your dad was not perfect. We also know who he is today. You are not going to damage his reputation, so get over yourself and get your plane ticket."

I had mixed up the dates and actually bought my plane tickets for the class a month ahead of when I was planning on going. This was my mix-up, but I decided I would go anyway. It was March 2010. I had an amazing experience. Humbling. My sarcasm, anger, and all was exposed as my defense mechanisms. We were paired up with buddies. My buddy picked me. The instructions were clear on who you were to pick as a buddy. When asked why he picked me, he said, "He's arrogant, disruptive and taking away from everyone else's experience!" Whoa! *Thanks for the brutal honesty,* I thought.

He was the perfect buddy for me.

During one of the exercises the lead facilitator asked me a question. I answered. She asked another question, I answered and started sobbing. "What are you afraid of?" she asked? I said, "That Ed will give me AIDS and I'll die." I sobbed and ran out of the room.

I went up to my room, freaked out. *Damn it! I knew this was going to happen. I am not faced with making a decision to leave Ed!* I heard a knock on the door. It was Kimberly. She asked me if I was coming back. I said yes, I just needed a moment.

I went back down to the room, and kept moving through the exercises. I had been recovering from my second back surgery in six years when we did an outdoor day. I don't want to give too much away, in case you go to Klemmer and Associates and take this series of seminars. But there was this exercise on "trust"—that was what it boiled down to. It was a physical exercise, but if you didn't trust your buddy, you would fall.

They didn't want me to do the exercise because of my back limitations. It would put a lot of pressure on my back. I didn't want to rob my buddy of this opportunity. He and I agreed we would go up and just do the first two steps and then drop. It was at that moment that I realized I could lean on my dad. I could trust him, and he would love me unconditionally. I have a large poster of that moment framed in my office today.

That was a defining moment in my relationship with my father. We became very close and started talking on the phone frequently. I had forgiven him for not telling me about my third-grade teacher. I didn't know that I was still carrying that baggage, but once I realized I had never really forgiven him for not telling me all those years, I felt this enormous sense of release. We were friends. For the first time in my life, I looked up to my father.

The next class in the series is only held twice a year. Turns out the next one was the following month. Had I not mixed up my plane tickets, I would have not had the opportunity to go to Heart of the Samurai for six months. But since it was the following month, I signed up and went.

Things were getting interesting. I noticed that there were more and more serendipitous moments in my life. Moments like the plane ticket. Moments like when I told my father what that poster I had on my wall meant to me—and when he told me he had the same poster and that he chose his buddy, who was gay, so that he could have a closer relationship with his gay son. We cried.

I went to Heart of the Samurai in April 2010. It was extremely moving. I learned my purpose in life, "To bring equality to the world." I learned so much at "Heart"—contribution, service, commitment, and integrity. I roomed with two guys who knew I was gay, but didn't care. I didn't need to share a room, but I wanted to help them out by reducing their expenditures for the week. It was out of my comfort zone to share a room, but I "got over myself" to make it cheaper for them to attend. They were from my Advanced Leadership class.

One of my roommates is an amazing man. His name is Matthew Courtright. He introduced me to his sister and her husband, Carolyn and Brett Stokes. They were very nice. I didn't get to know them, but I liked them.

I had a few defining moments at Heart. The first was when they asked each table to "bless the meal however you see fit." As my table held hands, I said, "Go ahead, I'm agnostic." My brain went "What?! You are an atheist!" Somehow my subconscious had taken over and I had shifted from believing there was not a God to not knowing if there was a God. I was okay with that shift. But it caught me off guard.

The second defining moment at Heart was when we did this grueling exercise and the end result was I realized I was a selfish and horrible brother to my sister. We rarely talked, I had taken very little interest in her or her family, and it hit me over the head like a ton of bricks. I immediately called her and told her I was sorry and that I loved her and would she forgive me. She did, because she is amazing and beautiful and forgiving.

The last class in the series is called "Samurai Camp"—it's where you take all the tools and lessons from Klemmer and Associates into practice in life. It's practical application. I had no intention of going. I knew how to set goals and achieve them. I didn't need that class. There was one more hour before the closing ceremony, and I signed up. I didn't know why, but I knew there was something pulling me to go to this class.

I came home and found out Ed had cheated on me while I was at Heart. Another trip away, and he was off playing. We went to therapy again. I started smoking in front of him.

Late June, we start our weekly calls to prepare for our first weekend of Samurai Camp. There were seventy-five students and we were all in groups of five or six. We had a leader, a leader buddy, and a senior leader on each call.

We worked on our goals and learned a lot about what we really wanted out of life. The idea behind "Sam Camp" is to create goals that you would not otherwise do if you weren't in camp. Goals that are a huge stretch for you. I thought I knew what my goals were going to be.

My professional goal was going to be to increase my commission on a particular client by 20 percent. When they asked me the "why" behind the goal, it became clear that I wanted to be right. Right about buying this software that was supposed to grow this client's account. Well, I couldn't make Ed agree that I was right. So this was not a good goal. I was stretched. If I couldn't use more money as a goal because the why behind everyone of those was "to be right," then what kind of professional goal could I have?

My team leader was Danielle Venne and her buddy was Lisa Darden (real name). They both asked me some deep questions. Lisa asked if I was religious. I said, "No, I'm agnostic." She told me it was hard for her to ask me that question, but that God was telling her to ask it anyway. She asked me some other questions about my job and what I wanted out of life. I said, "I want more joy in my life." I shared with her my experience of Ed cheating and how I was just stuck and I wanted to do things for me. I wanted joy and happiness, and I wanted that for my employees, too. So we came up with two goals.

We had just moved all our employees from their home offices after being home-office based for six years in our advertising agency, and they weren't all that excited about it. So I would do a baseline employee satisfaction survey and then increase it by 3 percent in ten weeks. My HR person said it was not possible.

My personal goal, to bring more joy into my life was to do thirty-six hours of things that brought me joy, by myself. This made me want to puke. How was I going to find thirty-six hours when I worked seven days a week and had three weeks of vacation planned in this ten-week period?

Late August we had our first weekend where we got to meet our Sam Camp groups and fellow students. It was an amazing weekend. We were standing in a circle and picking our buddies. They asked one person to pick a buddy, then another. I looked at Brett Stokes as he looked at me, and I was thinking, *Does he want to be my buddy?* I looked next to me, on both sides, and figured, *Yeah—I think he does.* So I walked over and said, "Let's be buddies."

S. Michael Edwards and Brett Stokes Copyright 2010 Courtesy of Sharp Designs Inc.

The idea behind buddies is they are someone to hold you accountable. We were given one-and-a-half hrs to get to know our buddy. You see, we were supposed to pick some-one that we didn't know. Well, I had met Brett, but I didn't know him. So one of the first questions I asked him was, "Are you religious?" He said, "Yes!" I was thinking, *Damn it!*

I had done a great job at keeping religious people out of my inner circle. They were usually not accepting of me being gay, thought they could change me, or basically thought I was going to burn in hell. So rather than being rejected, I just chose to keep them at arm's length (if not farther).

I asked him how his church reconciled the Bible and homosexuality. After all, if he's religious and I'm gay, how are we going to get along? He said his church actually goes to porn conventions and puts up signs with "Jesus Loves Porn Stars" printed on them. Brett later told me that his church was a hospital for sinners, not a sanctuary for saints. I was blown away. I said, "There is a church like that? I could totally go to a church like that!"

He went on to say that his preacher was very real, down to earth, and honest. "If you don't like how we operate, go find another church. If you don't like that we support AIDS, go find another church. If you think you are better than someone else, you must think you are Jesus because only God can judge." His church, he said, was a church for "everyone else." I asked the name of the church, and he told me it is called Eastlake Community Church.

I was okay with being his buddy. *This is one cool dude*, I thought to myself. So we spend the rest of the weekend working on goals, solidifying them, and working on other experiences. I found that my buddy is brilliant and loving and kind and one of the most amazing men I have ever met.

I stood up to share that I had been robbing myself of amazing people for twenty-one-and-a-half years because I did not allow religious people into my inner circle of friends and influence. I started to cry. I said, *I was missing people like Brett Stokes in my life because of this*. I committed to no longer judging people. I committed to letting down my walls against religion. I had stereotyped religion just like people stereotyped gays. Brett came over and gave me a hug and said he loved me.

The day I got back from the first weekend of Sam Camp, I found out that Ed had cheated on me while I was gone. It was the end of August. I left him that night. I told him I was done and that I deserved better and was worthy of so much more than he had to offer. I was empowered finally to stand up to his infidelity, and I walked away.

I asked people to pray for me. It was a huge step for an agnostic. But I needed all the help I could get. I could see amazing things happening in my life. If it was the prayers, then the more I could get the better.

Lisa Darden asked if she could pray with me on the phone, and I told her I wasn't ready for that. Not yet, anyway.

Over the next ten weeks I had weekly calls with Brett Stokes, calls with my small group, and calls with Brett's wife Carolyn and others on our bigger team. I was fully committed to doing what I could to help everyone get their goals.

I took up rock climbing as one of my activities that would bring me joy. Although you couldn't tell from my face, I was actually having fun.

I didn't go on vacation to the yacht as I had planned so that I could focus on my goals and my team. I was the second person to get their personal goal and the second person to get their professional goal. I got my professional goal of 3 percent increased employee satisfaction in five weeks. I thought, *Take that HR!*

I logged more than three hundred hours of activities that brought me joy, when I didn't see how I could get thirty-six. Rock climbing was a small part of my personal goal in terms of time. However, it was a huge part in terms of growth. My instructor was amazing.

In my first lesson, I thought the objective was to get to the top of the wall without falling. My instructor would yell up at me, "Why are you stopping?" I would yell back, "So I can decide where my next move should be!" He said, "When you stop, you get tired and you'll want to quit or fall. I'll have more respect for you if you get to the last step and don't think you can take another one, but take it anyway and fall than if you just give up without taking that last step!"

It was so true in my life. Why was I taking all this time to analyze my next step instead of just reaching for it? I was afraid to fall (fail). If you don't take it, you don't risk failure. But you also can't achieve greatness and success. It was a great lesson. It wasn't about getting to the top without falling, it was about the journey. If you fall, learn from it and try something different.

The majority of my alone time was spent embroidering. Janet Henze and Centa Terry asked me why I didn't sell my shirts that I wore. I had been embroidering shirts with my machine for years. People had always asked me why I didn't sell them. The thing was, my machine had one needle and a shirt would take ten to thirty-five hours to complete. I could make more money at McDonald's than selling my shirts.

Janet said, "Would you consider making a line of clothing for Klemmer and Associates Samurai Camp?" I said, "I don't have an embroidery business." Then I realized that I could very easily have one. I had met Kim Donaway who had multiple businesses. Why was I not worthy of owning more than one business? So I said, "Yes, I will put together a proposal for creating a selling a line of shirts for Sam Camp."

I bought a commercial embroidery machine that made my designs much faster. I put together a proposal for Sam Camp Shirts. It was accepted and I worked with a friend who is a wholesale embroiderer and flew her out to teach me how to use my new machine. Pat Brooks and I both made a ton of shirts to prepare for second weekend of Sam Camp (the final class in the series). We made over thirty shirts.

I found out that in December 2009 and January 2010, Ed's father had "gifted him" 50 percent of the company. That meant I was a minority shareholder now instead of being an equal shareholder. I didn't find this out until September. They kept it from me, because they knew it would upset me. I asked our corporate attorney for all the communication/emails regarding this gifting of the shares. She dragged her feet and eventually said I had no right to them.

I immediately began to prepare to sue Ed, his father, and the corporate attorney, for breach of fiduciary duty, ethics violations, among other things. I asked for more prayer. My dad asked me if he could pray with me and I said yes. I cried.

I had committed to going back to Heart of the Samurai to staff it, as my friends who didn't get to go when I went were going in October 2010. So I wanted to staff it. My mom hadn't staffed that class, she had staffed all the classes except that one. So she said, "I guess I know why now. The time is right for me to staff it with you." My dad rarely went to Heart, as he teaches the class before, which is quite taxing on him. However, he came to spend the week with us while we staffed.

At the last minute, I made a couple of designs of my shirts to sell at Heart of the Samurai. We took preorders for the shirts, since I didn't have time to have them produced. My embroidery business was growing before my eyes.

They chose me to be chief of staff over twenty staff members, and chose my mom to be my assistant chief of staff. It was a first. It was the first time I had staffed any of the Klemmer and Associates classes and they wanted me to be the chief? I was honored and humbled.

I met some amazing students at this seminar. I got to experience the exercises from a different perspective. I learned so much about myself that I hadn't known prior, even though I had been in the class before. I got to watch my friends go on their journey and grow. It was so beautiful.

I met a guy named "Charles" (not his real name) who had written me a letter. He was having problems with his sexuality. He wanted to talk. It took a couple of days for me to find time to read the letter, as I was extremely busy as chief of staff. Once I read the letter, I knew I needed to talk to Charles.

That night we had done an exercise on purpose. I decided to add the word joy to my purpose. My purpose in life is to bring joy and equality to the world. I wanted more joy, and I wanted to give more joy.

The next day we did an outdoor exercise. As chief of staff, I was wearing a headset/microphone so I could communicate with the facilitators. I decided that the timing was right to talk to Charles, so we had lunch together. We talked about my coming out story, his coming out story, and how he doesn't relate to how the media portrays gays. I told him that the media doesn't get to define who he is. He gets to define that. I suggested he surround himself with professionals who he could relate to. We had a great conversation.

During the conversation, Barbara Salerno, the producer of the seminar, asked me where I was over the headset. I told her I was serving a student and would be with her as soon as I was done. She said okay.

Once I finished lunch with Charles, I walked over to where Barbara was standing. One of the staff members, who had staffed a class I was in as a student, was talking to Barbara and asked her to pray for her. I immediately, without hesitation, bowed my head in prayer for her.

I then explained why I was missing in action, and turned to talk to Kim-Michelle Pullan (real name). Kim said she was impressed with my leadership and how much I had shifted from when she first met me. Kim-Michelle was also at first weekend of Samurai Camp when I stood up and said I was robbing myself of religious people by keeping them out of my inner-circle. She commended me on my growth and said, "Even your stance on religion is amazing." I said, "I know! I just prayed for the first time in twenty-one-and-a-half years!" She started crying and we hugged.

The facilitator that taught my Personal Mastery class—the one that told me to think of peanut butter when he talked about God, was also standing there. Michael Jr., a comedian, calls him Cryin' Brian. Brian Miller is very much in touch with his emotions. He heard my story, and that I just prayed and cried.

Someone had just spray painted a red heart on the back of Cryin' Brian's shirt and I gave him a hug. When I pulled my arm away, the word joy was stenciled on my arm. It was a clear modern day miracle. I turned to God and said, "I get it, you are with me. You have been with me all along, and I believe in you again." I thanked God for the joy from Brian's heart and the joy he was bringing into my life.

Cryin' Brian's Spray Painted Red Heart Copyright 2010 Courtesy of Forrest Corbett

The Hug Felt Round the World Copyright 2010 Courtesy of Forrest Corbett

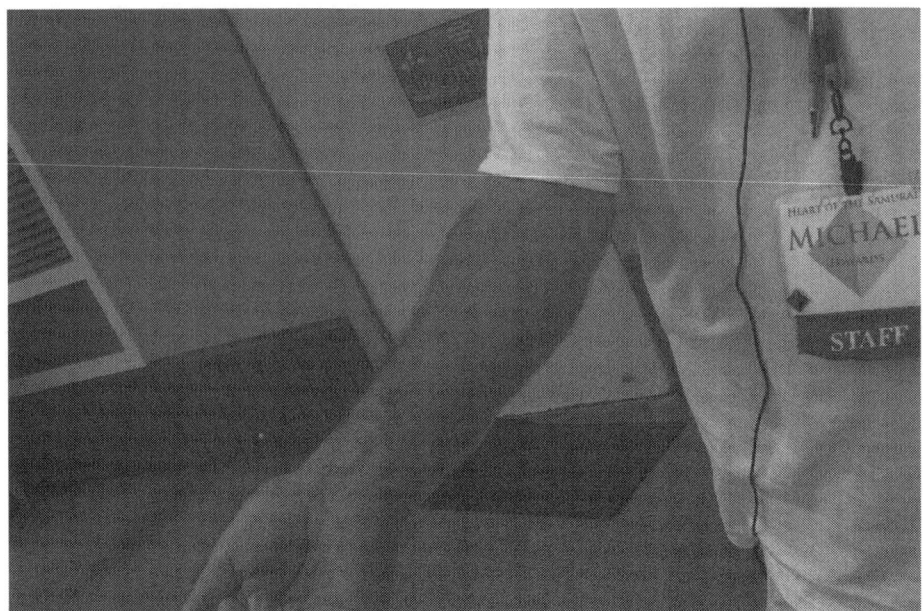

Joy Stenciled On My Arm From Cryin' Brian's Heart Copyright 2010 Courtesy of Forrest Corbett

We were all in awe, since I had just added the word joy to my purpose, and because when you see the picture of the heart and the word joy, it's just not possible that it be so clear. It was my modern-day miracle for sure. I was glad I finally got the sign. I might have ended up with a tattoo or a billboard!

When we finished the outdoor day, and came back to the resort to debrief the day, I stood up and shared my story of joy. I confessed to the room of over two hundred people, my dad included, that I believed in God again. There were tears of joy and hugs and happiness.

Now not everyone that attends Klemmer and Associates Leadership Seminars believes in God. You don't have to. I was able to get so much out of the classes without being a believer. I left the things I didn't agree with on the table and took the rest. So I want to be clear that if you are not a believer, that doesn't mean you can't get something out of these classes. Klemmer and Associates is the premier leadership and character development company. They believe in creating a world for everyone, with no one left behind.

I immediately called my buddy Brett, who was instrumental in getting me to see how God is love and that we're all sinners. But no one's sin is greater than another. There isn't an appendix to the Bible where sins are rated on a scale of 1–10. He helped me see that maybe the God he believes in is a God I could believe in. I wanted him to know he touched me, and that God spoke to me. It was an amazing call.

That week, Brett Stokes also reached his goal. He signed a contract worth $254K in new business. His goal was one or more contracts totaling $200K or more. I was so proud of him. When I knew what his goal was, I was a little worried, but I knew he could do it. He was driven, focused, and committed to making it happen.

With only a couple of weeks left before the end of Samurai Camp, and our second weekend together, I continued making the Klemmer shirts for the staff and to use as samples so we could do pre-orders. Pat Brooks and I got the shirts done and then the first weekend in November, I showed up for the final seminar weekend.

I was sitting on the van at the airport waiting to go to the hotel when another student named Jorge (not his real name) got on the van. He looked down and despondent. I said, "Hello!" He said, "Wow, I just talked to Gregory, who said I should call you!" I said, "Here I am!"

I asked him, "So how are you doing on your goals?" He said, "I am only at 50 percent." These goals are up and down goals. You either did it (100 percent) or you didn't (less than 100 percent). So he was down because he was not going to get his goal.

I asked him why he was down when the deadline for the goal was tomorrow at nine a.m. He still had plenty of time. It took him ten weeks to get 50 percent, he couldn't see how he could get the other 50 percent in less than twenty-four hours. I said, "What are you doing this afternoon?" He said, "Going skydiving." I said, "Don't you think you might find someone that wants to buy your product there?" He said, "Maybe." He started to perk up. I said, "Afterward, why don't you head over to the college campus, I'm sure there are students that would like to make a few bucks and since it is so cheap to get into your business, why don't you go there?" He lit up.

After getting settled at the hotel, a staffer suggested that we might want to set up a room to help people who hadn't gotten their goals. I jumped on it. Brett had already suggested we have a "war room" the last few weeks, where people who were complete on their goals could help others get over the wall on their own goals. So why not set up a war room at the hotel? We'd stay up as late as we needed to, in order to help everyone get their goals.

We asked the hotel staff to send all Klemmer students and staff, as they checked in, up to the war room to check in. We had computers, people, whiteboards, and spreadsheets. Who did we have left to help get over the wall on their goals? Then came word that Jorge had gotten his goal. Whoo-hoo! He did it. He just needed to believe in himself that it was not impossible and that anything is possible. He did it! I was thrilled. We helped at least eight to ten people get over the wall on their goals that night. When Brett and Carolyn arrived, they took the reins of the war room and I went to bed at one thirty a.m.

We had an amazing first day, celebrating the people that got their goals yet disappointed that we weren't 100 percent as a team. We did more exercises. I shared my experience about joy and staffing Heart and that I believed in God again. Tears and hugs followed. We had some great sharing from others about their journey over the last ten weeks, including the challenges, and triumphs.

I'm not sure what the exercise was, but I was totally in the moment with my small group. I was emotional and crying and I needed a tissue. I turned to the back of the room and there were my parents. They showed up to support me on my journey. What a gift. These are tears of joy. Thanks to Amanda Fillweber for capturing these priceless memories. I think you can tell from these pictures that my parents turned out to be amazing people, and they change people's lives on a daily basis. I love them with all my heart and wouldn't change a thing about the way things turned out. It was perfect the way God had this all planned.

Tears of joy when my dad surprised me by showing up to the second weekend of Sam Camp 20

Copyright 2010 Courtesy of Sharp Designs Inc.

Tears of joy when my mom showed up to surprise me for the second weekend of Sam Camp 20
Copyright 2010 Courtesy of Sharp Designs Inc.

We did an exercise where you write your vision in third person. Where do you see yourself in one year, five years, ten years, and twenty years? Now, I like to think big. You never know what you put out there, when it might come true. Miracles do occur. I have seen them. So I'm writing my vision and Brett's writing his, in total silence. When we finish, we wrote a note to each other, "Can I read your vision?"

As I read Brett's vision, I was in awe. We had never talked about it. I had written that Brett would have three kids. Brett wrote that he would have three kids. I had written that I would raise $1 billion over the next year for clean water in developing countries. Brett wrote that he would have a foundation to provide clean water in developing countries. I wrote that I would provide for sustainable communities and equal rights for women, children, and everyone, including gays. I also see myself personally sponsoring 100,000 people into Klemmer and Associates seminars. We had so much overlap in our visions over the next twenty years that it was mind boggling. Brett and I had never spoken about where we saw ourselves in 20 years. Yet both Brett & I saw our lives intertwined and being of contribution and service to the world.

God had put us together as buddies on purpose. Brett's calling was to get me to see God's love. I still think about that plane ticket that got me to Advanced Leadership where I met Brett's brother-in-law Matthew Courtright. If I hadn't gone a month earlier, I wouldn't have met Matthew, and then subsequently Brett. God is great.

The students all voted on who they thought was the most valuable player. Then they voted on who they thought was the person that represented the "Be, Do, Have" concept, and the person that surprised them the most.

I won the MVP Award. Brett won the Be, Do, Have Award.

There was a challenge put forth that I tap dance at the talent show. I haven't tap danced since high school. I said, "If you can find a pair of tap shoes in a size 13, I'll tap." Well, someone came up with the brilliant idea of putting tacks on a pair of shoes and they said, "Michael, we have your shoes." Not one to turn down a challenge, I did a little "tack dancing" number for the talent show.

Tack Dancing Copyright 2010 Courtesy of Sharp Designs Inc.

Tack Dancing Finale Copyright 2010 Courtesy of Sharp Designs Inc.

As soon as I was done, I found out my mom had bet Kim-Michelle $50 that I wouldn't do it. She lost the bet.

One of the most humbling experiences of my Samurai Camp experience was the closing ceremony. The room was filled with students, we were all given candles. They started with the lights off and lit my candle first, as the MVP, who touched so many. I then lit two candles, Brett's and Danielle's—my amazing buddy who changed my life, and my amazing team leader who created a space for me to lead. Brett sought out his wife, as he wanted to light her candle. It was dark, and he couldn't find her, and I remember hearing someone say, "Over here"—slowly the room became lit with light. A few words were said, and then one by one everyone blew out their candles except for me. I instantly saw how I had made a difference. I experienced how one person can impact so many. I also saw that moment when I was the only candle left to be blown out, that I choose to make a difference each and every day. It was a humbling moment.

Michael Edwards with the last candle burning Copyright 2010 Courtesy of Sharp Designs Inc.

I was asked to be a team leader for the next Samurai Camp, and the training started in November 2010 right as our camp ended. I was one of two students out of seventy-five to lead the next Sam camp. I was thrilled because I thought my journey had ended. Now I get to do it again, but from a leader position. I get to help create a space for my students to show up as leaders.

I have a new buddy now in my Sam Camp where I am a leader. He is a Christian and an amazing man. His name is Craig Waggenshutz. When I found out he was a Christian, I cried. I was so excited because I have shifted from not wanting religious people into my life to yearning for their guidance.

Craig and I worked on what our goals were going to be. This is where my 365 prayers came into play. I wanted a closer relationship with God. After twenty-one-and-a-half years of being an atheist, it was time for me to reconnect with God. It was past due, but all things happen for a reason, and being paired up with Craig was the perfect timing for me to reconnect with God.

We did an exercise where we scored ourselves on areas of our life. For the lowest score, we were to create a goal. My lowest score was in my relationship with God. So I said, "I will pray 150 times over the next seven weeks, not counting solicited prayers or prayers over meals." Craig asked, "Why not meals?" He then asked, "Can you give me an example of what a prayer for a meal is like for you?" So I told him about Thanksgiving, and how my mom had asked me to pray for the meal. I prayed for Ed, and others, and asked God to bless the meal. Mom was so moved and cried that I would pray for Ed, when he had cheated and stolen half the company from under my feet. Craig said, "So you are not just blessing the meal, but you are praying for others? Why not count those?"

So I knew where this was leading. If I counted those, then I was going to be challenged to increase the number of prayers. I got out my calculator, and in the period of time we're working on our goals, it took the prayers to 318. I told Craig that was not good enough—I didn't like the number. I said, "Let's make it 350!" So we agreed. Then my dear friend and former leader Danielle, who is also a leader in this Sam Camp, said, "Why not one for each day of the year?" I loved it. "Perfect! I'll do 365 prayers in seven weeks!"

"Where's the risk?" another leader named Adam asked. I said, "In documenting those prayers." He said, "What if you got a digital recorder?" My wheels started spinning. He said, "You could hook it up to your computer," and I finished his sentence and said, "and have them transcribed!" All of a sudden my goal of connecting with God was growing, and I was getting very excited about it!

Adam asked me if I was going to blog on it. I said, "I hadn't thought about that, but what an amazing idea! Then I can take that blog and write a book! Eventually that book will be made into a movie!" I told you I think big.

So that's the story of my life and where my 365 prayer blog came to be. I realize that's a lot of back story, but for you to really appreciate where I have come from, I thought you needed the raw, ugly truth about my life as well as the amazing miracles that have happened.

My goal doesn't start (the documenting prayers) until the first part of January. In the meantime, I now have my preamble to my blog and eventual book. I'll be documenting those prayers and the themes as well as the requests and the results of those requests.

Brett and I are still talking once a week (if not more often) to discuss our vision and how we can move forward. I decided that 50 percent of my profits from my Klemmer shirt sales will go to sponsor people into the Klemmer and Associates classes. I started S. Michael Edwards Designs, LLC and a website (www.smichaeledwards.com) to sell my non-Klemmer shirts, where 50 percent of my profits go toward providing sustainable communities through the charity Argros International and other non-profits that I want to support.

Brett and I met with a gentleman who has been through much of the Klemmer and Associates seminars. This man also has a vision of giving away $1 billion to charity. His vision is based on a ten-year timeline. Mine, a one-year. This man has a vision of 50,000 people sponsored into Klemmer and Associates, and when he heard my vision of 100,000, he said he was pissed. He needed to raise his numbers. I laughed. This gentleman introduced us to a man that would change our lives forever.

When you have a vision, and you focus on it and you pray about it and you are aware of your surroundings, amazing things will happen. The question is, do you let those opportunities go by? Or do you reach out and grab them?

So that is the preamble—the story, leading up to the story: An Atheist's Journey to the Most Unexpected Gift: A Lifelong Journey from Atheist to Believer.

I will Document 365 prayers to God in seven weeks. This journey will help me reconnect with God. I will document my progress during the seven weeks. My ultimate goal is to connect with God and be an inspiration for others to connect with God, too.

3 comments:

Anonymous said...

God's presence is clearly in and through you on this project of cultivating a prayerful life...the word says that in His Presence is fullness of joy...so I am excited to watch this process continue to unfold and see the joy manifest and grow. I still remember when I first met you and am amazed at what God is doing in your life...How He's brought you to Himself. I am inspired and honored to be your friend. What a powerful way to start your year!

Lisa Darden said...

AH-MAZ-ING!

I'm writing through tears...sadness, redemption...and tears of joy!

What an honor to journey with you and see how God is bringing you closer to Himself...

You are an incredible man, Michael Edwards, and I am sooooo thankful that you are a part of my life…

To many more amazing conversations and memories!

Craig Wagenschutz said…

Michael you are an absolutely amazing man! While I am anxious to see the end result of your journey through these weeks, I also realize it is only the beginning. God has worked miracles in each and every one of us throughout our entire lives. What a blessing for you to be able to recognize those miracles and share them with all of us! He truly has a plan for us all, and I am humbled and honored to be a part of that journey!

Monday, December 27, 2010

My Parent's Reaction

I sent my first post to my mom and dad, and a few of my close friends from Klemmer. My dad called, and said it was painful to read. He was choked up, I could tell. I told him I was grateful for the past. We both had to walk through the fire to get to where we are today. He still hasn't finished reading it yet. I am anxious for him to get to the part where we connect again, in my story. He is the most amazing man today. I am so proud of all that he does to change people's lives, including my own. His journey would not have turned out the same, had he not walked the path he took. I know in my heart that he did the best he could with what he knew how. Forgiving him at ALS was easy…Letting go of the past hurt, painless, loving him unconditionally, priceless.

My mom read the blog and this is her response below.

MOM—"Wow!! Painful and redemptive!! This question was asked in church today…"What is the essence of Christianity?" Your story truly reflects my answer of love and forgiveness. Loving God and loving people, too. I truly am sorry for causing you so much pain in your life. I love you and am so blessed to be a part of this amazing journey of yours. Thank you."

My response to my mom:

I hope that you are just seeing the pain, and not re-living it. Like I told Dad, it's really just the back story. No negative energy around it anymore, thanks to all the stuff I've done with Klemmer. I would hope you just see it for what it is…the path that we had to take to get to where we are today.

So my hope for you is that you would be grateful, as I am, for an amazing chain of events that has led me back to God. You played a vital role in that chain of events…and you should be proud of the steps you took in your journey to mend our relationship.

I love you, Mom. I know you did the best you could, and if we could do it all over again…I wouldn't change a thing. Because then I wouldn't be the man I am today.

I hope you feel the same way…because neither of us would be the same. We are better people because of the journey God put us on.

I love you, and I need your love.

S. Michael Edwards

Dear God,

I am so excited to be on this journey you have me on. I woke up today with renewed energy, and I thank you for giving me another day to make a difference. I choose joy today and every day. I pray you give me strength as I deal with Ed and our buyout negotiations. I ask for wisdom, and serenity for both Ed and myself. I am grateful for my amazing family, and thank you so much for your guidance in their lives, as they have guided mine. May you continue to bless my family and my extended family. Oh, and by the way, have I told you lately that I love you? I mean it, God, Love, like you were my father…my amazing father. You both rock! Talk to you later my friend.

P.S., Please be with Janet and her family—I know you know what's going on there, and I just ask that you give her strength and wisdom, and I lift her and her family up to you.

Chapter 5: 365 Prayers in 7 Weeks

Saturday, January 1, 2011

Prayers Answered

Well God, you did it again! I don't have to tell you, but for those who are reading this, another prayer answered. I asked for strength and wisdom during this "buy-out" process with Ed…and the other night he offered me a 50 percent pay raise to settle the lawsuit and give me an employment agreement! What a shift. I guess what they say, "Shift Happens" is no joke! Thank you, God, how amazing it is to have you walking beside me and lifting me up in strength and courage, holding me up so I don't back down, and giving me the wisdom to make choices that serve not only me, but my employees.

I am grateful! Gratitude is not even a strong enough word, but please accept my gratitude for your help in this matter. I'm so thankful.

Now, as we work to get this through the attorneys, I pray that Ed not back down from his verbal commitment and agreement to settle this matter amicably. And as we go through the division of assets and put the house on the market, please dear Lord, grant us both the serenity and allow our divorce to be amicable and calm. I know we have it in us, and with your help we can do this without pulling out the big guns. Well, you know we don't have guns, it was a joke, God. Unless you consider my attorney a Big Gun—I like to think of him as a pit bull. But I digress. We have a lot of change underway, and I am looking to you for strength, wisdom and serenity. I surrender to you God.

In your name,

Amen!

Thursday, January 6, 2011

God is Great

What an amazing day yesterday! It started with a meeting with Ed, while he vented and yelled and screamed about having to settle our dispute. I had reached out and asked for prayer, and I prayed to God that I stay serene, surrendered, and that whatever this meeting was about, that I surrender to God's will. I had no idea what the meeting was going to be about.

Turns out the meeting was about Ed getting all this anger out and then telling me he was ready to settle. I stayed serene the whole time.

The other founder who was in the room came into my office after the meeting and commented on how I stayed so calm. "That is the Michael I like," he said. "Nothing like the old Michael!"

The "old Michael"—yeah, I remember him. I would get in Ed's face and yell right back. I'd engage him like a wild animal tearing up a wounded bird. The "new Michael" stepped into serenity a few months ago. With God's help, it is serving me well.

Ed asked me to have my attorney draft the employment agreement that calls for a 50 percent pay raise over what I made last year, six-month engagement, signing bonus, among other things. *I'll take that any day*, I thought. *Better that my attorney draft it in my favor than Ed's attorney drafting it in Ed's favor.*

We put the house on the market late Monday night (January 1, 2011) and had our first showing yesterday. The family was here for forty-five minutes.

God, with your wisdom and plan, I am so grateful for all you have done for me. For this amazing journey you have me on. I am thankful for the meeting yesterday and grateful that you were with me, holding me up and lifting my spirits as I took the energy from Ed and then shook it off. You are amazing my friend. We should do lunch! Just not at the house today, as you know, we have another showing of the house. May we find the right buyer that is willing to pay the right price at the right time. Lord, I ask that we sell this house for +/- 4 percent of our asking price on or before March 31, 2011.

I also ask, dear Lord, that we sign the contracts with the two companies we are in talks with. You know who I'm talking about. It would be a huge coup and would help lighten things up at work, by helping our employees make more money and growing our business.

I am so thankful that you are blessing us with abundance. I praise you and give myself to you, dear God. Now, for an amazing day. Not sure what you have planned for me, but I'm sure it will be filled with joy. I choose joy every day. I start this day with joy in my heart and with you by my side.

In your name,

Amen

Thursday, January 6, 2011

Goal Date Set

I had an amazing conversation yesterday with Dan Asher, who was praying for me before my meeting. We talked about my goal of 365 prayers in seven weeks. That's a whole lot of praying! I told him my intention is to reconnect with God, turn my blog into a book, and eventually a movie.

The goal of completing 365 prayers by March 2 starts January 12, less than a week away. I'm ramping up and clearing the cobwebs to reconnect with God starting now. These prayers don't count toward my goal, but they do count toward my goal behind the goal (which is to reconnect with God).

I want my story and my journey to serve as an inspiration to all, to those who have walked a similar path and also to those "walking zombie Christians" who may not ever pray to God.

Dear Lord,

I pray that you give me the wisdom to touch hearts in my journey to reconnect with you. I pray that you fill me up and allow me to speak the truth that will allow others to see the greatness that you are! You are amazing. May you bless me on this journey in ways I can't even imagine. May you bless those for whom I pray. I am so grateful for all the Christians with whom you have surrounded me. I am learning so much, and what an inner circle I have! Thank you, God, for being my friend, my confidant, and my caretaker.

I pray that you fill Ed's heart with forgiveness, serenity, and joy. I know he's angry, you know he's angry, so I ask that we knock his socks off and bring him happiness and fun and joy. I ask that you allow him to put all the negative energy of the past behind him and that we continue to work together in a peaceful manner. I've seen what joy looks like on him. It looks good, God. May you bless Ed with an abundance of joy.

Passionately,

Authentic, Humble, Surrendered, and Spiritual Michael

Sunday, January 9, 2011

Bless My Dance Instructor's Family

I found out that my dance instructor from high school passed away this week. She was an amazing and gifted woman. She'd been in pain for a long time and had some condition that made life miserable for her. I will miss her, as she helped me come into my own skin and taught me how to tap dance and do jazz hands.

In remembrance of Jan Colleknon. An amazing woman who touched my life.

Father, please lift up Pink as she grieves the loss of her dear mother. May you lift up her entire family so they can remember the amazing woman who is their mother, friend, sister, and inspiration.

In your name I pray,

1 comments:

Just a Girl said…
    Amen.

Monday, January 10, 2011

You Rock God—Prayer #1

What an amazing day! I just want to thank you God for answering my undocumented prayer of how am i going to do 365 prayers in seven weeks? Turns out we were just granted approval to start our "goal" at Sam Camp 21 to start our goals tonight, January 10 instead of January 12. I don't have to tell you, as you already know, but I have been freaking out about the number of prayers in seven weeks. So thank you for the generous gift of a couple extra days (even if it's almost eleven p.m. Central on the 10th). You rock!

I just want to thank you for an amazing day. Every day I choose joy, and today was no exception. Thank you for filling my heart with joy as I trained who could be my replacement at the advertising agency I own with my ex-partner Ed. I could have chosen the "hard way," but with your grace and guidance, I chose to do the best I could to get who could be my replacement (we'll call him Todd) up to speed quickly and without malice. My intention is to train him to be my replacement, and if your will is that he is to replace me, at whatever time that may be, so be it.

I will be in integrity and authentic and share my knowledge with him as we grow our business…and if it's your will and I'm part of that business, then fantastic. If you have bigger plans for me, I'm ready. I surrender to you, God. You tend to know what's best for me, more than I do!

If I hadn't said it in the last twenty-four hours, let me just close by saying how amazed I am by your grace, generosity and love. You have amazed me daily and I look forward to our conversations between now and March 2, eleven p.m. Arizona Time, when I will have documented 365 prayers or more.

P.S., Of course, I am not going to stop then! Just a habit that I'm creating…for a lifetime of establishing a friendship with my creator.

Love you, mean it!

S. Michael Edwards

Tuesday, January 11, 2011

God Reads Email? Prayer #2
So I've struggled with how I was going to document my 365 prayers in seven weeks. It turns out God answers emails! I know, it's hard to believe, but prayers do not have to look a certain way. They can be eloquent, articulate, and the like, but that doesn't' mean that God doesn't hear them or answer them.

How many times have you prayed and the prayer wasn't documented? So it was perfect for me to create this blog. I thought I would video tape my prayers, then transcribe then write a book. But since God answers emails, why not blogs?

So my blog is my communication with my new BFF (Best Friend Forever). I'm sure if he answers emails, he'll answer my blogs, right?

God, I give great thanks for my buddy Brett Stokes and Carolyn Stokes and how they have moved me closer to you. Had it not been for them, and the way they walk the walk of Christ, I would have continued to be in denial of your existence. I'm so excited that I get to spend a few days with them next week as we meet with a major philanthropist to discuss Brett's and my vision of generating $1 billion dollars toward charity in the next year.

You've been amazing (but you know that) in how you have created the space to allow me to open my eyes to possibilities. Thank you! Thank you so much for the opportunity to meet such amazing Christians who allowed me to believe again. Thank you for giving me the opportunity to meet with like-minded people who want to change the world, one person at a time.

I am so looking forward to meeting with Jeff, who has an amazing nonprofit that is aligned with my vision of creating sustainable communities in developing countries.

My question for you, am I doing your will? Is there anything you want to teach me, tell me, or guide me that I am not currently hearing?

I'm listening...

Lord, let me hear your will and walk the walk you have in store for me. I pray that you will give me the wisdom to see the opportunity to work with Jeff and his organization and how we can raise $1 billion dollars in the next year.

In closing, thanks again for introducing me to Brett and Carolyn Stokes—I know you knew this and still know this, but they have changed my life forever. May my meeting with Jeff and Brett next Tuesday produce results that will rock your world as they hav

In your name, I pray, amen!

Passionately,

Authentic, Humble, Surrendered, and Spiritual Michael

Tuesday, January 11, 2011

Religious Lace | Prayer #3

So God, you did it again. Thank you for my dear friend Juanita King. She gave me this amazing book called *Solo, Based on The Message, An Uncommon Devotional* (copyright 2007).

Juanita knew my goal, and said I could start this daily devotional at the beginning of the year. Well, I hadn't started it yet. You knew that though. You had me wait until my goal started. So I open it up and one of the first three passages I read was about Religious Lace.

God, you know I struggled with prayer and how it needed to sound. What an amazing verse to speak to me this morning…not just about my prayers, but about my goal to pray to you.

Matthew 5:33–37

> "And don't say anything you don't mean. This counsel is embedded deep in our traditions. You only make things worse when you lay down a smoke screen of pious talk, saying, 'I'll pray for you,' and never doing it, or saying, 'God be with you,' and not meaning it. You don't make your words true by embellishing them with religious lace. In making your speech sound more religious, it becomes less true. Just say 'yes' and 'no.' When you manipulate words to get your own way, you go wrong."

Wow. So I guess you heard my prayer and now you just want me to be real with you. I mean, my pastor growing up would probably not like that I called you my new BFF. I am sure there might be others that think that's a little to sacrilegious for a prayer. But pious? Definitely not. Religious Lace? While I do enjoy some lace, my prayers are not about that. That's not who I am. Thank you, God. That takes the pressure off, and now we can just be down and real.

When I think about this journey I'm on, I think about the journey that my mom and dad are about to take this week. She traveling to San Francisco with my dad to staff and facilitate (respectively) the Advanced Leadership Seminar—I pray to you, my God, that you will watch over them and provide for their safe travel. That you will also instill in them your gifts of wisdom, and joy, and service. That they may be of contribution and that their students will have amazing breakthroughs. I pray for Kimberly Zink, an amazing woman in her own right. This was her first class back after having baby Timber. May the team come together and create an amazing shift in their thinking. Anything is possible, and miracles do occur. I got that, God. You have been quite clear on that. Now, let's see, with your guidance and help, if the students can get that too.

In your name I pray,

S. Michael Edwards

I am an authentic, humble, surrendered and spiritual man.

Tuesday, January 11, 2011

Really God? You are totally making me LOL! | Prayer #4

So I just went to go shower and the pressure was low. This is the result of Ed being up about two hours before he normally gets up. I know, we're not together any-more, but we're still living under the same roof, until our house sells. So I decided to skip ahead on the daily devotional, and what do I read?

> Matthew 6:5–6

> "And when you come before God, don't turn that into a theatrical production either. All these people making a regular show out of their prayers, hoping for stardom! Do you think God sits in a box seat?

> "Here's what I want you to do: Find a quiet, secluded place so you won't be tempted to role-play before God. Just be there as simply and honestly as you can manage. The focus will shift from you to God, and you will begin to sense his grace."

So God, I have an ambition, to turn my prayers into a book. I thought if I were real with you and added a splash of humor, this book might touch people's lives, their hearts, and their souls. I am curious, do you mean to tell me that I'm on the wrong path with my goal? Or are you just sending me another message about how prayer doesn't have to be this big show? I hope it's the latter. If you have some time, could you just get back to me on that? Because I seriously laughed out loud when I read that verse waiting for the hot water to be freed up!

While we're chatting (well, I am chatting, you are listening), I was wondering if you might find it in your heart to make the sale of the house happen quickly? I don't know where I will move, but I'm sure I'll be talking to you about that later. We've had four showings and some interest in a week, but no offers. How cool would it be, if I asked you for an offer this week and it happened? I mean, I'm just asking. If there is one thing I learned, it's that if you don't ask, you won't get. So I just thought, if it's in your will, that you might consider this request.

Thanks, and I'll talk to you later,

S. Michael Edwards

I am an authentic, humble, surrendered and spiritual man.

Tuesday, January 11, 2011

Draw Near to God and He Will Draw Near to You | Prayer #5

A great friend of mine, Lisa Darden, has intuition that is incomprehensible. Here's her email that she just sent:

> *Hey,*
>
> *I get this bulletin every day...and every once in a while I get the "urge" to send it to someone...and now that I know fighting God on this is silly, I do it. :) Thought of you today...hope this blesses you!!!*
>
> *Love you oodles!*
>
> *Lisa*

It's from Spirit of Prophecy Bulletin 1/11/11 (Okay, I just realized what a cool date today is!).

The scripture is perfectly in alignment with my goal of 365 prayers in seven weeks! As you know, my goal behind my goal is to reconnect with God. He has answered my prayer from earlier this am, about if my goal is his will.

James 4:8, "Draw near to God and He will draw near to you. Cleanse your hands, you sinners; and purify your hearts, you double-minded."

Thank you, God, for this message. It's clear that as I draw near to you in prayer that I will be near you and you near me. I love it when there is such clarity of purpose and when your Will is in alignment with my goals. I am so grateful for your watching over me and providing guidance on my journey to reconnect. You rock!

In your Name,

Passionately,

Authentic, Humble, Surrendered, and Spiritual Michael

Tuesday, January 11, 2011

Grant me the serenity and Ed, too, please | Prayer #6

I am sure I don't have to tell you, God, but it was an interesting afternoon. "Interesting" for those that are reading these prayers, is a southern way for saying "not great" or even "messed up."

Ed came into my office today on a rampage. He wanted to use the corporate credit card that he opened without my consent, using my Social Security number for business. Well, as you know God, I have been preparing for the worst and praying for the best possible outcomes. The worst, I had a personal guarantee on that card, even though I didn't open it. If Ed failed to make the payments, I would be responsible for the debt, personally.

Given Ed's lack of cash flow expertise, it's not been unknown for him to miss a payment when it comes to business. He's been better at personal credit, as he paid all the bills, only missing a payment on one of my cards. I gladly, as you know, God, took over payments on my own bills when we broke up after twelve-and-a-half years.

He didn't' like that I would not give him the card for the company. I told him that he could do a capital call if he needed cash flow (and since he claims that he owns 75 percent of the company, that means he would have to come up with 75 percent of the capital call). He cannot force me to make 25 percent of the loans to the company. So I told him "no" and to make a capital call. He screamed and yelled. Several times I asked him to tone it down, take it down a notch, calm down, etc. He was irate and said I should cut up the card or he'd call Chase and tell them I didn't work there anymore.

I asked him if he were firing me or if he were simply committing fraud. He didn't answer.

I thank you, God, for giving me the serenity to stay ground and center while under attack. We've had several emails back and forth about the card. After speaking with my attorney, since I never activated the card and the sticker was still on it, I just cut it up. That is what Ed requested. Either use it for company business or cut it up. So I cut it up in front of him and the emails between him, HR, and myself continued.

I had called Case and told them when I got wind of this new account that I did not open it, and I wanted this card cancelled and a new card issued. I never activated the new card. He was the only one that used it. The HR lady has been giving me hindsight insight. "If you received it, and didn't' open it, you could have thrown it away." Well, really? No kidding? Yeah, if I had received both the cards I could have...but I didn't. He received his card on my account, activated it and used it.

When I talked to Chase, they said I'd have to file a police report for stolen identity. I chose not to do that. I asked that they just remove him from the account and I didn't use the card.

I am still wondering, why his heart is so full of vinegar? Lord, can you please fill his heart with joy, serenity, and wisdom to stop this nonsense? Or is this a test of my surrender? I have surrendered to you, Lord. I think my actions today were a testament to that. I pray that you will work your magic on him and produce a miracle so he is a changed man, one of peace, harmony, and humility.

I know that may be asking for too much, but hey, miracles do occur.

Thinking of you,

S. Michael Edwards

Authentically, Humbly, Surrendered and Spiritually.

Tuesday, January 11, 2011

Did you know the toilet wasn't flushed? | Prayer #7
God, did you know that Ed hadn't flushed the toilet or opened the blinds to the master bedroom today? Is that why you cancelled the showing and rescheduled it for tomorrow?

Honestly (as my Grandma Myrtle King would say), it reminds me of my friend Al, who said when he didn't want the house he wanted to buy to sell (he was leasing at the time) he would cook Brussels sprouts before each showing. I am wondering if Ed doesn't want the house to sell, and that's why he didn't flush the toilet or open the plantation shutters?

I know you are in charge, thank you, because you rescheduled the appointment until tomorrow. I will most definitely have time tomorrow to make time to check all the toilets, blinds, and turn on the lights and candles because, as you know, I want this house to sell. My request to you was in forty-eight hours, and that was twenty-four hours ago, plus or minus a few hours.

The appointment/showing got rescheduled for tomorrow, and I'll be sure to make the house show ready. So what is it going to take to overcome Ed's resistance to selling the house? I just need some guidance there.

Any suggestions, signs, or wisdom would be greatly appreciated. I know it's best for us to get out of this house so we can move on with our lives. I just hope he isn't trying to sabotage the sale of the house. I do thank you for having him make his bed (huge win)! I just hope that we can get an offer and move on to our own lives and our own places…however that may look.

By the way, thank you for the courage you allowed me to step into and order a pair of tap shoes my size! Turns out my good friend and mentor Richard Caldwell knows how to tap as well. It's my intention that Richard and I will do a tap off with Viviane Martin singing…how fun will that be? A great tribute to my dearly departed dance teach Jan Colleknon, who passed away last week.

So I am praying for a quick sale, a quick employment agreement with Ed and settlement, and some practice time with Richmond so we can knock the socks off the staff/students at Sam Camp 21 in May! Tap shoes arrive in ten days. Practice TBD. I know you have given me gifts. I am so grateful, and I won't let you down, my God.

My purpose is to bring joy and equality to the world. I see this opportunity as being a win on both fronts with my purpose.

If you have other ideas, I'm listening…you seem to be on a hotline with me lately and I can't wait to see what tomorrow brings.

In your name,

Passionately,

Authentic, Humble, Surrendered, and Spiritual Michael

Wednesday, January 12, 2011

Oh No, He Didn't! | Prayer #8

I decided that instead of doing the daily devotional lock step, I would just flip it open and read the first verse that the book opens to. Spontaneous, and maybe, just maybe, it allows God to speak to me. Or maybe, just maybe it is sweet serendipity. (Lee DeWyze—Sweet Serendipity.)

Ephesians 2:1–6

> "It wasn't so long ago that you were mired in that old stagnant life of sin. You let the world, which doesn't know the first thing about living, tell you how to live. You filled your lungs with polluted unbelief, and then exhaled disobedience. We all did it, all of us doing what we felt like doing, when we felt like doing it, all of us in the same boat. It's a wonder God didn't lose his temper and do away with the whole lot of us. Instead, immense in mercy and with an incredible love, he embraced us. He took our sin-dead lives and made us alive in Christ. He did all this on his own, with no help from us! Then he picked us up and set us down in highest heaven in company with Jesus, our Messiah."

Whew…so true! It wasn't that long ago for me personally, God. You are so right. I did let the world tell me how to live. I did pollute my lungs with unbelief and exhaled disobedience. So amazing, your grace!

God, this is exactly what I told Brett Stokes when I "interviewed" him about his church. We are all sinners. Not one or the other is better. Thank you for putting this in front of me. You are with me, I see that, and I love it. I feel stronger because of your strength—it's like you've got my back!

Together we can accomplish things that I haven't even imagined yet! Together we can change the world. I say that from a place of service and contribution, knowing that you are with me and love me unconditionally and want me to live my purpose. To bring joy and equality to the world.

I'm on it God.

Catch ya later,

S. Michael Edwards, an authentic, humble, surrendered and spiritual man.

Wednesday, January 12, 2011

Two Lives Cross Paths | Prayer #9

God, I want to thank you for putting Sheri Gentry in my life. Thank you for Centa Terry, who recommended that Sheri call me. Turns out we have a lot in common—but alas, you knew that. That's why we're on this journey together. I pray that you fill Sheri with your Holy Spirit as she embarks on her journey. I can't wait to see what she creates. She is an amazing woman of contribution and service, and I hope in addition to that, that you will grant her peace and abundance and joy. May you watch over her and guide her on her journey as you have me, on mine. I know she'd love it!

Thanks, God.

Passionately,

Authentic, Humble, Surrendered, and Spiritual Michael

Wednesday, January 12, 2011

Buddy Pair Rating 10 Out of 10 | Prayer #10

Hey God! So I have my weekly call with Craig, my buddy from Sam Camp tonight. I can't wait to see him complete his goal before March 2. I pray that you will provide him with an abundance of opportunity to reach out and exceed his goal, to blow his goal out of the water! May you also fill his heart with purpose and joy and grati-tude once he achieves his goal.

Thank you for putting Craig in my life. What a blessing he's been. If it weren't for him, I wouldn't be doing this goal. He challenged me on areas of my life that were weak. That was the origination of this goal. I thought it was an exercise…one that eventually turned into reality, which is now. I do feel more connected to you, and it's because you had Centa and Dan Asher put Craig and me together as a buddy pair.

We have rated buddy pairs before, and I would rate Craig a 10 out of a 10. He's just the perfect buddy for me. I can't wait for when the students start and we can support one another on this journey with our students.

I so thank you for surrounding me with like minded people, with people of faith. Examples of all walks of life for Christians and spiritual beings. For so long I fought letting them in. You won. Now I am winning.

So thanks again, I owe you big time.

Passionately,

Authentic, Humble, Surrendered, and Spiritual Michael

Wednesday, January 12, 2011

Power of Intention | Prayer #11
Dear God,

As the Klemmer and Associates Personal Mastery in San Antonio approaches on January 21, 22, and 23, I gratefully request that the students attending see great value and choose to move forward in their journey. I am also requesting that my dear friends [names withheld] choose to attend and see value. This could be huge for Klemmer and Associates and is totally in line with my vision to personally sponsor 100,000 people into K&A.

You know I want to change the world for the better, and you know these friends have that enormous leverage and influence to do the same. It's because of K&A that I came to know you. So I'm hoping that you will honor my request and that not only the attendees see value, but that my influential friends attend.

Passionately,

Authentic, Humble, Surrendered, and Spiritual Michael

Wednesday, January 12, 2011

Thank You, God | Prayer #12
God, I just want to thank you for filling Ed's heart with serenity (I think he could use some more, but it was definitely a shift for him today).

Thank you for your grace and for allowing us to divide up our financial assets in a professional and agreeable manner. That means a lot to me, because it's been on my mind and I have been so worried about what it was going to look like. It looks amazing!

Now our next step is to divide up our assets. I pray that you will continue to fill Ed's heart with serenity, fairness and contribution so that we can do the asset division in a professional and calm manner without a lot of emotion or negative energy (Okay, how about no negative energy and just positive emotion? I like the sound of that better.).

It is so nice to be able to have an amicable divorce…and I pray that we continue down the path of harmony.

Love you, mean it!

S. Michael Edwards

I am an authentic, humble, surrendered, and spiritual man.

Wednesday, January 12, 2011

50 percent Answered | Prayer #13

So God, you work fast! 50 percent of the people I want to attend the Personal Mastery in San Antonio have committed to going (I'm carpooling so there will be no excuses). I talked to the other 50 percent, and they should get back to me tomorrow since they can't personally attend, but I'm asking that you allow their decision makers to attend.

Thanks so much for your support in these requests. You are all mighty and amazing.

BTW ["by the way," for those who aren't text savvy], I got permission from three out of four of my Master Mind team to pray for their requests (unless they explicitly say "not this one") by name. I think this will not only serve them, but me as well. It's a total win/win. So more to come on those as I get written permission to share their requests (which I was going to pray for anyway, but why not make them part of my 365 prayers in seven weeks?). So brilliant an idea you gave me, and I love you!

Now for my call with my amazing buddy Craig. Can't wait to see what we create!

Passionately,

Authentic, Humble, Surrendered, and Spiritual Michael

Thursday, January 13, 2011

WONKA Lesha Kitts | Prayer #14

Dear God, good morning! What a great call last night with my WONKAS, even though I broke my commitment and was late. I was actually talking to my friend whom I want to go Personal Mastery. He has plans that weekend, but was going to check into finding one or more replacements (and the legalities of it being free). So while you are not prepared for him to go, I do hope and pray that you will provide them the guidance and wisdom to send someone so they can see the power of Klemmer and the tools that led me back to you.

Now for my Master Mind team. I haven't really talked much about my amazing team, because we have this confidentiality clause. Well, I listened to your advice and asked them if they would allow me to pray for them by name and their requests to you. They agreed, and I was praying for them anyway, so now I can introduce to you three out of the four of them who have given me permission to pray for them and reveal their Master Min requests.

Some background for my readers. Master Minding is when you create an amazing group of people who hold the intention for certain requests. We meet on a weekly basis and go over a series of things that we learn in Sam Camp. My team is the team I was with in Sam Camp. We named ourselves the WONKA's—it was my dear and funny friend Lesha Kitts, a Willy Wonka fanatic, who came up with this name. Then as a team we created meaning for each of the letters in WONKA.

Warriors

Of

Noble

Kind

Acts

Lesha, knowing the movie like she knows her best friend, came up with a quote.

"We are the makers of music and dreamers of dreams."

Well, part of our dreams is Master Minding. There is a specific format for Master Mind "requests" or "asks" – that they be specific and have a timeframe. This may or may not be in alignment with God's will, but the idea is that these requests are what you want, in the time you want and if they are in alignment with God's will, be prepared to receive. The Master Mind team holds the intention that your requests will be honored. Master Mind teams are not new. Just read Napoleon Hill's book, *Think and Grow Rich*.

Lord, I pray for Lesha's requests this week. She has a beautiful opening, which I know you've heard.

With the love and support and integrity of this Master Mind team, and the knowledge that where I am...God is, I graciously make the following requests.

On or before January 31, 2011, she has completed fifteen hours of Gym Time.

That on or before January 31, 2011, the green houses are covered and ready to receive seedlings.

That Heather has completed Sam Camp 22.

I honor and support her requests, dear Lord. Her first is totally self-honoring, her second is totally contribution and service-related for her community garden that gives back to the community, and her third is selfless in that she wants her significant other, Heather, to attend Sam Camp 22.

So powerful, and yet so giving. She's an amazing blessing in my life, and I thank you for her and her gifts and talents. A true and powerful leader and giving woman.

I'll pray and introduce my other Master Mind members after I have some more coffee! Thank you, God, for coffee! LOL, you know the inside joke on that one. :)

Is it wrong to close a prayer with I'll be back? Or does it really need an Amen?

Amen (just in case),

Authentic, Humble, Surrendered, and Spiritual Michael

Thursday, January 13, 2011

WONKA Karen Sizelove | Prayer #15

Lord, thank you for introducing Karen Sizelove into my life. She is so fantastic. I can't help but smile when she is talking, she has such a gift for energy and enthusiasm and her creativity is out of this world. She finds beauty in everything. Leaves, clouds, chocolate, rain, snow, you name it. She gets it, appreciates it, and lets you and everyone around her know it.

Karen is an artist, and I think that is one reason I get along with her so well. We have both been blessed by you and the gifts you have given us, so we are in sync. We are of service, and we are of contribution.

Lord, I pray for Karen's requests this week as well. As she stated, "With the complete faith and trust in God, who is all love, and with the love and support of my Master Mind partners, I give thanks and ask: God has given me the gift to attend the Instructional Clinic at Crystal Peaks Youth Ranch, in Bend, Oregon, on or before March 12, 2011."

That her January 2011 Dove Chocolate Discoveries sales are $1,000 or more.

That God has guided her fiancé in playing full out in true choice during Sam Camp 21 on or before May 18, 2011.

I love Karen's Master Mind requests. She has great motivation and energy around each one. I would pray that you would provide for her the opportunity to self-fund, however that looks, her attendance at the Crystal Peaks Youth Ranch by March 12. She has the greatest of intentions and motivation behind this and is setting up her Y9 youth ranch to be of service and contribution to troubled youth.

She has started her own business and perhaps that is the vehicle you want her to use, dear God, to raise those funds, and $1,000 in January would be a great jump start!

And for her fiancé, who is an amazing man, that you grant him the wisdom and freedom to play full out that he focus on the possibilities and believe that miracles do occur. You are all powerful, God.

I thank you for your time (as Karen would say) and "Yow!"

Karen also would say, "How can I best support you?"

So God, in closing, I would ask, "How can I best support you?"

Thursday, January 13, 2011

WONKA Nelson Brandt | Prayer #16

God, my friend and Master Mind member Nelson Brandt is so amazing. What a gift you have given me in bringing him into my life. Our Master MindMaster Mind group is a powerful group of amazing people, and Nelson has stepped into being a great leader and mentor, not to mention your ability to fill his heart with forgiveness and joy. I thank you for bringing him into my life as we learn from each other to live a life of joy and a life of forgiveness.

It's been a great journey with Nelson. I am praying for his requests this week.

"I am grateful that I have been accepted into the H-65 helicopter First Pilot Syllabus on or before 31 January 2011."

"I am grateful that on or before 15 March 2011, God is providing Marvin Jemal, Robing Jemal, Robert Grossman, and Mark Berstein with the desire and ability to present a mutually agreeable settlement to me and my family."

"I gratefully request that on or before 31 January 2011 God would enable healing to occur in the aftermath of the tragedy in Tucson, Arizona."

Lord, Nelson is amazing, and I love that he is so caring and requesting healing for the tragedy in Arizona. Please, God, we need this healing more than anything. The political infighting is such that we could sure use a miracle and healing our great nation would be such a gift.

I pray to you, Father, that the lawsuit is settled for Nelson and his family and that he gets what is due and that the other parties find in their hearts the wisdom to settle the suit and that all parties find forgiveness in their heart. The wisdom to settle is powerful, and if it's your will as it's Nelson's request, I pray that you bring people into their lives that can facilitate that settlement.

Nelson is an amazing commander. Quite the pilot. You have given him talents and he is serving our nation. God, please provide the wisdom to those who pick the First Pilot Syllabus trainees to select Nelson.

I thank you for listening to these requests, and I pray that you will honor and support them as I do.

In your name, I pray,

Amen.

Authentic, Humble, Surrendered, and Spiritual Michael

Thursday, January 13, 2011

Testing and Results | Prayer #17

So I put a request out God that we'd get an offer on the house in forty-eight hours; well, as you know forty-eight hours has passed and I see you are teaching me a lesson in timing. Your will is not necessarily on my timeline. I totally get that. I guess I was testing the power of prayer, not to see if it works or doesn't, but to just ask and see what happens.

I am okay, God, that an offer hasn't been put down on the house yet. Our agent has been thrilled with the number of views on our listing, over 7,000 views to date in less than two weeks. We've had four showings in one-and-a-half weeks, and she is very happy with that. So there is interest, and I thank you God for that. I pray that the right family will find and fall in love with our house and that they will want to buy it with an offer of plus or minus 4 percent of our asking price.

It's time for me to move on, and I think this will be a huge step toward doing that. I don't know what you have in store for me, but I don't need to know. Your plan will be revealed to me in due time. I know that now. I can't wait to see what the plan is, as I know you have big plans for me and my future.

So I thought I would just follow-up and say, thank you for the lesson and ask that you reconsider my request for a quick sale of the house with an offer within plus or minus 4 percent of the asking price.

With gratitude,

Authentic, Humble, Surrendered and Spiritual Michael

Thursday, January 13, 2011

Daily Devotional Roulette | Prayer #18

LOL—so I just finished my prayer to you God, about the sale of the house…and decided I would do my daily devotional, Russian Roulette style.

Title: "A Loud No…A Quiet Yes" from *Solo, Based on The Message* (Copyright 2007).

James 4:7–10

> "So let God work his will in you. Yell a loud *no* to the Devil and watch him scamper. Say a quiet *yes* to God and he'll be there in no time. Quit dabbling in sin. Purify your inner life. Quit playing the field. Hit bottom, and cry your eyes out. The fun and games are over. Get serious, really serious. Get down on your knees before the master; it's the only way you'll get on your feet."

God, I surrender to you and continue to pray for your will to be done through me. I know you'll let me know if I'm not doing your will. In fact, I see it come through when I'm out of alignment with my purpose to bring joy and equality to the world. That is your will for me, as I understand it today.

I totally hit bottom, cried my eyes out, and now I am serious and I'm on my feet making a difference in this world, thanks to your wisdom and power. I thank you with all my heart for the talents you have given me and for allowing me to have the courage to make drastic changes in my life that will serve you better.

Thank you, God. You're amazing me every day…in so many ways.

I pray for my dad this week as he is changing lives and touching hearts. For Kimberly Zink, who is back from maternity leave, and baby Timber and her husband Tim that they are able to balance family and work. (Even though I don't like to call what they do work, God, because it's their passion.) I pray for my mom and her health and that she be filled with the wisdom to follow the doctor's advice and that you give the doctor the wisdom to speak to my mom and that she hear you and the doctor and do the right thing for her health.

I pray for my sister and her family as they are in my thoughts this morning. May she and her family be blessed, and may you watch over them with your gentle hand and guiding light.

In these things I pray to you my God,

Authentic, Humble, Surrendered, and Spiritual Michael

Thursday, January 13, 2011

Forgiveness | Prayer #19

Dear God,

I am so grateful for the feedback you are allowing others to provide to me. It's giving me time to reflect. I had feedback from two different people today on my story and journey. One was related to how I could write about my childhood and my parents. The other was about my relationships. Both elicited emotion. I am thankful that my blog and journey/story is making people think, and creatingn emotion.

I just wondered if it were necessary for me to include my painful past to support my current situation.

I think it is. As one person said, "It is all about forgiveness!"

I couldn't agree more, I told my dad that I would not change a thing about my childhood. He wouldn't either, he said. You see, we understand that had we not gone through what we went through in our past, that we wouldn't be where we are today. I will talk to my parents again about my journey and their feelings, God. I want to make sure that I am doing the right thing. I do feel I am speaking from my heart.

I forgave my dad long ago, then again in April 2010, when I was at Advanced Leadership. That was heartfelt forgiveness. I forgave my mom when I attended Personal Mastery. I forgave myself.

I had a hard time with forgiveness. Then I learned that it's just a choice. You just choose to forgive, it's that simple. Or you can choose to carry the burden of guilt, blame, shame. I carried that boulder of blame, shame, and guilt for a long time. I have since released it, and it is liberating. I thank you, God, for bringing people into my life that allowed me to see that forgiveness is a choice and for creating the space for me to release my demons.

I have the most amazing relationship with my parents today. They are such giving, caring, and loving people. They love me unconditionally, and I love them unconditionally. We talk all the time on the phone. I am so proud of my parents, for their contribution, service, and love of humanity. I love that they are changing people's lives, thousands of lives, and changing the world, one person at a time.

I am so grateful for you introducing them to the people that kept hounding them to go to Klemmer and Associates first seminar. It's where I first noticed a change in them. Over the years, they have become the most amazing people I know. I totally respect and adore my parents.

I just want everyone to know that sometimes you have to walk through the fire to get to the other side. You have to experience pain to really appreciate joy.

God, thank you for the amazing people in my life that help me understand and reflect on my purpose, and thank you for giving me the courage and allowing me to step into vulnerability. I see it as being vulnerable to the possible.

You rock, now I'm going to call my mom.

Love you,

S. Michael Edwards

Authentic, Humble, Surrendered, and Spiritual Michael

Thursday, January 13, 2011

Commitment | Prayer #20

Lord, I thank you for my amazing conversation with my mom tonight. I asked her about this blog and my future book/movie and how she really felt about it. I wanted to make sure we were clear. "Are you okay with my telling of how we started and where we are now?"

She responded, "If we weren't in the place we are now, I would have a hard time with it, but given where we are, I am totally okay with it."

So I have my mom's blessing on this blog and future book/movie. I want to get confirmation from my amazing father as well, as soon as he gets back from his class in San Francisco.

Lord, I pray that his class is amazing. That the students have breakthroughs and revelations and that they see the value in moving forward in changing their lives, and the lives of those around them. I pray for Kimberly Zink, Scott Pullan, and my father... all of whom have shown a commitment to changing the world one person at a time.

Which reminded me of this song...

"Commitment," LeAnn Rimes—the words totally resonate and I especially love the first verse.

by MascaraANDWhiskey

> *"What I'm lookin' for*
>
> *Is a love that's forever*
>
> *Someone who can capture my soul in a heartbeat*
>
> *And stay for all time*
>
> *What I'm prayin' for*
>
> *Is a match made in heaven*
>
> *Someone who will worship my body*
>
> *And still put his heart on the line"*

I hear and read the words to this song and realize that *you* are the one I have been searching for all these years. You will go the distance with me, you have the staying power, God. You make me go weak in the knees. You give me honor and love, and you are playing for keeps! You are a match made in Heaven!

Thank you, God!

In your name, I pray,

S. Michael Edwards

Authentic, Humble, Surrendered, and Spiritual Michael

Friday, January 14, 2011

Devotional Roulette | Prayer #21
Phillipians 1:3–6

> "Every time you cross my mind, I break out in exclamations of thanks to God. Each exclamation is a trigger to prayer. I find myself praying for you with a glad heart. I am so pleased that you have continued on in this with us, believing and proclaiming God's Message, from the day you heard it right up to the present. There has never been the slightest doubt in my mind that the God who started this great work in you would keep at it and bring it to a flourishing finish on the very day Christ Jesus appears."

Awesome God, what a mighty God you are. I love this verse. I am so grateful, God, that you heard my prayer and lifted my mom up. She listened to her doctor, and I thank you for that. She is too priceless, and I want her to be around for a long time. God, I pray that as she travels today to San Francisco to help Dad that you will watch over her and provide for a safe trip. I pray that you will fill her heart with service and contribution (not that she needs more, but we can all use a little top off every now and then).

God, may the students at Advanced Leadership be open to hearing how they can move forward in their lives and how much bigger and better their lives can be, if they get themselves out of the way. I pray that they hear and believe in trust, integrity, honor, and introspection and healing.

In your name I pray gratefully!

Authentic, Humble, Surrendered, and Spiritual

S. Michael Edwards

Friday, January 14, 2011

You Just Don't Give Up, Do You? | Prayer #22
God, I love how you are quite persistent at putting the right people together at the right time. I mean, you just don't give up do you? Thank you for allowing me to step into vulnerability...for reaching out to a friend who had a miscarriage. My grief counseling experience allowed me to offer an ear and a shoulder...and what I found out was that not only did we have a connection, but we have overlap in our visions.

I thank you for bringing her into my life. I pray that you will comfort her and her family, in their time of loss. That you will lift her up and allow her to pour her emotions on the table. I pray you will fill her heart with love and hope.

She is an amazing, strong, powerful force. She is changing the world. She has much to offer. I thank you, God, for putting her in my path and allowing me to connect with her.

I am so looking forward to working with her on her vision and her purpose in life. We will both learn from each other, as I suspect you knew all along.

What an amazing day it was yesterday. You put into motion an incredible chain of events…thank you!

TTYL God,

Authentic, Humble, Surrendered, and Spiritual Michael

Friday, January 14, 2011

Waiting With Baited Breath | Prayer #23

Okay, God, I don't' even know what that means, to wait with baited breath, but I am. I just delivered the settlement documents to "Ed" and pray that he signs and we put this whole matter behind us. I pray that he keeps his commitment and signs the deal we've agreed to in principle, without any changes. You know how my attorney is, he charges me for everything. Thanks for attorneys, God, they are amazing and provide me a great opportunity to practice serenity :)

May you fill "Ed's" heart with compassion and commitment today as he reads those documents. While I am leaving tomorrow, my desire is to have these all signed by the end of the month!

Thanks for your help in getting this matter solved, you are a blessing in my life and I couldn't have gotten through this trying time without your love and support.

In your name,

Authentic, Humble, Surrendered, and Spiritual

S. Michael Edwards

Friday, January 14, 2011

Breaking Up Is Hard To Do | Prayer #24

Lord, I ask you to be with my dear friend who is going through a break up. May you lift her up and guide her. I ask that you surround her with love and friends and supportive people as she grieves the loss of her relationship. I ask that you provide healing and strength as she goes through this difficult time.

She means the world to me, and I don't like to see her suffer. I know she will come out of this a stronger woman, but it's just hard to understand why things like this happen.

I know you have a plan for her, and I can't wait for her to see that plan. It will be amazing, I'm sure.

Thank you, God, for your grace!

Authentic, Humble, Surrendered, and Spiritual

S. Michael Edwards

Friday, January 14, 2011

Employee Satisfaction | Prayer #25

God, thanks for the inspiration that Lisa Darden and Danielle Venne gave me in tackling employee satisfaction as part of my Sam Camp goal. As you know we got an 83 percent; my goal was to increase it by 3 percent, which I accomplished in five weeks, much to the chagrin of our HR department, who said it couldn't be done.

I love the latest results! You rock my world God. We got 89 percent—so we're doing something right! That's a 7 percent increase since I started. We still have work to do, as I want to get to the mid 90 percent range.

I ask that you give me the wisdom on how to do that, God. What can I do differently to help motivate and get our employees excited about work and what they do? They do such amazing work, but we're clearly missing something if we're not in the 90 percent range. Or are my expectations too high?

Looking for guidance—you seem to know the right time and place to provide it, so I'll just wait and listen.

Thankfully yours,

Authentic, Humble, Surrendered, and Spiritual

S. Michael Edwards

Friday, January 14, 2011

Grace Like Rain | Prayer #26

God, one of my favorite songs is "Amazing Grace"…and then I found Grace Like Rain from a CD I bought at Eastlake Community Church. I prefer their version of Grace Like Rain over the original.

The lyrics speak to me, loud and clear, and I thank you, God, for filling Todd Agnew's heart with this song and for Todd sharing his talents with the rest of us. My favorite part is the mix of the old "Amazing Grace" with the new "Grace Like Rain" lyrics.

> *"Amazing grace, how sweet the sound*
>
> *That saved a wretch like me*
>
> *I once was lost but now I'm found*
>
> *Was blind but now I see so clearly"*

I think the part that gets me in this song is the part about being lost, God. I was lost, for twenty-one-and-a-half years, but now I'm found. I was totally blind and now I can see so clearly. Your grace saved me. Your grace appeared the hour I first believed. I was a sinner by birth, saved by the grace of God. (Ephesians 2:8.)

I am thankful for your grace, dear God. You're a loving God, and you have graced and blessed me and I'm forever grateful.

Can't wait to do lunch with you one day. I'd love to pick your brain on a few things I have questions about. I guess I don't have to wait though. So I'll put those questions to you now.

Why the tragedy in Arizona? Why the inequality in the world? Why the poverty? Is it man's unwillingness to change these things?

What do you suggest I do to make a difference? I am already on a mission to change the world. To create an army to tackle these problems. I want to raise $1 billion dollars in the next year to fight for equality and to build sustainable communities, and I know I can do it with the help of others.

I thank you for providing me access to those people, and pray that you will give me the wisdom to connect with them on a heart level so we can make change happen at a rapid pace. I know it's impossible for some to believe, but I believe that in you, everything is possible.

Just my thoughts, just my concerns, just my being with you.

By the way, the goal behind my goal was to connect with you at a deeper level, and I am feeling it, God. I am feeling that connection like I never had as a child going to church. Maybe I wasn't old enough to be aware of your grace, but I see it clearly now and appreciate it like no other.

I praise you God for your amazing grace.

In your name,

Authentic, Humble, Surrendered, and Spiritual

S. Michael Edwards

Friday, January 14, 2011

I Just Wanna Praise You | Prayer #27

I am on a roll, God, listening and jamming to your believer's music. I was exposed to this song at Klemmer and Associates Samurai Camp by my dear friend Hannah Stetson, who is the epitome of a Christian, walking the walk and living the life Christ had in mind for her. That's my experience of her.

When she sang and danced to "Shackles," by Mary Mary, I was captivated, in a trance at how beautiful the song was. I had never heard it before, God, but I thank you for giving her the inspiration to share her talents with us. An amazing song… and the message, I just want to praise you! Amen, what a great message, and rings so true (sorry for the pun).

In your name I praise you God!

Passionately,

Authentic, Humble, Surrendered, and Spiritual

S. Michael Edwards

Saturday, January 15, 2011

I Am with You | Prayer #28

Good morning, God! What an amazing day yesterday, as I was thinking about you more and more and lay in bed last night praising you and your glory. I was reflecting on my first week of my prayer goal and realized that not only am I praying often, but I am thinking about you often. In fact, if I could just invent some Bluetooth technology that would take my thoughts and put them onto my blog, I would have had thirty or forty prayers yesterday just thinking about you and how grateful I am that we are on this journey together.

I love that this mechanism of 365 prayers is actually connecting me with you in a powerful way. That you are constantly on my mind. That I can feel you with me, every step, every day, all the way.

Lord, thank you, and I pray that you will bless me on my flight to Portland, Oregon, today. Watch over me, God, as I travel to the northwest and meet with family and friends and potential new clients.

In your name I pray,

Authentic, Humble, Surrendered, and Spiritual

S. Michael Edwards

Saturday, January 15, 2011

Devotional Roulette | Prayer #29

Pour on the Blessings, dear God. As I did my morning ritual of Russian Devotional Roulette, I came upon 2 Corinthians 9:8–11.

> "God can pour on the blessings in astonishing ways so that you're ready for anything and everything, more than just ready to do what needs to be done. As one psalmist puts it,

He throws caution to the winds,

> giving to the needy in reckless abandon.

His right-living, right-giving ways

> never run out, never wear out.

"This most generous God who gives seed to the farmer that becomes bread for your meals is more than extravagant with you. He gives you something you can then give away, which grows into fully formed lives, robust in God, wealthy in every way, so that you can be generous in every way, producing with us great praise to God."

Another amazing moment brought to you by God, LOL. Lord, your sense of timing is impeccable. As you know my trip to the northwest is scheduled around a meeting with the man who is connected with Agros International, a Seattle-based NGO working to break the cycle of poverty among the world's rural poor, helping landless poor families in Central America purchase farmland and develop sustainable livelihoods, empowering rural, poor families to work their way out of poverty and develop self-sustaining villages.

This is totally in alignment with my vision and Brett's vision, who helped set up this meeting. So how perfect, that as I prepare to pack my bags and fly out to meet with this amazing man, who has a heart of gold, that you give me this reminder of how these blessings can support me in my journey to develop sustainable communities in developing countries.

Thank you, God! Your timing is perfection.

Authentic, Humble, Surrendered, and Spiritual

S. Michael Edwards

Saturday, January 15, 2011

Answered Prayer | Prayer #30

God, as you know, I had requested my friends attend the Personal Mastery on the 21, 22, 23, and you have answered those prayers. They are all committed to attending, including the influential ones that I have been praying would go.

Thank you so much for answering this request. When I got the first no, I was not giving up. I know that you can move mountains. I had put it out to my Master Mind group and said to myself that if it's your will, it will still happen. We must be on the same page. I am not sure if it's because you feel the time is right for these people or because I didn't give up or just because I held the faith…whatever the reason, I am grateful that they are committed and will be attending.

I pray they see value and want to take this to the next level. It changed my life and I know it will change their lives, if they allow themselves to get out of the way.

Thank you, God! Prayers answered! I love typing that and saying it to you.

Authentic, Humble, Surrendered, and Spiritual

S. Michael Edwards

Sunday, January 16, 2011

Do You Believe? | Prayer 31
Oh God,

What a blessing you are in my life. I thank you for my safe trip to Portland yesterday. It gave me time to read *The Shack*, by William P. Young. The inscription on the inside was given to my dad, and signed by Richmond. I only know one Richmond, who is also an author and a friend. I wonder, God, is this Richmond Caldwell who gave my dad that book? The book my mom let me borrow, the book that Lisa Darden suggest I read?

I wonder these things because the book had such a tremendous impact on me. I will be praying more about the parts of the book that spoke to me. I dog-eared the pages, and there are many. I am grateful for the book, dear God. I write this with tears streaming down my face,

I believe that God is love and forever with me in my life.

I believe that God is forgiving and has not left my side.

I believe that God is grace, which I choose to embrace.

I believe that God is good, and loving and kind,

and as I wash the rust of disbelief from my mind,

I believe that God is my friend, my confidant, and my life.

Dear God, thank you for you love, forgiveness, grace, and greatness.

Authentic, Humble, Surrendered, and Spiritual

S. Michael Edwards

Sunday, January 16, 2011

The Shack and Forgiveness | Prayer 32

God, I thank you for touching my heart in such a deep way, for speaking to me in a language that I can clearly understand…for being real with me.

I was touched by *The Shack*, written by William P. Young. How appropriate, God, that I read a story set in the Pacific Northwest and find so many words that resonate with my past. I'd like to thank you for the people you put into my life who encouraged me to read this book. Lisa Darden, for one…whom I resisted. I know you knew all along that I would read this book, in due time. You had a count of how many times it would take before I finally read it. To Richmond, who gave the book to my dad. To my mom, who let me borrow it. Finally, to you, who told me yesterday to take it on the plane for my flight to Portland.

I think the best place to start is with forgiveness. It truly touched my heart.

"So forgiveness does not require me to pretend what he did never happened?"

"How can you? You forgave your dad last night. Will you ever forget what he did to you?"

"I don't think so."

"But now you can love him in the face of it. His change allows for that. Forgiveness in no way requires that you trust the one you forgive. But should they finally confess and repent, you will discover a miracle in your own heart that allows you to reach out and begin to build between you a bridge of reconciliation. And sometimes—and this may seem incomprehensible to you right now—that road may even take you to the miracle of fully restored trust."

Wow, God! This was so true for me. I had forgiven my father longago and prayed about it in my daily prayers. What is written above is exactly what happened with my father and me. I forgave me and knew that I could trust him and that he loved me unconditionally. That is only possible if he had forgiven himself.

What is even more amazing is that I had carried around this burden of "forgiveness" with Ed's father and wife. I was not willing to let it go, until Shane McGuire asked me how my forgiveness was coming along. He asked me what I was getting out of it. Surely I was getting something out of it, or I would have forgiven them. Then my phone went dead.

I was driving an embroidery machine, which had been generously loaned to me by an-other Compassionate Samurai that I met at Heart of the Samurai 31, and I had spotty reception. God, you were working miracles that day, because I had been carrying my burden on forgiveness for so long, since September 2010, when I found out what Ed's parents had done. I'm sure God, that you had my phone die so I could ponder what I was getting out of not forgiving them. It was then that I realized what I was getting…I was choosing suffering. As I learned through Klemmer and Associates, "Suffering is Optional."

As soon as I realized that this choice of forgiveness was that easy, just a choice, I for-gave them in my heart. Immediately you gave me cell coverage and I called Shane and thanked him and told him I had thrown the boulder over the edge. I grinned for one-and-a-half hours. What a weight had been lifted.

Lord, I thank you for giving me this passage, because it shows that I can forgive and still be angry. I can forgive on a daily basis until that anger goes away. Forgiveness is not the same as forgetting. I can build a bridge of reconciliation.

This applies not only to Ed's family, but to Ed himself. I can even have the experience of a miracle of restored trust.

Now *The Shack*, it's just fiction…but God, I know you are speaking to me, I know you are with me and that you hear my pain and suffering and you are healing my wounds.

I just thought of saying, "God bless you!" But then you are God! So bless you, my God! LOL, bless you as you bless me. What an amazing God you are.

Authentic, Humble, Surrendered, and Spiritual

S. Michael Edwards

Sunday, January 16, 2011

The Shack and As One! | Prayer 33

God, we often say at Klemmer and Associates, "As One!" I read in *The Shack*, by William P. Young, the section of how Jesus talks to the main character Mack and says that he wants to be the center of everything and live inside of Mack. No hierarchy, but the center of a mobile, where all is interconnected, but nothing is greater than the other.

That is powerful, God, that you are with me, and in me, and I am with you and in you. We are as one. Even when I turned my back on you twenty-one-and-a-half years ago, you were with me. You knew how many times it would take to get through to me. Happy days are here again! Lord, you are with me, and as I stated before, I cannot stop thinking about you being with me. All the glory that you bring my way, the joy and the strength and the serenity. I feel you inside and beside me on this journey. I feel your heart beat with my heart.

Lord, I am so grateful for your love and for watching over me. I could have easily died of AIDS, but you watched over me. That's not to say that if I ever did get AIDS that I would blame you. I know that everything happens for a reason. But I thank you, God, that I have been blessed with a full life and that my life has been filled with more joy in the last six months, than I had in the last twelve years.

Thank you, dear God, for your gifts of joy, love, grace, and for being with me…footprints in the sand…as one.

Authentic, Humble, Surrendered, and Spiritual

S. Michael Edwards

Sunday, January 16, 2011

It's NOT YOUR JOB TO CHANGE THEM | Prayer 34

God,

I thank you again for allowing my mom to attend that workshop where she realized it was not her job to "get me into heaven" but to love me unconditionally.

I believe that was you working through her, on my journey back to you. Then God, I read in *The Shack* a passage where they say Jesus said, "All I want from you is to trust me with what little you can, and grow in loving people around you with the same love I share with you. It's not your job to change them, or to convince them. You are free to love without an agenda."

God, I pray that you will continue to spread this message to all the believers out there, that they see it's their job to love everyone, without an agenda. It is this love without prejudice that allowed me to see your shining light through Brett Stokes. He loved me without an agenda, as did his wife Carolyn. They weren't trying to convince me to come to you. They were just loving me.

God, I am so blessed by you. Each and every day, I thank you for the gifts you have given me. For Brett and Carolyn Stokes and the way they loved me, through you. For Lisa Darden and Amanda Fillweber, for the way they loved me through you. For Brian Miller, a man I despised for knowing who I was, for calling me on it, and not letting me get away with playing small. I love you, Brian Miller. You are like a brother to me. For Brian Klemmer and his legacy, Sona Vanderhoof, Kim-Michelle Pullan, Kimberly Zink, Scott Pullan, and Krystal Klemmer. For Mom, Dad, and my sister. God, I especially thank you for Janet Henze and Centa Terry, who love me for who I am, without agenda. For Patty Huesers, Paulette Hansen, Jeff Pelizzaro, Pat and Brent Brooks, and Craig Waggenshutz…all of whom, without judgment, love me unconditionally.

I thank you for my friend Shiela, whom I was able to fellowship with last night. We had an amazing time. We go way back, and while I changed her name in the beginning, it's time I call her by her name, because she is one amazing woman who is making a difference and changing lives—the lives of her children and the lives her children touch. She is an inspiration to motherhood and friendship. Thank you for bringing her into my life. I pray you surround her with your love, and her family as well.

Thank you, God. You totally bless me in all the amazing spiritual people with whom you surround me.

Authentic, Humble, Surrendered, and Spiritual

S. Michael Edwards

1 comments:

Just a Girl said...

You made me cry. Thank you. I have too many blessings to count. Thank you for being part of my life and being such an inspiration to me. Part of who I am is because of you.

Love, Shi

Sunday, January 16, 2011

Jesus Take the Wheel | Prayer 35

God,

I am praying at a rapid pace this morning. I am totally in my zone, and thank you for allowing me to read *The Shack*. It is such an amazing book!

I often think about fear. I hear others with the same fears or fears in general. I wondered how you would feel about them. Now, I don't know if *The Shack* was inspired by you, but I trust that it was. It has spoken to me at a level so deep and so timely that I cannot imagine that you did not inspire William P. Young to write it.

Another passage that I dog-eared was the passage on fear and why we keep it all hidden inside. It's a coping mechanism, learned at an early age. The key, according to *The Shack*, is to learn to live loved. God will, "Make a home inside of you, then share. The friendship is real, not merely imagined. We're meant to experience this life...together, in a dialogue, sharing the journey."

Whoa! Yeah, that hit me like a ton of bricks, God. That is exactly what we are doing. We are in dialogue, and I am constantly thinking about you now. My 365 prayers was a mechanism to reconnect with you, but in fact, it's created this constant dialogue and friendship. So when I called you my BFF (Best Friend Forever), and wondered if that was okay to say, I had no idea about this written word in *The Shack*.

We are on this journey together God. I am blessed to have you on this journey. And when times get tough, I am reminded of "Jesus Take the Wheel," written by James/Lindsey/Sampson. Listen to the lyrics. It's amazing.

Sunday, January 16, 2011

Devotional Roulette—Judgment | Prayer 36

Great work God, I love my devotional roulette and it ties in nicely with what I've been sharing about my issues I had around religion.

Luke 15:1–7

"By this time a lot of men and women of doubtful reputation were hanging around Jesus, listening intently. The Pharisees and religion scholars were not pleased, not at all pleased. They growled, 'He takes in sinners and eats meals with them, treating them like old friends.' Their grumbling triggered this story.

"Suppose one of you had a hundred sheep and lost one. Wouldn't you leave the ninety-nine in the wilderness and go after the lost one until you found it? When found, you can be sure you would put it across your shoulders, rejoicing, and when you got home call in your friends and neighbors, saying, 'Celebrate with me! I've found my lost sheep!' Count on it—there's more joy in heaven over one sinner's rescued life than over ninety-nine good people in no need of rescue.

God, this is beautiful. May all the people of faith understand and take this to heart. May you fill their hearts with love and understanding and allow them to see their judgment is not what you seek.

This is what I was struggling with, for so long…judgment, against me, being gay, and yet 99 percent of the people doing it were not reaching out to me, like Jesus would, they were judging me. I had a problem with that God, as you know. It was a big time road block for me.

Then I realized God, that we're all sinners. Those who judge and those who live. No one sin is greater than another…at least as far as I can see.

So thank you for this passage, God. It reminds me to reach out to those who may or may not be saved. To love everyone, regardless of their faith, condition, or attitude. To be a loving man. To be an example of love.

I have surrounded myself with people of faith, and may we surround others with our love, without judgment. What a great gift we will giving, a gift that we have been given.

Thank you, God. I love you and respect you and I'm loving this journey with you. Another great song that touched my heart this day, "Petra—Jesus, Friend of Sinners."

Authentic, Humble, Surrendered, and Spiritual

S. Michael Edwards

Sunday, January 16, 2011

Jesus Has a Lead Foot | Prayer 37

So I posted "Jesus Take the Wheel," and on my travels to Bothell Washington, I get a speeding ticket. I see your sense of humor, God. Honestly, I think Jesus has a lead foot. If it's okay with you, I'll drive and let Jesus sit in the passenger seat. I'd like him to be with me, and to watch over me, but two speeding tickets in less than two weeks is a bit much.

So I hope you see the irony, as I certainly do. I am not sure if there is a lesson here, because I don't want to slow down. I want to speed up and make a difference. But it did strike me as hilarious that I got the ticket after listening and posting "Jesus Take the Wheel" by Carrie Underwood this morning.

Love you, mean it! Hope you see I'm teasing you a bit.

Authentic, Humble, Surrendered, and Spiritual

S. Michael Edwards

Sunday, January 16, 2011

Jesus Held an Open Bar | Prayer 38

Psalm 23:6 (The Message)

Your beauty and love chase after me

every day of my life.

I'm back home in the house of God

for the rest of my life.

What an amazing service at Eastlake Community Church tonight God. I thank you for the shift in the service, as the message that was planned was postponed until next week. As you know, Eastlake had a tailgate party for the Seahawks game. It was all over the news, and so Pastor Meeks wanted to talk about the two camps. "Oh, that's the church that parties," or the other camp, "Oh, that's the church that doesn't follow the rules."

Your message was loud and clear to me. He said that Jesus turned water into wine. I knew that already. I've heard it a million times. Why there are churches that don't believe in drinking is beyond me. But Pastor Meeks said, why do you think he turned water into wine? His mother came to him, as only she could, and asked him what to do. So Jesus, being Jesus, turned 150 gallons of water to wine, to "keep the party going." Jesus likes to party. Jesus had an open bar! I loved that he said that, because "institutionalized religion" in my experience has never talked like that.

Pastor Meeks asked, "Dude, why don't more people go to church? Well, it's because it's like a funeral every week!" I couldn't agree more, God. But that's not been my experience the two times I have been to Eastlake. This is about 1,500 miles away from my home.

He asked, why would the news care if we partied? The Bible doesn't say, "Thou shall not ferment barley." God, what a way you have with Pastor Meeks to allow him to be real with his congregation. No wonder they have grown so fast in just six years.

God is forgiveness, grace, mercy, hope—this is the message we should be spreading.

Pastor Meeks talked about how people who were nothing like Jesus liked Jesus. It was institutions that didn't like him. A tailgate party at the church? Seriously?

People loved it. They had over 2,000 people attend to celebrate. Why not be known as the church that likes to party, to celebrate, and to fellowship? Does it have to be boring? Where is this church in Texas God?

Institutions thought Jesus was a drunk and a glutton.

Jesus was celebration, festival, and joy.

Jesus is resurrection, life, power, not funeral or death.

This life matters, kind words, acts, and people are affected around the world due to our kind acts and words. It's the ripple effect.

If you are disconnected and bored, that means you are not connected with God; if you are connected, celebrate and party and share your joy.

This message is the message that I have been seeking, Eastlake is truly the church for the rest of us. After reading *The Shack*, this message totally resonated with me. It's about our relationship with you, God, not about the institution or man's will, and I thank you for speaking to me, through the pastor.

What a glorious night and a celebration. You totally rock.

So I've been to church two times since believing in you again, both times at Eastlake with Carolyn, and once with Brett in attendance. Thank you, God, for bringing them into my life and allowing me to see that religion can be hip, cool, and not judgmental. I praise you, God, for your grace, mercy, love, and beauty.

> Psalm 100:5 (The Message)
>
> For God is sheer beauty,
>
> all-generous in love,
>
> loyal always and ever.

In your name, I pray with praise,

Authentic, Humble, Surrendered, and Spiritual

S. Michael Edwards

Sunday, January 16, 2011

Happy Birthday Brent | Prayer 39

God, what an awesome day with Brent and Pat Brooks. They opened their homes to me and their family and allowed us to share in Brent's birthday. They asked me to bless the meal, which I did. I am still not quite comfortable praying in public, but I am taking all the opportunities to make myself get over that fear.

After church tonight at Eastlake Community Church, I was like, "Wow, that's a cool conversation with God." Why can't I do that out loud? But I can totally do it when I'm blogging my prayers.

I know I'll get there, but thank you for the opportunity to stretch and to fellowship with my amazing friends and their family. Thank you for bringing them into my life.

It was really weird to have my aunt, to whom I rarely speak, write to me today and tell me that her friend knows Pat Brooks! What a small world. I love how you are introducing me to people who know people I know.

Turns out that friends of Pat and Brent's were at his party, and they know the guy (or the company) that we're meeting with…the philanthropist. It could turn out that Laura's uncle is part of what we're looking for. Maybe that's why I was there, I don't know yet. But what another amazing serendipitous moment (or God Wink) if it turns out that I met the niece of the philanthropist's business and she asked, "How can I help you with your vision?"

I told her I would get back to her after our meeting, because God, I don't know what you have in store for Brett and me at that meeting.

I pray you give us the wisdom, as you always have, to have the right answers to how we can spread your word, and be of contribution and service. It's going to be an amazing meeting, and I thank you for giving Brett the connections and will to make this meeting with Jeff Ericson happen.

I love you, God, more now than ever. Your grace and beauty are simply awe-inspiring.

With all my love,

Authentic, Humble, Surrendered, and Spiritual

S. Michael Edwards

Sunday, January 16, 2011

Get Home Already Brett | Prayer 40
So Brett's flight is delayed; maybe that is your plan God. I just pray that you get him home safely. I can't wait to hear about his trip and for him to be back with his

amazing wife Carolyn. I thank you for bringing them into my life, and I am so grateful that they allow me into their home, as a brother and friend.

I am truly blessed, and I thank Carolyn's brother Matthew for introducing me to these amazing people. Have I told you how grateful I am that I met Matthew Courtright? So many pieces to the puzzle to bring us all together, and Matthew was a piece of that puzzle.

I pray that you will watch over Brett and Matthew and surround them with your love and wisdom. Two amazing men that I respect.

I pray that you watch over Carolyn, and surround her with peace and your grace.

In your name,

Authentic, Humble, Surrendered, and Spiritual

S. Michael Edwards

Monday, January 17, 2011

I've Got a Friend in You | Prayer #41

Hey God, it's me. Thank you for the safe travels home of my buddy and friend and brother in Christ, Brett. It's so energizing to be with him. I am so grateful each and every day for the greatness you have given him and the strength and leadership he steps into each day.

God, you are also speaking to me, and contrary to what others might think, it's not just voices in my head. These daily Devotional Roulettes tell me otherwise. Today's Title, "The Friend"—I think it's not a coincidence, nor serendipity, that as I wake up in my friends Brett and Carolyn's house, having just read *The Shack*, where William P. Young talks about how "I am with you, inside of you"—that you would have me open the devotional to the page titled "The Friend"—the verse, is what caught me off guard.

John 14:15–17

"If you love me, show it by doing what I've told you. I will talk to the Father, and he'll provide you another Friend so that you will always have someone with you. This Friend is in the Spirit of Truth. The godless world can't take him in because it doesn't have eyes to see him, doesn't know what to look for. But you know him already because he has been staying with you, and will even be in you!"

God, I just ask that the Holy Spirit guide me today. That in what I say, think, do, and where I go…that my Friend, is always inside me and guiding me. Today I listened to this song, "Holy Spirit," by Nate Sallie. Awesome lyrics.

Your amazing, my friend, and I'm blessed to have you in my life.

Authentic, Humble, Surrendered, and Spiritual

S. Michael Edwards

Monday, January 17, 2011

Kingdom and the King | Prayer #42

God, when I first attended Eastlake Community Church, I was so moved by their "realness"—they lack of "institution" and their music. As you know, God, I rarely sang in church as a child or young adult. If I did it was out of compliance.

Then I bought four CDs of Eastlake's band, and have listened to them religiously. (Sorry, pun intended.)

It was last night that when the music started that I knew I knew this song. I had heard it fourteen times before, at least. With words on the screen, I was moved to sing along. What glory and grace and an amazing song, and in it, the lyrics "For His glory we will sing."

And sing I did…and praise, I did, and in gratitude, I thank you for being my Father, my guardian, my friend. I was moved by "Kingdom and a King," by Robbie Seay Band.

Authentic, Humble, Surrendered, and Spiritual

S. Michael Edwards

Monday, January 17, 2011

Who Is Jesus? | Prayer #43

God, thank you for inspiring my friend to send me the You Tube video of the young man who explains who Jesus is…God, you have blessed this child, and blessed me through him. Simply awesome.

Authentic, Humble, Surrendered, and Spiritual

S. Michael Edwards

Monday, January 17, 2011

Ooops. Skipped a Prayer | Prayer #44

God,

Please forgive me, I totally stepped into fear and didn't bless the meal for lunch today. I don't know what got into me. I can't claim I "forgot"—I just simply didn't step into my beingness and ask if we could bless the meal.

It was a great meal, with Adam and Carolyn, and I thank you for the opportunity to meet Adam in person. I pray you will forgive me for not praying over the meal. I'm not sure if that is a ritual that you care about, if our conversations are enough, or if you really want both. I do feel you are with me, and yet, I chose to not thank you for the blessings in front of my friends.

I do hope you bless that amazing meal to my body, and I thank you for the abundance you have given me and my family.

Humbly yours,

Authentic, Humble, Surrendered, and Spiritual

S. Michael Edwards

Monday, January 17, 2011

Do You Like Prayer Spam, God? | Prayer #45

God, I was just wondering if you liked spam in the form of a prayer. I got one today and rather enjoyed it. I read it and liked it—but it wasn't my prayer from my heart. I wonder if that matters. Prayers from the heart vs. those that are rehearsed or scripted?

You can let me know when you get a chance.

Dear Lord, I thank you for this day,

I thank you for my being able to see

and to hear this morning.

I'm blessed because you are

a forgiving God and

an understanding God.

You have done so much for me

and you keep on blessing me.

Forgive me this day for everything

I have done, said, or thought

that was not pleasing to you.

I ask now for your forgiveness.

Please keep me safe

from all danger and harm.

Help me to start this day

with a new attitude and plenty of gratitude.

Let me make the best of each and every day

to clear my mind so that I can hear from you.

Please broaden my mind

that I can accept all things.

Let me not whine and whimper

over things I have no control over.

And give me the best response

when I'm pushed beyond my limits.

I know that when I can't pray,

You listen to my heart.

Continue to use me to do your will.

Continue to bless me that I may be

a blessing to others...

Keep me strong that I may help the weak...

Keep me uplifted that I may have

words of encouragement for others.

I pray for those who are lost

and can't find their way.

I pray for those who are misjudged

and misunderstood.

I pray for those who

don't know you intimately.

I pray for who that will delete this

without sharing it with others

I pray for those who don't believe.

But I thank you that I believe

that God changes people and

God changes things.

I pray for all my sisters and brothers.

For each and every family member

in their households.

I pray for peace, love, and joy

in their homes; that they are out of debt

and all their needs are met.

I pray that every eye that reads this

knows there is no problem, circumstance,

or situation greater than God.

Every battle is in your hands for you to fight.

I pray that these words be received

into the hearts of every eye that sees it

in Jesus' name. Amen!

Authentic, Humble, Surrendered, and Spiritual

S. Michael Edwards

Monday, January 17, 2011

I Can Only Imagine | Prayer #46

God, The song *I Can Only Imagine* totally touched my heart.

"I can only imagine, when the day will come, when all I'll do is to worship you"…
While I am not there yet God, where it's all I can do, I am making some amazing
strides in connecting with you as one.

Thank you for giving the gift of song to Wynonna, and for helping her touch my
heart in such an amazing way. I give you the glory, God…and praise you as you
bless me in all that you have given me. Another great song today, that the lyrics
speak loud and clear. I can only imagine.

Tuesday, January 18, 2011

Devotional Roulette | Prayer #47

Morning God,

I think I've decided that my favorite part of my morning is no longer biscuits and
gravy, but my devotional to you. I look forward to it each day, knowing that you are
with me and that we'll be talking often.

I am so excited for this day ahead, whatever it is you have in store for Brett and me,
as we meet this afternoon with Jeff Ericson, our new philanthropist friend.

I pray that your will be done, that we be filled with wisdom and ideas to help bring
our visions together as one.

Now for the daily devotional:

2 Corinthians 9:8–15

"God can pour on the blessings in astonishing ways so that you're ready for
anything and everything, more than just ready to do what needs to be done.
As one psalmist puts it,

He throws caution to the winds,

giving to the needy in reckless abandon

His right-living, right-giving ways

never run out, never wear out

"This most generous God who gives seed to the farmer that becomes bread for your meals is more than extravagant with you. He gives you something you can then give away, which grows into full-formed lives, robust in God, wealthy in every way, so that you can be generous in every way, producing with us great praise to God.

"Carrying out this social relief work involves far more than helping meet the bare needs of poor Christians. It also produces abundant and bountiful thanks-givings to God. This relief offering is a prod to live at your very best, showing your gratitude to God by being openly obedient to the plain meaning of the Message of Christ. You show your gratitude through your generous offerings to your needy brothers and sisters, and really toward everyone. Meanwhile, moved by the extravagance of God in your lives, they'll respond by praying for you in passionate intercession for whatever you need. Thank God for this gift, His gift. No language can praise it enough!"

God, thank you for your blessings in my life and most importantly for the vision to work with others to support a common goal of giving away $1 billion dollars over the next year. How appropriate that on the day we are to meet with a major philan-thropist, you provide me with this reminder about how important it is to carry out social relief work. Thanks for reinforcing my vision, and I pray that others will also see the vision and support it as well!

As I get more information on this charity, and add it to the arsenal of charities I sup-port, I pray that as many people as I touch will do the same to give back. It's only through you and your generous gifts that we have anything, and so with gratitude I give back in a life of service and contribution.

Love in prayer, God,

Authentic, Humble, Surrendered, and Spiritual

S. Michael Edwards

Tuesday, January 18, 2011

This Little Light of Mind | Prayer #48
God,

I just want to thank you for creating in me a most unique man. I carry your light, and I pray that you fill me with courage to be the authentic man that I am. I pray to you, God, that I let others see in me the glory that is you. May my life serve as an example to others, and may they come to know you through me.

May my journey be an inspiration to many and a calling to arms for the masses. That we are here to glorify you and to love one another!

I pray these things, in your name,

Authentic, Humble, Surrendered, and Spiritual

S. Michael Edwards

Tuesday, January 18, 2011

It's Nearly Time to Prepare | Prayer #49
God,

We had a most amazing call last night for Sam Camp. We're preparing our fields for the students who will arrive before they know it. May you continue to watch over the leaders of this Sam Camp, ensuring they have their fields ready to receive your blessings. I pray that each of my peers and seniors and facilitators watch over each other and provide accountability, honesty, integrity, and commitment to help each other and the entire Sam Camp team achieve things bigger than they ever thought possible.

I pray these things, knowing that your plan is bigger and greater than anything we could ever know. Your plan for each of us will be revealed in due time. It's exciting, God. It's exciting to see the growth of my peers, and I am looking forward to seeing the growth of those around me and the world as our students go out and make shifts.

We love the saying "Shift Happens." To put it into context, miracles do occur.

Yeah Yeah,

Authentic, Humble, Surrendered, and Spiritual Michael

Tuesday, January 18, 2011

Compliance or Kindred Spirits | Prayer #50

God,

I wonder how many people pray out of compliance and not because they want to really know you? Not out of judgment, but out of curiosity. I had dog-eared a page in *The Shack,* and the passage that spoke to me was about going and talking to God out of obligation vs. talking to God because you want to. The part that was so powerful for me was that the author said that if you go out of obligation, "You won't get any points

My takeaway from that was that it must be authentic and real. When you throw those rituals in and do it because you have to, that is not what it's all about. It's about connecting and loving and being love. It's about being open and honest.

I am seeing that in my daily life with you now, God. I am sharing my innermost thoughts, which you already know and knew well before I had them. But I am free to make choices, and your Son died on the cross for me. So how can I glorify you and praise you for such an amazing sacrifice?

It's truly *The Ultimate Gift*, a movie I will watch this week, written by Jim Stovall. Jim Stovall is amazing, and I met him on a plane on the way to Staff Heart of the Samurai 31. So it's perfect that we watch that movie this week, to prepare for our students who are getting ready to start Sam Camp 21, many of whom came from Heart 31 and heard Jim Stovall speak.

He sat on the plane next to me, and I reached over and introduced myself to him. His story is truly inspirational, his motivational speaking is inspiring, and he continues to impress me with all he does in this world. Lord, I am blessed that you keep creating the space for me to make choices to meet people like Jim Stovall. I have much to learn from them, and your plan is perfect.

I will talk to you later, God,

Authentic, Humble, Surrendered, and Spiritual

S. Michael Edwards

Wednesday, January 19, 2011

God, I Love Coffee | Prayer #51

God,

Thank you so much for an amazing meeting yesterday. Brett and I learned so much about AGROS International, and it fits in with our vision like pieces to a larger puzzle, but of course you knew that, which is why you created the space for Brett to get us the meeting with an amazing philanthropist and business man, Jeff Ericson who gave us over four-and-a-half hours of his time—his idea.

He is in the coffee business, and my brain is full of ideas on how we can help him and AGROS. God, please help Brett and I distill these ideas and with clarity understand the best possible way to move forward with this kind and God-loving man.

What a blessing it was to learn all Jeff Ericson had to share, to pray over a meal, to get a tour of his coffee roasting plant, Camano Island Coffee Roasters, and to hear about his vision on sustainability and charities (he's not a fan), and you, dear God.

I think I can mark 1.18.2011 down as a day that my life changed. I see huge things happening as a result of being introduced to this man, who is so well-connected, so full of ideas, and so generous. Brett and I couldn't stop talking about all the possibilities and it became clear to us both that this meeting was divine intervention. Thank you!

It's a big day for me, and I'm behind. I pray that you allow me to get clarity and caught up on all things, and that I glorify you in all I do today.

In your name, I pray,

Authentic, Humble, Surrendered, and Spiritual

S. Michael Edwards

Wednesday, January 19, 2011

Devotional Roulette | Prayer #52

God, you crack me up. Title of today's daily devotional is, "Holding Everything Together." I just prayed that I get caught up, as I'm behind, and this is the devotional I read today.

Cha

Hebrews 1:3

This Son perfectly mirrors God, and is stamped with God's nature. He holds everything together by what he says—powerful words!

God, I strive to mirror your son, and thus you. I honor you, glorify your name, and am grateful for all that you have given me. I am totally blessed in you and know that I too can hold everything together with what I say, as I am made in your likeness.

In your name,

Authentic, Humble, Surrendered, and Spiritual

S. Michael Edwards

Wednesday, January 19, 2011

Cab Ride | Prayer #53

God,

What an amazing story my friend Susan sent me. It reminds me that life is precious and that the little things matter. The acts of kindness matter and make a difference. I thank you for the message, and I appreciate the reminder that in doing these acts of kindness daily, we can be more like you.

For my friends who haven't read the story of "The Cab Ride," author unknown, I've copied it below.

I arrived at the address and honked the horn. After waiting a few minutes I walked to the door and knocked. "Just a minute," answered a frail, elderly voice. I could hear something being dragged across the floor.

After a long pause, the door opened. A small woman in her nineties stood before me. She was wearing a print dress and a pillbox hat with a veil pinned on it, like somebody out of a 1940s movie.

By her side was a small nylon suitcase. The apartment looked as if no one had lived in it for years. All the furniture was covered with sheets.

There were no clocks on the walls, no knickknacks or utensils on the counters. In the corner was a cardboard box filled with photos and glassware.

"Would you carry my bag out to the car?" she said. I took the suitcase to the cab, then returned to assist the woman.

She took my arm, and we walked slowly toward the curb.

She kept thanking me for my kindness. "It's nothing," I told her. "I just try to treat my passengers the way I would want my mother to be treated."

"Oh, you're such a good boy," she said. When we got in the cab, she gave me an address and then asked, "Could you drive through downtown?"

"It's not the shortest way," I answered quickly.

"Oh, I don't mind," she said. "I'm in no hurry. I'm on my way to a hospice."

I looked in the rear-view mirror. Her eyes were glistening. "I don't have any family left,' she continued in a soft voice. "The doctor says I don't have very long." I quietly reached over and shut off the meter.

"What route would you like me to take?" I asked.

For the next two hours, we drove through the city. She showed me the building where she had once worked as an elevator operator.

We drove through the neighborhood where she and her husband had lived when they were newlyweds. She had me pull up in front of a furniture warehouse that had once been a ballroom where she had gone dancing as a girl.

Sometimes she'd ask me to slow in front of a particular building or corner and would sit staring into the darkness, saying nothing.

As the first hint of sun was creasing the horizon, she suddenly said, "I'm tired. Let's go now."

We drove in silence to the address she had given me. It was a low building, like a small convalescent home, with a driveway that passed under a portico.

Two orderlies came out to the cab as soon as we pulled up. They were solicitous and intent, watching her every move. They must have been expecting her.

I opened the trunk and took the small suitcase to the door. The woman was already seated in a wheelchair.

"How much do I owe you?" she asked, reaching into her purse.

"Nothing," I said.

"You have to make a living," she answered.

"There are other passengers," I responded.

Almost without thinking, I bent and gave her a hug. She held onto me tightly.

"You gave an old woman a little moment of joy," she said. "Thank you."

I squeezed her hand, and then walked into the dim morning light.. Behind me, a door shut. It was the sound of the closing of a life.

I didn't pick up any more passengers that shift. I drove aimlessly, lost in thought. For the rest of that day, I could hardly talk. What if that woman had gotten an angry driver, or one who was impatient to end his shift?

What if I had refused to take the run, or had honked once, then driven away?

On a quick review, I don't think that I have done anything more important in my life.

We're conditioned to think that our lives revolve around great moments.

But great moments often catch us unaware—beautifully wrapped in what others may consider a small one.

Wednesday, January 19, 2011

No Speeding Tickets, Please | Prayer #54

Hey God,

I'm packing up and getting ready to leave Bothell for Vancouver, Washington, and I pray you will keep me safe and focused on obeying the laws and the speed limit as it changes every time I blink. I'd rather not give the State of Washington any more of my money. They have nice roads and all, but I think my money is better spent elsewhere. :)

So as I travel this road, I'll be thinking about you and how I can make a difference in this world. I'll be listening if you have any wisdom to provide on my journey…both the drive and my journey in life.

Love you, God,

Authentic, Humble, Surrendered, and Spiritual

S. Michael Edwards

Wednesday, January 19, 2011

Safely Home to Mom and Dad's | Prayer #55

God,

Thank you so much for the conversations we had on the way home from Bothell to Vancouver. I arrived safe and sound, and had great company with you and no radio or other distractions for three hours. I enjoyed just "being with" you—my head was focused on driving and yet, I was still able to talk to you about what you want me to do. While I don't have a clear picture, I have some amazing ideas…so thanks for that!

I am excited for Sam Camp to start. We get to start calling the students next week to get to know them. I pray that we rock this camp out and that "Shift Happens."

Thank you, God, for the blessings in my life, and for "being with" me on my journey.

Authentic, Humble, Surrendered, and Spiritual

S. Michael Edwards

Wednesday, January 19, 2011

Support For Friend | Prayer #56
God,

A dear friend is having difficulty right now, and I pray that you will lift him up and show him the light. Lead his heart and fill him with possibilities. I pray that you will allow him to see the greatness in himself that you have given him and that others see in him. I pray that he makes the decision to move forward in his life, rather than backward.

In your name, God, I pray,

Authentic, Humble, Surrendered, and Spiritual

S. Michael Edwards

Wednesday, January 19, 2011

She Will Be Missed | Prayer #57
God,

Amazing call tonight, and we thank you for your presence. Unfortunately, we lost a member today, and she will be dearly missed. She was a true blessing in my life and the lives of our group. I pray that you will fill her and heal her and surround her with love and blessings. She is in my thoughts, and I know that you are taking care of her and her family.

God, may you bless her and let her know how impactful she's been in all she has done to help me grow.

Authentic, Humble, Surrendered, and Spiritual

S. Michael Edwards

Wednesday, January 19, 2011

Master Mind Brandt | Prayer #58

Hi God,

It's me again, I am praying to you on behalf of the requests that Nelson Brandt has put out there for us to hold the intention, and for me that means a discussion with you. His requests follow:

> *I am grateful that on or before 18 January 2011 that I have the knowledge and wisdom to effectively serve as the department head of the aviation engineering department at USCG Air Station Atlantic City.*

> *I am grateful that on or before seven p.m. on 23 January 2011 God provides me with the ability to assist Cooper Brandt (my eight-year-old son) with the "focus" to complete his Pinewood Derby project (from Cub Scouts).*

> *I gratefully request that on or before 31 January 2011, God would enable healing to occur in the aftermath of the tragedy in Tucson, Arizona.*

Father, I know that Nelson has what it takes to be an effective department head, and I pray that you will continue to bless him with his leadership and wisdom as he serves the USCG. I pray that you provide him the wisdom and ability to help his son Cooper focus so he can complete his Cub Scouts project. (Remember when I did mine God? How cool was that?) I also honor and support his requests that the nation be healed this month in the aftermath of the tragedy in Tucson, Arizona.

Father, I honor and support all his requests and pray that you will bless him in his requests as well.

Authentic, Humble, Surrendered, and Spiritual

S. Michael Edwards

Wednesday, January 19, 2011

Master Mind Lesha Kitts | Prayer #59

Dear Father in Heaven, my dear friend Lesha Kitts has the following requests, and I honor and support them and pray that you will honor her requests as well. As you know, we are the Warriors of Kind Noble Acts (WONKA)

Wonkas,

With the love, support and integrity of this Master Mind team, and the knowledge that where ever I am…God is, I graciously make the following requests.

That on or before January 31, 2011, I have completed 2010 accounting for the orchard.

That on or before March 15, 2011, Grow Green is organic certified.

That by July 4, 2011, I have met Eva Mozes Kor.

I also pray that you will give Lesha the wisdom and guidance on her journey and discovery for her vision to create sustainable communities, however that may look. She has a gentle heart and a giving spirit, and I ask that you surround her with love, wisdom, and the ability to step into vulnerability and share her gratitude with others that may or may not know how grateful she is for the impact they have had on her life.

Amen,

Authentic, Humble, Surrendered, and Spiritual

S. Michael Edwards

Wednesday, January 19, 2011

Master Mind Karen Sizelove | Prayer #60
Father in Heaven,

I pray that you honor and support Karen on her journey to abundance and prosperity and happiness and that you honor and support her requests which are pasted below:

Personal: With complete faith and trust in God, who is all love, and with the love and support of my Master Mind partners, I give thanks and ask that I have sold 100 or more Dove Valentine Dessert Truffle Collections on or before January 31, 2011.

Professional: With complete faith and trust in God, who is all love, and with the love and support of my Master Mind partners, I give thanks and ask that I have donated $500 or more to Crystal Peaks Youth Ranch, (CPYR) (rescues horses, mentors children, brings hope to families and empowers ministry) from the sales of my Dove Chocolate Discoveries Valentine Fundraiser.

Esoteric: With complete faith and trust in the abundant, all-loving God and with the love and support of my Master Mind partners, I give thanks and I ask that Crystal Peaks Youth Ranch (CPYR) and all ranches inspired by CPYR experience daily abundance in health, finances, love and joy for themselves and their loved ones throughout 2011 and thereafter.

In your name, I pray these things,

Authentic, Humble, Surrendered, and Spiritual

S. Michael Edwards

Thursday, January 20, 2011

Midnight Cry | Prayer #61
God,

I thank you so much for the time I had with my mom today. What a blessing she is in my life. How amazing she is, and what a great morning I have shared with her.

She wanted me to hear a cassette tape. Yep, that's right, she still owns a cassette tape. In fact, she said she had thrown most of them out, but kept this one that had "Midnight Cry" on it, because it was so special for her.

We listened to the song together, and while I couldn't understand the words, she recited them to me as the singer sang the words. I went and found the lyrics and this version by Michael English, and Mom told me that when she and Dad would listen to this song, they would cry when the singer sang the lyrics, "Oh, I can almost see the Father as He says, 'Son, go get my children.'"

It was very touching, and later we laughed when she told me that she has, on many occasions, said, "I will specifically see you on the other side. But you gotta be there, in order for me to find you!"

Lord, I thank you for my parents not giving up on me, and so wanting me to come back into your arms.

My mom said, "I always wanted it for you so much, but I never envisioned what it would look like but to see it. It is so amazing, so happy, talking to him, the joy, singing praise music, spending time with him, and it's beyond my wildest dreams to see you so in love with Jesus. Joy unspeakable. For you to take my hand at the restaurant last night and bless our food out loud was like, 'wow.' It's a privilege to pray, so if someone asked me to pray, I would be honored to."

Lord, I am so blessed and thank you so much for my mom and dad. What a gift I have in them and in you.

I rocked out to Midnight Cry with the Brooklyn Tabernacle Choir and Michael English.

I'm going home to Texas today...I pray you will be with me on my journey, as you always are, and that you provide for safe travels and that I glorify you in my actions and words.

Amen.

Authentic, Humble, Surrendered, and Spiritual

S. Michael Edwards

1 comments:

Linda Edwards said...

Talk about quickly changed...the changes we see in you look good on you. I love you so much and am so proud of the godly man you have become. I would love to just sit back and watch you change the world and smile proudly, but you challenge me to dream bigger, too.

Thank you Father God for not giving up on Michael. Thank you for your faithfulness and amazing grace. Thank you for filling Michael with a joy that comes from you and flows out to everyone he comes in contact with. I pray in agreement with Michael for safe travels home today and then off to San Antonio tomorrow. May your angels go before him, with him and after him. In Jesus' name I pray, Amen.

Thursday, January 20, 2011

Please Place Your Seats | Prayer #62

Lord,

I thank you for in-flight WIFI! I am amazed at the technology that has been created by such brilliant minds. I am actually in the air now, and praying much closer to you than when I am on the ground, how cool is that? Well, I assume you are up here, but maybe that is my own sunglasses thinking that you are up here, when in fact you are always with me, no matter where. Hmmmm, I guess that is something I could look up. What is my idea of where you are…is it heaven on earth, or is it celestial? I don't know. Don't need to know I guess.

Thank you for the opportunity to see my dad and give him a hug as we had about twenty minutes in the airport to visit while he landed and before I had to go through security and board the plane. It's always great to see my dad, and give him a big ol' hug. He told me how incredibly proud he is of me, and that sure does feel good.

I sought my dad's approval for years as a child and early adult, and now that I have it, it fills my heart with joy.

Thank you, God, for such amazing parents, who love me unconditionally, provide fuel to my fire and encourage me to make a difference in the world.

That's what I'm doing, will continue to do, and if you are willing, one person at a time, change the world and glorify you along the way.

In your name, these things I pray to you,

Authentic, Humble, Surrendered, and Spiritual

S. Michael Edwards

Thursday, January 20, 2011

New Client with Big Wallet | Prayer #63

So I'm playing catch up, God. It's not that we haven't talked at all today, but I haven't had the opportunity to document our conversations.

I just wanted to say thanks for the amazing call from a prospect today. I was referred to him by another client, which is always a great feeling, and I have been nurturing the relationship for about two months. He called me today, and we had a great discussion about their needs. It's a $4.5 million account to start, but could be even bigger based on the opportunities I saw. He talked like it was a done deal, they just have to get it past the CEO for his approval. God, I pray that you will provide wisdom to the CEO to let them focus on what they do best, and let our company focus on what we do best, which is Internet advertising.

I pray that we'll know in the next couple of weeks if we get this new client, and I thank you for the abundance you are sending our way. I feel like the closer I get to you, the more you are rewarding me. Maybe it's just that I am changing for the better, and my beingness is shifting and that is helping. Either way, I'll take what you are dishing up, and with gratitude I thank you.

In your name,

Authentic, Humble, Surrendered, Spiritual

S. Michael Edwards

Thursday, January 20, 2011

Payday and Pay Raise | Prayer #64

God, today was payday, and I've been told my 50 percent pay raise showed up. While I haven't seen proof, I'll trust that they did the right thing and held their commitment even though we don't have a signed employment agreement.

It was a very interesting conversation with Ed this morning, as he was a little irritated, but I thank you for surrounding me with love and serenity and for allowing me to step into a calm, responsive and gentle being. We were able to work things out, and I pray that you continue to fill my heart and soul with serenity as I surrender to you.

Thanks for doing that today, it was a potential road block to our future, as I had no idea if "this time" I would actually get what was promised. I'll see when I get home and ask for a copy of the deposit slip.

Passionately,

Authentic, Humble, Surrendered, and Spiritual

S. Michael Edwards

Thursday, January 20, 2011

San Antonio | Prayer #65

Lord,

I pray that you will provide for safe travels to San Antonio tomorrow as I attend the Klemmer Personal Mastery with my friends. I ask for you to watch over them, giving them calm and allowing them to get over their fear of the unknown and step into possibilities for the future.

These are two amazing women in their own right, and I see this as being a turning point in each of their lives. I pray you watch over them, guide them, and allow them to let go and play full out, seeing and finding value in all that they experience.

I am also excited because it's my first experience to staff a Personal Mastery. I was pretty much shut down, as you know, the last time I went, walking out, and wanting to leave. Whoa, am I glad I didn't. My life would not be the same. So to experience this class again, with a new set of values, and a whole new perspective on life is exciting for me. It'll be like it's my "first time" (again).

I can't wait to see what's in store for me and the students, and pray that you watch over us all and allow the facilitator (an amazing man in his own right) to rock some worlds and change hearts...he certainly has done that to mine!

We leave at nine a.m. CT, but you knew that, just asking that I don't get another ticket in my haste to change the world. :) LOL. It's going to be a long weekend, but the payoff is priceless.

Love you, Lord,

Authentic, Humble, Surrendered, and Spiritual

S. Michael Edwards

1 comments:

Linda Edwards said...

Michael, I know you're really busy this weekend...staffing your first PM and all. I've got your back. Many prayers are going up for everyone involved. May there be ah-ha's and forward movement for everyone. May God's presence be felt and embraced. Thank you, Father, for the abundance of energy you supply. Thank you for everyone in the class moving forward (however that looks). Thank you for safe travels home with your angels protection. I love you, Lord, and lift this day up to you. Amen.

Tuesday, January 25, 2011

Personal Mastery | Prayer #66

God,

Thank you for the prayer army and an amazing experience in San Antonio. I realize that it wasn't the right time for two of my friends to go, but that time will come and it will be perfect when they do. The two who did commit to going played full out and were so grateful it was amazing.

I thank you for answering the prayers of the army that was praying for my friends who went and the other students in the room, including me. It was like a whole new class for me. Even though nothing has changed with the class, so much has changed with me in almost three years since I first went.

I teased Brian Miller about the class, telling him how much I liked the newer version better...fully knowing that it was me who was open and not resisting what he was sharing.

It was a perfect time for me to attend the class and get familiar with the foundation of all things that Brian Klemmer teaches and writes about.

God, I thank you for the amazing people you have put in my life, and I am grateful for the experiences we were able to share together this past weekend.

In your name I pray,

Authentic, Humble, Surrendered, and Spiritual

S. Michael Edwards

Tuesday, January 25, 2011

Alligators up to My Neck | Prayer #67
Oh God,

I feel like I have alligators up to my neck. I am praying to you, knowing that you are within me and that I can do it with your help. I have been choosing to say "yes" to so many things, and not honoring myself by choosing to say "no" when it comes to my goals and needs. I pray for strength to be able to say "no" and to choose to stay focused.

I know now, that if you are within me, and I say, "I can't," that I am saying that "You can't." Can't is not a word in my vocabulary. I also know that saying "no" is far different than "can't."

Lord, please lift me up as my life starts speeding up. I pray for support, drive, passion, energy, and possibilities.

In your name, I pray these things,

Authentic, Humble, Surrendered, and Spiritual

S. Michael Edwards

Tuesday, January 25, 2011

Meal Prayers | Prayer #68
God,

It's so funny, I'm sure, that I haven't documented any meal prayers. When I started this journey, I was not going to include meal prayers, because those are just a given, and then Craig asked me why, and we agreed I wasn't just blessing the meal, so we bumped up the number of prayers I would do, and here it is, Prayer #68, and I haven't documented a single meal prayer.

Lord, you know I have been praying for meals. I just haven't documented them. I prayed for every meal I had while I was in San Antonio, yet they were silent and between you and I.

I haven't gone back to my computer to pray for a meal after the fact, but I will pray for a meal today ahead of schedule.

Lord, I have a meeting with a very important client today. We talked about them raising their budget. I told the chief marketing officer that if she found any quarters in the sofa, we could spend it and generate more revenue for her company. Today we are going to lunch, and I pray that she raises her budget. That she "found some quarters" metaphorically speaking of course. Maybe a quarter is 25 percent more? Who knows, but I pray she sees the value and raises the budget.

God, in addition to that, please bless the meal we have together. We are of different faiths and I'll be introducing them to the "new guy" today, who is an atheist. I don't know how you feel about me praying for the meal ahead of time, but I want to honor my client as I know that her faith believes in a different kind of prayer than mine.

Could be interesting to ask her to bless the meal. I'm not sure how that would go over either. So God, I am asking the blessing early, in your name, I pray,

Amen

Authentic, Humble, Surrendered, and Spiritual

S. Michael Edwards

Tuesday, January 25, 2011

Quarters In The Sofa | Prayer #69
God,

Thanks so much for answering my prayer about my client spending more money (aka, finding quarters in the sofa)! She raised her budget 21 percent (not quite a quarter, but I'm thrilled). Then I had another client meeting, and they doubled their budget.

I am so grateful for the abundance you are providing. The lunch was amazing and I prayed for the food and the connection with our client. We had a great discussion, and I love working with them!

Thank you, God!

Authentic, Humble, Surrendered, and Spiritual

S. Michael Edwards

Tuesday, January 25, 2011

A Calm Washed over Me | Prayer #70
Hey God,

Thanks so much for an amazing day. I really felt your calming energy wash over me today, and it was powerful. I am so grateful for the conversation I had with Ed, who also seemed so serene about our contract discussion. It was totally amazing that he was coming from a place of serenity. I ask that we get the contract and settlement signed by 31 January 2011. He's had it for a while, but didn't have the money to pay the attorney to review the contract. I just ask, God, that we are able to knock this contract out of the way and move forward with a civil co-existence in work and home.

I pray God, that we find a buyer for our house, too. We've had great interest, but no offers yet. While I don't really want to leave the house, I know it's for the best. I don't know where I'll move when it sells, but I surrender to you, that you know, and that it's your timing, not mine.

Thank you, God, for your gracious generosity and love. What a blessing, and the serenity is priceless!

Amen.

Passionately,

Authentic, Humble, Surrendered, and Spiritual

S. Michael Edwards

Tuesday, January 25, 2011

Devotional Roulette | Prayer #71
God, your sense of humor makes me LOL. I just opened up my daily devotional, randomly, and it was 2 Timothy 2:22–26

"Run away from infantile indulgence. Run after mature righteousness—faith, love, peacejoining those who are in honest and serious prayer before God. Refuse to get involved in inane discussions; they always end up in fights. God's servant must not be argumentative, but a gentle listener and a teacher who keeps cool, working firmly but patiently with those who refuse to obey. You never know how or when God might sober them up with a change of heart and a yearning to the truth, enabling them to escape the Devil's trap, where they are caught and held captive, forced to run his errands."

How perfect is that? I just got through praying about the amazing serenity in Ed and the wave of calmness in me, and then this is my devotional roulette! You amaze me, God. I am so grateful for faith, love, and peace. Ed and I would almost always have arguments, not able to communicate in a professional or loving manner, until I went to Klemmer and Associates' training.

I am so thankful and grateful for your grace and amazed at how you are answering my prayers. Thank you, God, you are awesome!

In your name, I pray,

Amen.

Authentic, Humble, Surrendered, and Spiritual

S. Michael Edwards

Tuesday, January 25, 2011

Legacy | Prayer #72

The Ultimate Gift was truly an inspirational movie, by an inspirational writer. God, I thank you for introducing me to Jim Stoval, on my flight to Heart of the Samurai in October. I sat across from him in First Class, stepped outside my comfort zone, and said hello. We had a great conversation. I had heard him speak at my first Heart of the Samurai experience in April 2010, but I had not seen the movie based on his book. It is an amazing movie.

Thank you for introducing me to the movie and to Jim Stovall. He is truly inspirational, and I enjoyed talking to him about his new movie, starring Lou Gossett Jr., titled *The Lamp*.

The song at the end of the movie really inspired me. It's titled "Legacy" and it's funny (well, to me, probably not to you, as you had this all planned out), that I was talking to someone today who talked about my legacy. WE talked about how my vision to sponsor 100,000 people into Klemmer and Associates would translate into millions of people who had the same vision I have and that Brian Klemmer has, which is to change the world, with no one left behind, one person at a time.

That is my legacy, and I'm just getting started.

Thank you, God.

Passionately,

Authentic, Humble, Surrendered, and Spiritual

S. Michael Edwards

Tuesday, January 25, 2011

Devotional Roulette—Salvation | Prayer #73
God,

I opened another passage for more inspiration today, in my daily devotional. What a great reminder of living a God-filled life. Thank you!

Titus 2:11–14

"God's readiness to give and forgive is now public. Salvation's available for everyone! We're being shown how to turn our backs on a godless, indulgent life, and how to take on a God-filled, God-honoring life. This new life is starting right now, and is whetting our appetites for the glorious day when our great God and Savior, Jesus Christ, appears. He offered himself as a sacrifice to free us from a dark, rebellious life into this good, pure life, making us a people he can be proud of, energetic in goodness."

I appreciate the reminder, God, and how appropriate that when I turned my back on you, you showed me how to turn my back on a godless, indulgent life. I am forever grateful that you have shown me how to take on a God-filled, God-honoring life. I do pray that you are proud of me and what I am doing to glorify you.

I am especially fond of the last three words, "energetic in goodness." May that give me strength as I reshuffle my responsibilities and make room for more God-honoring ways.

In your name, I pray,

Authentic, Humble, Surrendered, and Spiritual

S. Michael Edwards

Tuesday, January 25, 2011

She Shall Be Confident | Prayer #74
Father God,

I pray today that my dear friend and employee stand in her power today at our client meeting, that she be filled with confidence as she provides a recap of the client's account and performance. I pray that you bring her a stillness in her heart and that she realize how amazing she is, in her strength and courage.

I know she has it in her, and I pray that she will come to know that as well. Father, watch over her and guide her to be the best she can be today and all days.

In your name I pray,

Authentic, Humble, Surrendered, and Spiritual

S. Michael Edwards

Tuesday, January 25, 2011

Come Let Us Adore Him | Prayer #75
Morning God,

My devotional roulette is perfect for this amazing day you have in store for me today. A great reminding to adore you, which of course I do!

1 Peter 3:13–18

"If with heart and soul you're doing good, do you think you can be stopped? Even if you suffer for it, you're still better off. Don't give the opposition a second thought. Through thick and thin, keep your hearts up and tell anyone who asks why you're living the way you are, and always with the utmost courtesy. Keep a clear conscience before God so that when people throw mud at you, none of it will stick. They'll end up realizing that *they're* the ones who need a bath. It's better to suffer for doing good, if that's what God wants, than to be punished for doing bad. That's what Christ did definitively; suffered because of others' sins, the Righteous One for the unrighteous ones. He went through it all—was put to death and then made alive—to bring us to God."

Lord, what an amazing message. It reminds me to stay ground and center, and serene, and to adore you. "Adoration" by the Newsboys. Amazing song, with touching lyrics.

In your name I pray,

Amen.

Authentic, Humble, Surrendered, and Spiritual

S. Michael Edwards

Tuesday, January 25, 2011

And So It Was | Prayer #76
Hi God,

Great meeting today. My friend and employee was not nervous and did an amazing job. Her goal is to be more self-confident, and she prayed, I prayed, and I think Lisa Darden even prayed for her. She was confident and did a great job conveying the value of her work and the value to the client. They were pleased.

Thanks for keeping her in your loving arms. I see growth before my eyes, and it's awesome.

Passionately,

Authentic, Humble, Surrendered, and Spiritual

S. Michael Edwards

Tuesday, January 25, 2011

She's Got the Blues | Prayer #77
God,

I just got off the phone with a dear friend who could sure use your help. I see the greatness in her, and yet she is doubting herself. She could sure use a boost of some "God love" to help her see how amazing she is. I am just praying that you fill her heart and mind with confidence, courage, power, energy, love, motivation, passion, and joy.

I know that was a big ol' run-on list, but it just flowed out. Please keep her on your radar. I know she'd appreciate all the help she can get to get out of her funk!

Amen.

Authentic, Humble, Surrendered, and Spiritual

S. Michael Edwards

Wednesday, January 26, 2011

Heart | Prayer #78
God,

My friend Karen told me about my friend Tim who is having problems with his pacemaker, and I prayed for him, with him on the phone and my amazing Master Mind team. I pray to you again, that his doctor's appointment tomorrow goes well and that he doesn't require major surgery to correct the issue he's having. I pray that his friends and family are lifted up and surrounded in strength and faith, that you will take care of him, and that you will lift him up and give him a great big hug and correct his heart condition.

He's a very special man to me, and I know he's a child of yours. We both have a vested interest in him continuing his work on earth. May he be blessed with healing, courage, and strength tomorrow as he finds out what the problem is. May you also provide his doctor with the wisdom to diagnose the issue and resolve it quickly.

In your name I pray,

Authentic, Humble, Surrendered, and Spiritual

S. Michael Edwards

Wednesday, January 26, 2011

Master Mind Gratitude | Prayer #79

God, I am so grateful to you for putting our Master Mind team together. We are family and have bonded in such a way that we really get each other. We're connected at a heart level and have history, and I am thankful for the friends I have in Lesha, Karen, and Nelson.

We had a great call tonight. As soon as I get their revised requests, I'll be praying to you on each one. I wanted to thank you for putting such a powerful group together. We are "as one," and you are so much a part of our group. Go figure, because when I started with them, I was an atheist, or at least an agnostic, and now we actually all mention God in our requests.

Powerful, and I thank you from the bottom of my joyful heart!

Authentic, Humble, Surrendered, and Spiritual

S. Michael Edwards

Thursday, January 27, 2011

Whale of a Client Opportunity | Prayer #80

God,

You are gifting me with such abundance, and opportunities are around me like I have never seen before. I am so grateful for all that you have given me. I know that as I get, I give back. I'm pretty sure that's why you are blessing me in such a magnificent way...because I am focusing my efforts on a life of service and contribution.

I thank you, God, for the "whale of a client" that you have put before us. We just had our fourth meeting with them, and I'm so excited for the opportunity to help them grow their business. I thank you for the wisdom that our team has, which is moving this client forward.

Father, I pray that you will provide the wisdom to put together a powerful presentation that shows the value we bring to the table for this client.

I thank you for healing my friend Tim. Praise to you God for healing his heart.

In your name,

Authentic, Humble, Surrendered, and Spiritual

S. Michael Edwards

Thursday, January 27, 2011

Praying For Lunch | Prayer #81

God,

I thank you for an amazing meal today and that you bless it to my body, nourishing my body and soul. I love the message I received at lunch today...thanks for the reminder! My cup from a fast food restaurant was labeled with "Refresh with joy."

You know that joy is a powerful word for me. I thank you from my heart for reminding me that I asked for more joy in my life, and you are definitely providing.

In your name,

Authentic, Humble, Surrendered, and Spiritual

S. Michael Edwards

Thursday, January 27, 2011

Spread the Word | Prayer #82

God,

I have a big meeting next week and wanted to reach out and ask for your support. I need just a smidge of wisdom so I can enroll this amazing client into spreading the word to his distributors. He has already said that based on our preliminary results, he mentioned it to his top distributors and they are very interested.

The best customer is one who refers us to other customers. I love it! Thanks for watching over me, and I pray that our meeting next week is fruitful.

Thanks for the abundance of opportunities, God. You are pushing me forward at a rapid pace, and if I just had a pair of roller skates, the friction would be minimal. :)

Love ya!

Authentic, Humble, Surrendered, and Spiritual

S. Michael Edwards

Thursday, January 27, 2011

Devotional Roulette | Prayer #83

God, I love the devotion for today, you have answered so many of my prayers and then today's scripture:

Romans 10:11–13

"Scripture reassures us, 'No one who trusts God like this—heart and soul—will ever regret it.' It's exactly the same no matter what a person's religious background may be: the same God for all of us, acting the same incredibly generous way to everyone who calls out for help. 'Everyone who calls, Help, God! gets help.'"

So I guess that's why I am seeing an abundance of my requests come to fruition, and I am truly grateful God. It's amazing how you work. I shouldn't be amazed, but you reassure me and I am grateful. Reminds me of the song by Bette Midler, "Wind Beneath My Wings."

In your name,

Authentic, Humble, Surrendered, and Spiritual

S. Michael Edwards

Friday, January 28, 2011

Guess Who's Coming to Dinner | Prayer #84

God,

What a blessing to have dinner with an amazing woman last night. She is a woman who changed the lives of so many, whose lives touched mine. It's funny how life goes full circle sometimes. Kimberely Borgens has touched so many lives of my loved ones, and I was able to fellowship and break bread with her.

I thank you, God, for surrounding me with spiritually minded people, who have so much to offer, and that I can, in return, offer my talents.

I asked her to pray for the meal, as I wanted to hear how it sounded coming from her. It was beautiful. Dinner was fantastic, and I thank you for allowing me the opportunity to connect with her on a heart level.

May you continue to bless her as she blesses others with her gifts of coaching.

In your name I pray,

Authentic, Humble, Surrendered, and Spiritual

S. Michael Edwards

Friday, January 28, 2011

Alligators vs. Abundance | Prayer #85

God,

I apologize for not being grateful for the abundance. I know I said I was, and then I turned around and said, "I'm up to my eyeballs in alligators"—which, as my friend Amanda Fillweber pointed out, sounds a lot like a victim.

I truly am grateful for the abundance, and I'm up to my eyeballs in abundance. That sounds better.

Now God, as I wade in this abundance, I pray that you will give me the energy to spin the plates of opportunity that you have in front of me. I pray that you will give me the wisdom to shift things around so that my priorities are in line with your purpose. I pray that you will give me strength and fill my heart with creativity and possibilities.

Through you all things are possible.

I pray these things, in your name,

Authentic, Humble, Surrendered, and Spiritual

S. Michael Edwards

Friday, January 28, 2011

Coffee Man Revealed | Prayer #86

Lord,

Today is the day that Brett Stokes and I have a follow-up call with Jeff Ericson, the president of Camano Island Coffee. I pray that you will give us both the wisdom to present some amazing ideas on how we can all work together to grow his businesses and in turn change the world by supporting Agros International, Land, Love, Hope.

I believe we have a great value that we bring to the table, and I pray that we can all create a win/win/win/win/infinity by working together to bring about change.

I pray that you will be in me and with me as we have this meeting and that your light shine through me.

In your name, I pray,

Authentic, Humble, Surrendered, Spiritual,

S. Michael Edwards

Friday, January 28, 2011

Abundance x 2 | Prayer #87
God,

You keep blessing me with abundance! Thank you! I'm so happy that my client called this morning, you know the one that I prayed would find a quarter in her sofa (metaphorically speaking). Well, today she called and found another quarter. In one week she upped her budget 50 percent! Significant in terms of spend, putting her back at the top three of our client-spend list.

Thanks for blessing me and our business. Thanks for the abundance, it's awesome!

Gratefully yours,

Authentic, Humble, Surrendered, and Spiritual

S. Michael Edwards

Friday, January 28, 2011

Answered Prayer #86 | Prayer #88
Whoa, God, you are great! The meeting with Camano Island Coffee was fantastic, and they are very excited to work with Brett and me. They were so excited at what we presented, and I am grateful to you for giving me the wisdom to present this in a way they saw value and were ready to sign on the dotted line.

Thank you, God, for your continued blessings and for just being with me on my journey. You are great!

In your name, I pray,

Authentic, Humble, Surrendered, and Spiritual

S. Michael Edwards

Friday, January 28, 2011

Is There Hope? | Prayer #89

Lord, with all the violence in the world today, in Egypt, and elsewhere, I wonder if there is hope for every person. It's through you that I know there is, and I pray that you will watch over those who are violent, and provide wisdom to those that are in power, and peace to those that are powerless. Thanks for an amazing song by Casting Crowns, "Everyman," which is awesome.

I pray these things in your name,

Authentic, Humble, Surrendered, and Spiritual

S. Michael Edwards

Saturday, January 29, 2011

Commitment AGAIN | Prayer #90

God,

I am not sure why I can't seem to get this down, commitment. I committed to something and didn't follow through. I truly feel queasy about not following through, as it's not a trait I wish to be known for not keeping. Lord, I pray that you will help me keep my commitments and help me see how my choices are affecting my commitments.

I know I am not perfect, and maybe this is a lesson in humility? I get it, God.

In your name,

Authentic, Humble, Surrendered, and Spiritual

S. Michael Edwards

Saturday, January 29, 2011

Light at the End of the Tunnel | Prayer #91

God,

I am looking at the light at the end of the tunnel but all I can see is a train. I know that with you, all things are possible. I pray for my mind to open up to possibilities and not defeat. I pray that you provide me the confidence that together we can do what we set out to do. I pray for conviction and motivation and determination. I also pray that I don't have to "earn" these the hard way... Lord, if you would, lift me up and encourage me that my mission is noble and that my vision is clear and help me to see that the light at the end of the tunnel is not a train, but it's you, with your open arms, ready to hold me tight and to say, "Child, well done" on the end of this journey. That is my wish, and my prayer to you God.

In your name,

Authentic, Humble, Surrendered, and Spiritual

S. Michael Edwards

3 comments:

Linda Edwards said...

"The apostles then rendezvoused with Jesus and reported on all that they had done and taught. Jesus said, 'Come off by yourselves; let's take a break and get a little rest.' For there was constant coming and going. They didn't even have time to eat" (Mark 6:31).

Father God, my heart goes out to Michael right now. He's so busy and so in love with you and humanity. He has so much on his plate. I pray you will surround him with your love, your energy, your strength, your power and may he take time to rest in you, too. You are worthy and as your child so is he. Thank you for hearing and answering my prayer. In Jesus' name, I pray, amen.

January 29, 2011 9:38 AM

Dad said...

Michael,

I've read your prayer and heard your heart. There is no doubt about your mission being noble. (See scripture below.) You have already experienced conviction. What you do with that is the question. You are brilliant and highly motivated to make a difference for others. Remember to sew into your life, casting off those shackles that you know are anchoring your energy to the past.

I love you and know that you will hear from the King of Kings, "Well done, my good and faithful servant." And I'll be standing there with a huge smile, clapping and whistling the loudest.

Love,

Dad

Matthew 25:34–40

New International Version

"Then the King will say to those on his right, 'Come, you who are blessed by my Father; take your inheritance, the kingdom prepared for you since the creation of the world. For I was hungry and you gave me something to eat, I was thirsty and you gave me something to drink, I was a stranger and you invited me in, I needed clothes and you clothed me, I was sick and you looked after me, I was in prison and you came to visit me.'

"Then the righteous will answer him, 'Lord, when did we see you hungry and feed you, or thirsty and give you something to drink? When did we see you a stranger and invite you in, or needing clothes and clothe you? When did we see you sick or in prison and go to visit you?'

"The King will reply, 'I tell you the truth, whatever you did for one of the least of these brothers of mine, you did for me.'"

January 29, 2011 10:36 AM

S. Michael Edwards said...
Thanks for the encouragement Mom and Dad! I can especially visualize you, Dad, whistling and cheering me through the gates of Heaven. Mom, your prayer is so beautiful. It chokes me up to know that you are with me on this journey!

Thank you both, from the bottom of my heart!

Saturday, January 29, 2011

Devotional Roulette | Prayer #92

God,

You got it! Light flooded the room in my devotional, when I prayed about the light at the end of the tunnel. I do love your sense of humor and timing.

Today's scripture:

> Acts 12:7–9
>
> "Suddenly there was an angel at his side and light flooding the room. The angel shook Peter and got him up: 'Hurry!' The handcuffs fell off his wrists. The angel said, 'Get dressed. Put on your shoes.' Peter did it. Then, 'Grab your coat and let's get out of here.' Peter followed him, but didn't believe it was really an angel—he thought he was dreaming."

Lord, I pray you take my handcuffs off my wrist and my mind, as I know I am not dreaming and that you are with me. I pray that my mind open up and my heart flow through so we can connect on an even deeper level.

Sometimes I feel like we're having coffee and talking, and sometimes I feel like we're having a formal first date. I just want to be real with you, God. You know how I love coffee and maybe I'm trying too hard to make my prayers be profound. Maybe that's why I am not on pace to complete all my prayers by March 2?

I am going to toss aside the shackles on my mind and I am going to get real. It doesn't have to look a certain way, I know this.

A good friend of mine asked me if I prayed over the clothing that I embroider, for the person who is going to wear it. I thought that was rather profound, and I hadn't even considered it. What a blessing to those that receive my garments.

Today I will honor you in my first garment. A garment full of crosses. I will get up and get dressed, with the shackles off my wrists, and I will honor you today, God.

I'll keep you posted on my progress. It's off to the fabric store to get some fabric for my new design…I am pretty sure you will be proud of it, as it is to honor you and the person I will be praying for who will receive this garment is me.

In your name,

Authentic, Humble, Surrendered, and Spiritual

S. Michael Edwards

Saturday, January 29, 2011

Bless My Sister | Prayer #93
God,

I just got an email from my sister that made me laugh out loud and nearly choke on my coffee. She's so awesome. I pray you bless her and her family, and that you provide them with opportunities for abundance, joy, and happiness.

I do miss her and want the best that life has to offer her.

Give her a big hug for me today God. I know she'll feel it!

In your name,

Authentic, Humble, Surrendered, Spiritual

S. Michael Edwards

Saturday, January 29, 2011

God Bless My Parents | Prayer #94
God,

I am so grateful for such supportive and amazing parents. I feel like the luckiest son in the world. Their encouragement and faith is inspiring and motivating me.

My dad wrote:

Matthew 25:34–40

New International Version

"Then the King will say to those on his right, 'Come, you who are blessed by my Father; take your inheritance, the kingdom prepared for you since the creation of the world. For I was hungry and you gave me something to eat, I was thirsty and you gave me something to drink, I was a stranger and you invited me in, I needed clothes and you clothed me, I was sick and you looked after me, I was in prison and you came to visit me.'

"Then the righteous will answer him, 'Lord, when did we see you hungry and feed you, or thirsty and give you something to drink? When did we see you a stranger and invite you in, or needing clothes and clothe you? When did we see you sick or in prison and go to visit you?'

"The King will reply, 'I tell you the truth, whatever you did for one of the least of these brothers of mine, you did for me.'"

Whoa, did that strike a chord. It is like an energy bar that fills my soul and propels me forward.

God, may I continue to honor my fellow mankind and womankind, and in doing so honor and glorify you.

In your name,

Authentic, Humble, Surrendered and Spiritual

S. Michael Edwards

Saturday, January 29, 2011

Robin Sharma | Prayer #95
God,

I am sitting here, embroidering a statement of my love for you. I look up and see this quote above my desk, and it hit me…

"What other people think of you is none of your business…Leadership is about having unshakeable faith in your vision and unrelenting confidence in your power to make positive change happen!" Thanks to Robin Sharma for the quote, and God thank you for reminding me to look up and see what's around me.

Clearly I had a little trembling in my faith and vision and confidence and yet, you showed me, that I can do this and it doesn't have to be hard. "Choose easy," is what I keep hearing. True choice.

Thanks, God, for my parents, my buddy Craig, and for your love,

I say, I'll ride the train tracks to the end of the tunnel, why not be on the train but going the other way—so that when I get there, that light will be you? That's my choice, that's my final answer.

Love, peace, harmony,

In your name,

Authentic, Humble, Surrendered, and Spiritual

S. Michael Edwards

Saturday, January 29, 2011

Is That Really Him? | Prayer #96
God,

You are truly blessing me today. Ask and you shall receive. I just got a call from Ed, and he is going to loan me money from the company to pay my property taxes. I was waiting on the settlement money to pay the taxes, and wanted that settlement to be done by the thirty-first. I guess it doesn't have to look a certain way, and the fact that Ed is willing to help me out, just to save me $500 in interest, is pretty amazing and so out of character for who he used to be.

God, I thank you for filling Ed's heart with compassion and generosity.

In your name,

Authentic, Humble, Surrendered, and Spiritual

S. Michael Edwards

Saturday, January 29, 2011

Dance Dance Dance | Prayer #97

Hey God,

You're on a roll today! Ask and you shall receive? Yep, I am so getting that concept today. Ed just called me and asked if we could play some music and dance before the staff meeting on Monday.

I did that for a while, but he chose out of dancing to get the energy flowing—which set the context for the rest of the staff. Yesterday our office suite neighbor said, "You don't dance anymore?" We had gotten back into the rut of work in lieu of fun, when I really want work to be fun.

So out of the blue, Ed calls and asks if I'll play some music and put something together for a little dance before the meeting. He sees value in it! I asked if he was open to feedback and he said yes, and I told him that he helps set the context, and his participation is key to raising the energy, too. He said he would participate!

So, Monday should be fun!

In your name I pray,

Authentic, Humble, Surrendered, and Spiritual

S. Michael Edwards

Saturday, January 29, 2011

Breaking Thread With God | Prayer #98

God, I feel so much love and encouragement now. It's been awesome spending the day with you and "breaking thread"—I made this shirt to glorify you and to put myself out there and honor me. Know you were in my thoughts as I created this shirt, and I thank you for sending your Son to die on the cross for our sins.

In your name I pray,

Authentic, Humble, Surrendered, and Spiritual

S. Michael Edwards

Saturday, January 29, 2011

Broken and Spilled Out | Prayer #99

God,

What an amazing God you are. I thank you for my mom who sent me this song, after she read my prayers this morning. It really helps me understand how much you love me, by what you were willing to give up for me. All in the name of love, sparing no expense. Thanks for touching my heart today and for surrounding me with an army of prayer warriors who have lifted me up and given me strength today. You are with me, and through you the power of your warriors are with me. I have been lifted up and honored today. The song for the day is "Broken and Spilled Out."

Words by Gloria Gaither, Music by Bill George.

1 comments:

Linda Edwards said...

Michael, thank you for your openness and vulnerability. I know that I've been with Jesus all day in a sweet, sweet way that might not have happened this way had I not been reading your prayers. I cannot get that Steve Green song, "Broken and Spilled Out," out of my head. That has really kept me connected to Him in a very real way. There's that Win/Win/Win again. Have a great evening and thanks for making a difference in my life. Your proud Mom

Saturday, January 29, 2011

Arms of an Angel | Prayer #100

Hey God,

Thank you for reminding me about this amazing song, and inspiring my latest creation, which is being embroidered as we speak.

I have found my comfort. I felt filled with joy today. Quiet time with you is clearing my mind. Talking to my parents fills my heart with joy. An email from my sister reminded me of family. Friends called, and I supported them in their "stuff."

I'm choosing to surrender, and you are reminding me that I am not alone today. Thank you, God, for an amazing day…"It's got to be love, I've never been so sure of this before." The lyrics to "Angel," by Sarah McLachlan, made my day. The music was icing on the cake.

Gratefully yours,

Authentic, Humble, Surrendered and Spiritual

S. Michael Edwards

Saturday, January 29, 2011

Angels Watching Over Me | Prayer #101

God, here is the creation inspired by you and reminding me of the song "In the Arms of an Angel."

I'll be wearing this shirt proudly as your son. I was going to say "Son of God" but since I'm talking to you, that seemed odd.

Thanks for inspiring me today. I enjoyed your company today.

In your name I pray,

Authentic, Humble, Surrendered, and Spiritual

S. Michael Edwards

Saturday, January 29, 2011

Pre-Meal Prayer | Prayer #102

God,

As I prepare to go to dinner with a friend, I pray that you will bless the meal, my friend, and my family today. May your wonder and grace surround us all in your arms. I pray that you will be with my friends and watch over the world with your love in this horrendous time of turmoil across the world. May you fill the hearts of our leaders and Ed with love, compassion, and forgiveness.

In these things I pray,

Amen.

Authentic, Humble, Surrendered, and Spiritual

S. Michael Edwards

Sunday, January 30, 2011

When I Get Where I'm Going | Prayer #103
Hello God!

What a glorious day today. I wanted you to know that I was thinking about you. In fact, I did a lot of thinking yesterday…and it was perfect. I just wanted to thank you for an amazing day and a wonderful dinner with my friend. I'm ready for another great day today.

My friend Dan sent me a book to read, called *Jim and Casper Go to Church*, and I think I'll start reading that today. A believer, an atheist, an unlikely friendship…frank conversation about faith, churches and well-meaning Christians. Sounds right up my alley!

In the meantime, I wanted to share this song that hit me this morning, and I'm sure it was no surprise to you. You are reminding me to focus on where I'm going, and when I get there. The big goal. That's what I can focus on. Thank you.

I rocked out to Brad Paisley, "When I Get Where I'm Going," and it made my day.

In your name, I pray,

Authentic, Humble, Surrendered, and Spiritual

S. Michael Edwards

Sunday, January 30, 2011

Devotional Roulette | Prayer #104
Oh God, what an amazing God you are. I enjoyed the devotional today, and it reminds me to not be skeptical, reinforcing the power and awesomeness you have and provide.

Mark 2:1–12

After a few days, Jesus returned to Capernaum, and word got around that he was back home. A crowd gathered, jamming the entrance so no one could get in or out. He was teaching the Word. They brought a paraplegic to him, carried by four men. When they weren't able to get in because of the crowd, they removed part of the roof and lowered the paraplegic on his stretcher. Impressed by their bold belief, Jesus said to the paraplegic, "Son, I forgive your sins."

Some religion scholars sitting there started whispering among themselves, "He can't talk that way! That's blasphemy! God and only God can forgive sins."

Jesus knew right away what they were thinking, and said, "Why are you so skeptical? Which is simpler: to say to the paraplegic, 'I forgive your sins,' or to say, 'Get up, take your stretcher, and start walking'? Well, just so it's clear that I'm the Son of Man and authorized to do either, or both (he looked now at the paraplegic), "Get up. Pick up your stretcher and go home." And the man did it—got up, grabbed his stretcher, and walked out, with everyone there watching him. They rubbed their eyes, incredulous—and then praised God, saying, "We've never seen anything like this!"

I love the last line, "We've never seen anything like this"! So does that mean it's not possible? No! Thanks for reinforcing that everything is possible through you.

In your name,

Authentic, Humble, Surrendered, and Spiritual

S. Michael Edwards

Sunday, January 30, 2011

Jim and Casper Go to Church | Prayer #105
Hey God,

Finished the book sent to me by Dan Gaub. Amazing book. Really struck a chord with me, as a former preacher and an atheist travel the country to "secret shop" churches. I could totally relate to the atheist's point of view (Casper).

Why is it that Christian's say one thing and do another? (Love thy neighbor yet hate gays?)

Are these mega churches really what Jesus asked us to do?

I struggled with these issues for decades, and what I came to know after reading this book was that I am not alone. I pray, God, that more Christians will read this book and see how they are perceived by outsiders. I pray that they walk the walk of Jesus instead of the institution, that they spend their tithes to help the poor, the needy, and not the superstar evangelist.

I pray these things in your name,

Authentic, Humble, Surrendered, and Spiritual

S. Michael Edwards

Sunday, January 30, 2011

My Purpose | Prayer #106

So God,

As I was reading the book *Jim and Casper Go to Church*, I realized that my purpose in life to is to bring joy and equality to the world. Yet, I have not once prayed for that. Interesting, huh? If that is truly my purpose, why have I been so wrapped up in all this other stuff? Why haven't I asked you to hear my cry?

Lord, I so want the world to be a place of joy and equality. For everyone, not just the rich, the white, the males. I want equality for women, men, children, gays, lesbians, Muslims, etc. I am reminded of the saying, "Why can't we all just get along?"

God, it's more than getting along for me, why can't we all "love thy neighbor as thyself"? That is my request of you. To fill our hearts with compassion and joy and that we treat everyone as we would want to be treated.

In your name, I pray (albeit, a little late in the game).

Authentic, Humble, Surrendered, and Spiritual

S. Michael Edwards

Sunday, January 30, 2011

Dinner Prayer | Prayer #107
God,

I just got through watching *Dinner with Schmucks*…and it made me think about my purpose and equality. The premise of the movie is a dinner where you bring someone who is an idiot (for an "idiot-off")—not really in line with my vision. However, it did make me wonder, where in my life have I chosen judgment? It was painful to watch, and funny at times, but the message was solid. We're all humans, and we are all equal.

Lord, I pray that you will fill the hearts of those who are in judgment against anyone…that they will see and want equality for everyone.

In your name I pray,

Authentic, Humble, Surrendered, and Spiritual

S. Michael Edwards

Sunday, January 30, 2011

Religion? | Prayer #108
God,

I'm still processing the book *Jim and Casper Go to Church*, and I am wondering what your thoughts are on the various forms of religion. I guess I think of them like different accents of the same language. I'm sure there are plenty of people that would not agree with me. I guess I'm wondering about what the book says about church, and since your Son only mentioned church two times in the Bible, and yet we've institutionalized it, made it a business, and spend tons of money keeping the machine running.

What are your thoughts on this? Do you want us to be doing good in the world or building mega churches? Or can it be both? I'm just curious.

The concept of "church planting" has this bitter taste for me. Does it have to look that way? Couldn't it be about relationship between me and you?

I'll look forward to your response, as it's been on my mind lately. As you know, I haven't gone to church here in Texas. I do enjoy Eastlake Community Church. Am I better off having a relationship with you and doing good deeds, or is it your desire that I go to an institution and follow tradition? I'm not much of a tradition kind of guy.

I just want to praise you, glorify you, and do good things for people in need. Is that enough?

In your name,

Authentic, Humble, Surrendered, and Spiritual

S. Michael Edwards

Sunday, January 30, 2011

Street Kids | Prayer #109

God,

I just watched *20/20* from Friday night, and I was saddened by the story of these kids living on the street. I pray that you will surround all the kids in the world who are homeless with your love and protect them from harm. I pray that you hold them in your arms and bring people into their lives who can reassure and provide for them with love and encouragement. My heart goes out to these kids, and I pray they will come to realize that their situation does not define them. I pray that they make choices that will assimilate them back into society and build their self-esteem. I pray that I am able to make a difference in their lives through you, God.

In your name I pray,

Authentic, Humble, Surrendered, and Spiritual

S. Michael Edwards

Sunday, January 30, 2011

Say What You Need To Say | Prayer #110

Hey God,

I was touched by that story on homeless kids and the song at the end reminded me of what I want with you: "Say" by John Mayer.

It's exactly what I've been thinking about all day—what do I say to you, God? Then this song said, "Say what you need to say."

I am so grateful for the abundance you have given me. I am blessed beyond measure, and I am so thankful for you in my life. You have given me talents that I am using to help others. You have given me life and love and an amazing family.

Every day, my alarm plays a ringtone of John Mayer, with the song "Say." Say what you need to say.

Say what you need to say?

I think thank you!

In your name, I pray,

Authentic, Humble, Surrendered, and Spiritual

S. Michael Edwards

Sunday, January 30, 2011

Yet I Live | Prayer #111

God,

Thank you for blessing me with a mom who shares such amazing stories, songs, love, and support. She just sent me this song, which I love—I love the powerful message! I am alive!

"As I look back on what I thought was living

I'm amazed at the price I choose to pay

And to think I ignored what really mattered

Cause I thought the sacrifice would be too great

But when I finally reached the point of giving in

I found the cross was calling even then

And even though it took dying to survive

I've never felt so much alive."

Philips, Craig and Dean—"Crucified with Christ"

In your name, I pray,

Authentic, Humble, Surrendered, and Spiritual

S. Michael Edwards

1 comments:

Linda Edwards said...

Again, so thrilled that this song spoke to your heart. A few years ago a gal from Kim's church sang this song with her teenage son at her husband and his dad's funeral. The son's basketball team was there, and it was standing room only. I can't help but think of that when I hear this song. She must truly know that God will be with her no matter what!!

My love and prayers are with you this week. I'm so proud of you and know you'll be a blessing and also be blessed. Hugs, Mom

Sunday, January 30, 2011

In Christ Alone | Prayer #112

God,

I feel like I may have gone to church today by proxy of mom, they sang this song in church…which surprises me, because when I went to that church, it was all hymns. The lyrics speak volumes and definitely lift me up. I think I love this band! Thanks for inspiring them so they can inspiring the rest of us. I love this song, "In Christ Alone" by Newsboys.

Lord, I am grateful that you gave your only Son, so our sins could be washed away. In the power of Christ I stand, and in your name I pray,

Authentic, Humble, Surrendered, and Spiritual

S. Michael Edwards

---

1 comments:

Linda Edwards said...

You did go to church today. You were with me in my heart! When Pastor Jed-dediah said we are crucified with Christ…I thought of the other song and knew I wanted to send it to you. This song spoke to my heart, too, and since we're connected…voila!! I'm so thankful and happy that you were blessed, too. God is good.

Sunday, January 30, 2011

Small Groups | Prayer #113

God,

Tomorrow our small group calls start, and I pray that you will be with me as we get to know each other. I pray for the wisdom to create the space for amazing leaders, who will step up and make a difference in Sam Camp and in the world at large. May they be rocked to their core with an undeniable confidence that anything is possible and miracles do occur. Camp is on!

In your name I pray,

Authentic, Humble, Surrendered, and Spiritual

S. Michael Edwards

Monday, January 31, 2011

Beautiful Day | Prayer #114
God,

Thank you so much for another beautiful day! I count each day as a blessing, and I'm am grateful for all that you bring my way.

Thank you for giving me the wisdom to have an amazing call with my small group today. It was powerful and definitely set the mark for where we are going to go. Amazing people, and a profound call.

In your name I pray,

Authentic, Humble, Surrendered, and Spiritual

S. Michael Edwards

Monday, January 31, 2011

Bless This Beef | Prayer #115
God,

I pray that you will bless the meal I just had, an amazing beef tenderloin sandwich. May it nourish my body and provide energy to move forward and get stuff done! I pray that you will be with Ed this week as he finalizes the contracts for our settlement and as he gets started in his own Sam Camp experience. May he be open, honest, and vulnerable to the possibilities.

Lord, I ask that you fill his heart with opportunities to shift and move forward.

In your name I pray,

Authentic, Humble, Surrendered, and Spiritual

S. Michael Edwards

My Buddies Rock | Prayer #116
God,

Thank you so much for surrounding me with amazing buddies. Craig was amazing on the call today and supported me and our students. He is a blessing, and I'm so thankful for you putting him in my life.

I also want to thank you for my buddy Brett, who arranged a meeting with another potential client today. The meeting was without an objective, but the call went great and there are opportunities to help serve and provide contribution.

I pray that you will continue to bless me with the wisdom on how to move things forward and grow our business as this potential client is all about giving back to the community. I love having clients with a servant's heart.

In your name I pray,

Authentic, Humble, Surrendered, and Spiritual

S. Michael Edwards

Monday, January 31, 2011

Scarcity of Time |Prayer #117
Oh God,

I have been fretting about scarcity of time, not sure why. Fretting gets me no-where. All the sudden I feel this sense of empowerment. I pray that you help keep in grounded in abundance of time. Fake it till you make it seems to have worked so far, and now I am not feeling that sense of scarcity anymore.

Thanks for helping me shift my priorities. I will continue to lean on you for support as things continue to ramp up and take off like a rocket ship.

Ask and you shall receive, tenfold…yep, I get that, got that, and I'm loving it!

In your name I pray,

Authentic, Humble, Surrendered, and Spiritual

S. Michael Edwards

Monday, January 31, 2011

Got Life? | Prayer #118
God,

Thanks for the daily devotional.

> John 12:24–26

> "Listen carefully: Unless a grain of wheat is buried in the ground, dead to the world, it is never any more than a grain of wheat. But if it is buried, it sprouts and reproduces itself many times over. In the same way, anyone who holds on to life just as it is destroys that life. But if you let it go, reckless in your love, you'll have it forever, real and eternal.

> "If any of you wants to serve me, then follow me. Then you'll be where I am, ready to serve at a moment's notice. The Father will honor and reward anyone who serves me."

So I guess that's where this abundance is coming from…I've chosen to serve you and glorify you, and I am being rewarded. Pretty good deal, if you ask me. So again, I can't thank you enough for life, for abundance, and for bringing the people into my life who allowed me to let go of life and serve and follow you.

I'm here to honor you, and I am reaping the rewards.

I'm counting my blessings, but need a calculator or an Excel spreadsheet to keep track. Too many to count on my fingers and toes.

Thanks, God. Great devotional!

In your name I pray,

Authentic, Humble, Surrendered, and Spiritual

S. Michael Edwards

Monday, January 31, 2011

Come On Ride The Train | Prayer #119

So God,

Remember when I was praying about the light at the end of the tunnel and feeling it was a train? Loved this passage I read today.

John 3:19–21

"This is the crisis we're in: God-light streamed into the world, but men and women everywhere ran for the darkness. They went for the darkness because they were not really interested in pleasing God. Everyone who makes a practice of doing evil, addicted to denial and illusion, hates God-light and won't come near it, fearing a painful exposure. But anyone working and living in truth and reality welcomes God-light so the work can be seen for the God-work it is."

I am working and living the truth, God, and I welcome your light at the end of the tunnel and now in the present. I pray the work I am doing is seen as the God-work it is. May you continue to shine your light on me and the work I am doing to help others.

In your name I pray,

Authentic, Humble, Surrendered, and Spiritual

S. Michael Edwards

Monday, January 31, 2011

Luke 17:17–19 | Prayer #120

Great passage Lord,

Luke 17:17–19

"Jesus said, 'Were not ten healed? Where are the nine? Can none be found to come back and give glory to God except this outsider?' Then he said to him, 'Get up. On your way. Your faith has healed and saved you.'"

I feel saved, I feel blessed, and I feel gratitude beyond measure. Thank you, God, for all you have done in my life. I thank you, then I read about the importance of gratitude and thanks. I love it when a plan comes together!

In your name,

Authentic, Humble, Surrendered, and Spiritual

S. Michael Edwards

Savior Please | Prayer #121
God,

Mom is such a blessing. She's blessed me with this amazing song today by Josh Wilson, titled "Savior, Please." I can relate to the lyrics. I work so hard, I live so fast. Lord, I know I can't do this alone. God, I need you to hold onto me. I am nothing without your love. Amazing, and I am so grateful for Mom and for you holding onto me.

In your name I pray,

Authentic, Humble, Surrendered, and Spiritual

S. Michael Edwards

Tuesday, February 1, 2011

Honestly, as Grandma Would Say | Prayer #122
God,

I got the legal documents back from Ed's attorney yesterday, basically undoing and building in trap doors to invalidate what we had agreed to. I told him I was not inclined to sign the documents and that I would prefer, if he was unwilling to go along with my agreement that I had drawn up, to not settle and undo everything.

God, I pray you will bless Ed and allow him to see his commitment and word mean something and that he is better off agreeing to settle this matter as we agreed. I pray that you will provide a gentle nudge to get this settlement finalized in a timely manner. It's been lingering on so long, I just want to finalize the deal and be done with it.

In your name I pray,

Authentic, Humble, Surrendered, and Spiritual

S. Michael Edwards

Tuesday, February 1, 2011

Ice | Prayer #123

God,

It's beautiful outside, but it's icy and treacherous on the roads. I pray that you will watch over the drivers and pedestrians in North Texas and watch over them today as people make their way. I love the beauty of it all, and I also realize that with that beauty comes danger. Please watch over everyone today and help them make the right choices in travel.

In your name I pray,

Authentic, Humble, Surrendered, and Spiritual

S. Michael Edwards

Tuesday, February 1, 2011

Samurai Camp 21—As One | Prayer #124

God,

As I connected "virtually" with every student last night, I prayed and continue to pray that you will bless the students in Sam Camp 21. That they work as one, and are blessed with growth and learning beyond measure. I pray that you open their hearts and minds and that they are able to experience an amazing breakthrough (or more than one) in their personal and professional lives that move them forward in ways they could never imagine or dream possible.

Lord, I pray that you will be with all the leaders and seniors and facilitators as we set the context for the students. I also pray that we all give 110 percent and create the space to allow the students to step into their own leadership.

In your name I pray,

Authentic, Humble, Surrendered, and Spiritual

S. Michael Edwards

Tuesday, February 1, 2011

Soup or Bowl | Prayer #125
God,

I find it humorous that people pray for their favorite football team playing in the Super Bowl. I guess we all have our passions and desires, so why not pray for them, right? I'm reminded of the book *Jim and Casper Go to Church*, and how Casper, the atheist, wondered why people were praying for the pastor of one church to get a meeting with Bono of U2, when all these people are dying all over the world.

He makes a good point. Should our prayers be so focused on things like football and Bono, or on things that might actually help change the world?

How about we pray for the poor, the hungry, the homeless? That you would provide them with shelter, food, and a way out of poverty? I pray for that today, God.

The Super Bowl is so off my radar, but I do enjoy the commercials!

In your name I pray,

Authentic, Humble, Surrendered, and Spiritual

S. Michael Edwards

Tuesday, February 1, 2011

How HE Loves Us | Prayer #126
God,

Thanks for the reminder about how much you love us. I pray that you will love on the people of Egypt today and forever, as they go through political turmoil and violence and death. I pray that you fill their hearts with compassion, forgiveness, and joy and remove their anger and violence. May this song serve to remind others how you love us. David Crowder Band—"How He Loves."

Thank you for your love and grace, God.

In your name I pray,

Authentic, Humble, Surrendered, and Spiritual

S. Michael Edwards

Tuesday, February 1, 2011

Lift Her Up | Prayer #127

God,

I pray that you lift up Janet Henze and family today and surround her and her family in your love and arms. I haven't heard how she is doing, but I know that she could use some love and support, and maybe today or this moment is the moment she needs it most. She's on my mind, and I just want to ask that you comfort her and give her strength as her father is so ill.

In your name I pray,

Authentic, Humble, Surrendered, and Spiritual

S. Michael Edwards

Tuesday, February 1, 2011

Ghost Town | Prayer #128

God,

I guess you heard my prayer this morning about safe travels. Only one employee showed up to the office. The rest had the wisdom to stay home. Not sure what that says about me and the other employee who showed up? Hee hee.

It's been really quiet without all the people here and has given me time to ground and center myself.

I had a great call with a potential client, who said he was going to sign the contracts and put the checks in the mail. Thank you, God, for giving me the ability to enroll him in the value of our services.

Thank you for an amazing month we had in January. Typically not a great month for advertising agencies, but we had a banner month (online marketing pun intended).

In your name and with gratitude,

Authentic, Humble, Surrendered, and Spiritual

S. Michael Edwards

Tuesday, February 1, 2011

Ice Ice Baby | Prayer #129
God,

I am going to head home, as the blizzard conditions are getting worse and nobody is here. I pray that you will keep me safe on my drive and also keep anyone else on the roads here in North Texas safe (and away from me).

Hmmm, I guess this is what it would be like to live in Colorado? I think I prefer the sun. :)

Thank you in advance for the safe trip home!

In your name,

Authentic, Humble, Surrendered, and Spiritual

S. Michael Edwards

Tuesday, February 1, 2011

Safe and Sound | Prayer #130

God,

Thanks for the amazing ride home…slip sliding away. I never knew how long it could take to ski home in a car when I don't live that far away. I'm just glad you gave me the wisdom to leave early, rather than wait for the temperature to drop even further on these already icy roads.

I thank you for allowing me to get home safe and sound and without a single scratch (on my car)—the tires did scratch the ice.

In your name I pray,

Authentic, Humble, Surrendered, and Spiritual

S. Michael Edwards

Tuesday, February 1, 2011

Sizelove Prayers | Prayer #131

God,

My dear friend Karen Sizelove has the following requests for Master Mind:

1. With the love, support, and integrity of the Master Mind team and knowledge that wherever I am…God is, I graciously make the following request that: I have been accepted to staff Wilderness Awareness School, on or before February 27, 2011, by noon EST.

2. With the love, support, and integrity of the Master Mind team and knowledge that wherever I am…God is, I graciously make the following request that: I have received $2,000 in orders from Dove Chocolate Discoveries on or before February 20, 2011, by noon EST.

3. With the love, support, and integrity of the Master Mind team and knowledge that wherever I am…God is, I graciously make the following request that: all those around you health happiness, peace, promotion, wealth, and all the blessings of life on or before February 2, 2011, by noon EST and thereafter.

God, I pray that your will is in alignment with Karen's requests and that she be accepted into the Wilderness Awareness School, which is in perfect alignment with her purpose. I also pray they she rock the Dove Chocolate Discoveries and generate $2,000 or more in orders and that all those around you, God, have health, happiness, peace, promotion, wealth, and all the blessings of life.

In your name I pray,

Authentic, Humble, Surrendered, and Spiritual

S. Michael Edwards

Tuesday, February 1, 2011

John 3:16 | Prayer #132

God, I got this from a friend, another God Spam email…but the message is so profound, I wanted to post it and ask that the message spread far and wide. I used to delete these types of emails, but this one struck me, as I'm not ashamed to profess my love for you and your love for me and all mankind. May those who find this message, send it out to create an army of prayer warriors!

John 3:16

I don't understand it.

A little boy was selling newspapers on the corner, the people were in and out of the cold.

The little boy was so cold that he wasn't trying to sell many papers.

He walked up to a policeman and said,

"Mister,

you wouldn't happen to know where a poor boy could find a warm place to sleep tonight would you?

"You see, I sleep in a box up around the corner there and down the alley, and it's awful cold in there for tonight.

"Sure would be nice to have a warm place to stay."

The policeman looked down at the little boy and said, "You go down the street to that big white house and you knock on the door. When they come out the door you just say John 3:16 and they will let you in."

So he did. He walked up the steps and knocked on the door, and a lady answered. He looked up and said, "John 3:16." The lady said, "Come on in, son."

She took him in and she sat him down in a split bottom rocker in front of a great big old fireplace, and she went off. The boy sat there for a while and thought to himself:

John 3:16… I don't understand it, but it sure makesa cold boy warm.

Later she came back and asked him, "Are you hungry?" He said, "Well, just a little. I haven't eaten in a couple of days, and I guess I could stand a little bit of food."

The lady took him in the kitchen and sat him down to a table full of wonderful food. He ate and ate until he couldn't eat any more. Then he thought to himself: *John 3:16…*

Boy, I sure don't understand it but it sure makes a hungry boy full.

She took him upstairs to a bathroom to a huge bathtub filled with warm water, and he sat there and soaked for a while. As he soaked, he thought to himself: *John 3:16…*

I sure don't understand it, but it sure makes a dirty boy clean. You know, I've not had a bath, a real bath, in my whole life. The only bath I ever had was when I stood in front of that big old fire hydrant as they flushed it out.

The lady came in and got him. She took him to a room, tucked him into a big old feather bed, pulled the covers up around his neck, kissed him goodnight, and turned out the lights. As he lay in the darkness and looked out the window at the snow coming down on that cold night, he thought to himself: *John 3:16…I don't understand it but it sure makes a tired boy rest.*

The next morning the lady came back up and took him down again to that same big table full of food. After he ate, she took him back to that same big old split bottom rocker in front of the fireplace and picked up a big old Bible.

She sat down in front of him and looked into his young face. "Do you under-stand John 3:16?" she asked gently. He replied, "No, ma'am, I don't. The first time I ever heard it was last night when the policeman told me to use it." She opened the Bible to John 3:16 and began to explain to him about Jesus. Right there, in front of that big old fireplace, he gave his heart and life to Jesus. He sat there and thought: *John 3:16…don't understand it, but it sure makes a lost boy feel safe.*

You know, I have to confess I don't understand it either, how God was willing to send His Son to die for me, and how Jesus would agree to do such a thing. I don't understand the agony of the Father and every angel in heaven as they watched Jesus suffer and die. I don't understand the intense love for me that kept Jesus on the cross till the end. I don't understand it, but it sure does make life worth living.

John 3:16, "For God so loved the world, that he gave his only begotten Son, that whosoever believeth in him should not perish, but have everlasting life."

If you aren't ashamed to do this, please follow the directions. Jesus said, "If you are ashamed of me, I will be ashamed of you before my Father." Pass this on only if you mean it.

I do love God. He is my source of existence. He keeps me functioning each and every day.

Take sixty seconds and give this a shot!

Let's just see if Satan stops this one.

All you do is:

1) Simply say a small prayer for the person who sent you this, "Father, God bless this person in whatever it is that You know he or she may be needing this day.

In Jesus' name,

Amen!"

2) Then send it on to ten other people.

Within hours, ten people have prayed for you, and you caused a multitude of people to pray to God for other people. Then sit back and watch the power of God work in your life for doing the thing that you know He loves.

In your name I pray,

Authentic, Humble, Surrendered, and Spiritual

S. Michael Edwards

Wednesday, February 2, 2011

Power Down and Prayers Up | Prayer #133
God,

As the power just went out, I was thinking about all the people who cannot afford heat. The roads are icy, and I pray that you will provide wisdom to the people seeking warmth. I pray that they not use the oven or outdoor heating devices. I pray that they seek shelter and warmth in a safe environment. I pray you will be with the linemen and -women who repair lines and that we get our power back as soon as possible.

As soon as I hit publish on this post, my Internet went down. So I plugged in my iPhone to use it as my Internet, not knowing how long the power would be out. As soon as I was ready to publish again, the power came back up!

Thank you, God!

In your name I pray,

Authentic, Humble, Surrendered, and Spiritual

S. Michael Edwards

1 comments:

Linda Edwards said...

Father God, thank you for Michael's compassionate heart. I honor and prayerfully support his requests. Please help those who are out in this weather; protect them and keep them safe and warm. I lift this day up to you and pray that you will be honored and glorified by all we do and say. In Jesus' name, amen.

Wednesday, February 2, 2011

Bible Roulette | Prayer #134

God,

I left my daily devotional at the office, and since it's so icy I decided to open the Bible to do a little Bible Roulette. I've found that it's always perfect, no matter what page I turn to in the devotional, and I love the verse that popped open today.

Psalm 35: 27–28

But those who want the best for me, Let them have the last word—a glad shout!—and say, over and over and over, "God is great—everything works together for good for his servant." I'll tell the world how great and good you are, I'll shout Hallelujah all day, every day.

Hallelujah, God! Power is on, heat is on, and the song that my parents were singing when they met is on. (Dad accidently did a Hallelujah when it was supposed to be silent; Mom, of course noticed the rebel across the room...the rest is history.)

Great psalm, God,

In gratitude and praise,

Authentic, Humble, Surrendered, and Spiritual

S. Michael Edwards

Wednesday, February 2, 2011

Screenwriters Prayer | Prayer #135

God,

A dear friend of mine has written a screenplay, and her dream is to win the competition for screenwriters and get an agent. She is extremely talented, and I pray that she will win the competition and touch hearts. She is a compassionate samurai and has a servant's heart. I pray you will watch over her as she looks for a new career and moves forward with a mission.

In your name I pray,

Authentic, Humble, Surrendered, and Spiritual

S. Michael Edwards

Wednesday, February 2, 2011

Hallelujah—You Make Me Smile | Prayer #136
God,

My Bible roulette and my mom and you are all in sync today. I just read her Facebook email where she sent the following message and video. You make me laugh and smile when you give me these "God Winks."

"I love that God puts a song in my heart and I, in turn, can share it with my two beloved 'children.' I'm blessed, and I love you both so much. May God continue to hold you close!"—Mom

Thanks for the song by Heather Williams, titled "Hallelujah," Mom. Amazing.

So again, I shout Hallelujah! I'm in need of your grace today and every day God.

In your name I pray,

Authentic, Humble, Surrendered, and Spiritual

S. Michael Edwards

Wednesday, February 2, 2011

Chili | Prayer #137
God,

With all this cold and the power cycling on and off, I think it's time for some chili…I love the idea of "it's chilly, so I'll have chili"—may you bless my food to my body, giving me strength, energy, and warmth. May you also bless those who are without food and shelter today, so that they may find the shelter and nourishment they need.

I pray you will continue to bless with me the wisdom to keep moving forward in life, making wise decisions for business and my personal life.

Hallelujah!

In your name I pray,

Authentic, Humble, Surrendered, and Spiritual

S. Michael Edwards

1 comments:

Just a Girl said...
Stay safe in your crazy Texas weather. Unbelievably it is sunny here in Oregon, although quite "chili," too!

Wednesday, February 2, 2011

Client Saved | Prayer #138
God,

Thanks for the wisdom when I had a client who wanted to move hosting to another provider. I was able to enroll him in staying and actually added in consulting hours, which I was not getting before. You gave me the wisdom to stay ground and center, not be defensive, and save the account.

Thank you!

In your name I pray,

Authentic, Humble, Surrendered, and Spiritual

S. Michael Edwards

Wednesday, February 2, 2011

New Client Opportunity | Prayer #139

God,

I pray that you will be with me today as I have a call with one of our new clients who is referring us to one of his distributors. This is one of over 250 distributors, and we've done so well with the main client that he's already referring us on to his main distributor. I pray for the wisdom to enroll him and then look forward to the referrals coming all around for the other distributors. This could really be a big win for our business!

In your name I pray,

Authentic, Humble, Surrendered, and Spiritual

S. Michael Edwards

Wednesday, February 2, 2011

Happiness is a Choice | Prayer #140

God,

I think you know who I'm talking about, and I could really use your support in providing me the wisdom to help this friend see how happiness is a choice and that suffering is optional. It's been a challenge to enroll him, and I feel like I'm fighting instead of guiding. I could sure use some guidance on how to deal with this controller who is stuck.

In your name I pray,

Authentic, Humble, Surrendered, and Spiritual

S. Michael Edwards

Wednesday, February 2, 2011

Square 1 | Prayer #141

God,

Looks like we're back to square one on the settlement with Ed. Basically my attorney doesn't like his attorney's agreement, and his attorney doesn't like our agreement. Neither of us wants to spend more money on attorneys, and I'm just not sure what I should do next.

My inclination is to go back to square one and just sue to undo the whole ownership transfer. Is that out of fairness or revenge? The more this drags on, the more I think the settlement offer, as far as money goes, is too low. Maybe I ask for more money and just sign the deal presented by his attorney?

Any advice, God?

Thanks for your guidance!

In your name,

Authentic, Humble, Surrendered, and Spiritual

S. Michael Edwards

Wednesday, February 2, 2011

My Buddy Rocks! | Prayer #142

God,

I want to thank you again for my buddy Craig. He rocks. He's such an inspiration and amazing support for me. I'm so thrilled that he is closing in on his goal…that was a stretch for him. He'll be one of the first to complete his goal, and that totally makes me happy.

May you continue to bless me on this journey with amazing people like Craig. I honestly feel a heart connection with him and love connecting with him and being a part of this amazing journey together.

In your name I pray,

Authentic, Humble, Surrendered, and Spiritual

S. Michael Edwards

Wednesday, February 2, 2011

Referral Call Was Amazing | Prayer #143
God,

Thanks so much for the wisdom that allowed me to enroll another client today. I love that we have done such a great job for a client that he was doing most of the enrolling for one of his distributors. They asked for contracts, and I pray that they will sign up as a client. As goes one, so go all. And with over 250 distributors, this could be a big win for our agency.

Thanks again, and I'm completely grateful for the abundance!

In your name I pray,

Authentic, Humble, Surrendered, and Spiritual

S. Michael Edwards

Wednesday, February 2, 2011

I'm Not Alone | Prayer #144
God,

I thank you for the support of my leaders and seniors who helped me navigate a difficult situation today. The guidance and wisdom of the whole is far greater than the wisdom I had alone. In the end, the advice worked. The situation was course corrected, and all is good.

I pray that you will continue to bless me on this leadership journey, challenges and all, as it's a learning experience for me and the students.

In your name I pray,

Authentic, Humble, Surrendered, and Spiritual

S. Michael Edwards

Thursday, February 3, 2011

Matthew 23:8-12 | Prayer #145

God,

In my Bible roulette this am, I found this passage: Matthew 23:8–12.

> "Don't let people do that to you, put you on a pedestal like that. You all have a single Teacher, and you are all classmates. Don't set people up as experts over your life, letting them tell you what to do. Save that authority for God, let **him** tell you what to do. No one else should carry the title of 'Father,' you have only one Father, and he's in heaven, And don't let people maneuver you into taking charge of them. There is only one Life-Leader for you and them—Christ.

> "Do you want to stand out? Then step down. Be a servant. If you puff yourself up, you'll get the wind knocked out of you. But if you're content to simply be yourself, your life will count for plenty."

Father God, I think this speaks volumes about my contract statement that I sign every prayer with at the end. It's the perfect passage to remind me that I am an Authentic ("simply be yourself"), Humble (if you puff yourself up, you'll get the wind knocked out of you), Surrendered ("There is only one Life-Leader for you"), and Spiritual (one Life-Leader for you and them—Christ).

May you lead me in the right direction as I try to hear your voice on how I should move forward, God. May I be a humble servant, and glorify you in my actions today.

In your name I pray,

Authentic, Humble, Surrendered, and Spiritual

S. Michael Edwards

Thursday, February 3, 2011

Above All | Prayer #146

God,

I love getting these videos and messages from my mom. It's so inspirational and a great way to start my day! She wrote this morning:

"Thinking of you both this morning and praising God that He thought of you… and you thought of Him! Have a glorious day! Love, Mom"

She sent the song "Above All," by Michael W. Smith. Great lyrics and music.

Father, thank you for my mom and dad and their unconditional love for me. Thank you for loving the world so much that you gave your Son to die for our sins. That above all, you thought of me, my family, and my fellow man.

In your name I pray,

Authentic, Humble, Surrendered, and Spiritual

S. Michael Edwards

Thursday, February 3, 2011

Shine | Prayer #147
God,

I am thinking about the people in Egypt this morning. I am praying that you will lift them up, the whole world needs it. I am thankful you gave me a sign, the sign of joy on my arm, and you brought me the light. It reminds me of this song, "SMS (Shine)," by David Crowder, of which the lyrics are so profound.

I love you, God,

In your name I pray,

Authentic, Humble, Surrendered, and Spiritual

S. Michael Edwards

Thursday, February 3, 2011

#91 vs #147 | Prayer #148
God,

I just realized that I had prayed about the "light at the end of the tunnel" (Prayer #91) and then you reminded me of "Shine," Prayer #147. I'd say that's an answered prayer. The shackles are off, your light is shining through, you have done exactly what I asked, and I am grateful. It's so much easier coming from the heart rather than trying to be profound. It's awesome how you move me, love on me, and shine your light on me.

Thank you for answering my prayers,

In your name I pray,

Authentic, Humble, Surrendered, and Spiritual

S. Michael Edwards

Thursday, February 3, 2011

Group Hug | Prayer #149
God,

It was amazing to watch my buddy's team connect as a group from the get go! What an amazing group of people, who were open and vulnerable and sharing honestly. I am excited to be on this journey with them and looking forward to what they create.

I pray you will continue to bless them and allow them to dream dreams bigger than they thought possible, to expect the unexpected, and to realize that miracles do occur.

What a great day!

In your name I pray,

Authentic, Humble, Surrendered, and Spiritual

S. Michael Edwards

Thursday, February 3, 2011

Bless This Food | Prayer #150
God,

I thank you for the amazing abundance and pray that you will bless this food to my body, to nourish my body and soul and provide me energy to move forward to glorify you in all that I do. I am so grateful that Ed came up to me this morning, still trying to figure out a settlement, and I am thankful that you are helping push this along.

I pray that you will continue to fill his heart with wisdom, compassion, and resolve to finalize this deal, which I thought was dead yesterday.

Lord, I pray you give me the wisdom to stay ground, centered, and compassionate and that I make the right choices to create a win/win for both Ed and myself.

In your name I pray,

Authentic, Humble, Surrendered, and Spiritual

S. Michael Edwards

Thursday, February 3, 2011

Everything Glorious | Prayer #151
God,

I thank you for making everything glorious! I can choose to suffer, or I can choose to be grateful in all you provide for me in my life. I believe in glorifying you and that through you all things are possible. You do not give me more than I can handle. I am grateful for all that you have giving me and give thanks. I love this song, "Everything Glorious," David Crowder Band.

You are glorious, and I believe, God,

In your name I pray,

Authentic, Humble, Surrendered, and Spiritual

S. Michael Edwards

Thursday, February 3, 2011

Ugh Lawyers | Prayer #152
God,

I just got the bill from my attorney, and at this point, the bills from him are more than the settlement. So I'm giving up all my rights to pay my attorney and not getting anything out of it. I'm a little queasy about the whole thing. Maybe this is you showing me where I should go, and maybe I just need more clear direction. It's certainly not making me want to stay, it's making me want more money for the settlement or to just go full force ahead and sue to undo the whole deal. Maybe you want me to just take the buyout and walk away?

Any advice would be appreciated. I hope I didn't overreact when I told the attorney that I was done with his services...but at this point I'm not sure what direction you want me to take.

Help please?

In your name I pray,

Authentic, Humble, Surrendered, and Spiritual

S. Michael Edwards

Board of Directors | Prayer #153
God,

I have been asked to serve on the board of directors for a non-profit. I am totally good with most of their mission, and while not 100 percent committed to the mission statement, I feel I could be of contribution and service in the areas where I am in agreement. I was wondering if you could provide some guidance on this. I have voiced my opinion and I'm awaiting a reply as to how they feel about my feelings on the mission, but was wondering what you thought?

Or maybe you already told me, by my reaching out and letting them know ahead of time my concerns?

Any thoughts would be appreciated. Of course, I could use some wisdom around this decision.

In your name I pray,

Authentic, Humble, Surrendered, and Spiritual

S. Michael Edwards

Thursday, February 3, 2011

Prayers Answered | Prayer #154
God,

Thanks for the guidance on my prayers regarding the non-profit board. We had our meeting tonight, which was my first introduction to the board, and it was amazing. I'm so blessed to be a part of this organization, and after "showing my cards" it became clear that this non-profit is totally in alignment with my vision of contribution and service.

Thank you, God!

In your name I pray,

Authentic, Humble, Surrendered, and Spiritual

S. Michael Edwards

Thursday, February 3, 2011

Freezing! | Prayer #155
God,

I want to thank you for the abundance and opportunities you are putting forth in my life. I had a great meeting with my buddy Brett and Jeff Ericson that could take us to the next level of our lives in both abundance and contribution and service. I'm so excited to see how this plays out. It may very well be my exit plan from the ad agency. The value of the company, with all these new clients will be a huge windfall for me. Thank you, God for the gift and abundance of money and opportunities.

The meeting was amazing, and I can't wait to see what we can create to change the world!

In your name I pray,

Authentic, Humble, Surrendered, and Spiritual

S. Michael Edwards

Friday, February 4, 2011

He Is with You | Prayer #156
God,

The joy of waking up and reading a note from Mom—usually accompanied by a video—continues. This morning, she wrote:

> "Good morning, this is the day that the Lord has made. I will rejoice and be glad in it. No matter what you're going through…please know that God is with you. You are in my prayers. I pray that God will give you peace…His peace. With love, Mom and Auntie Coffee"

What's funny, is that joy "will come in the morning" is in the lyrics…and that's exactly how I feel when I get her daily messages and videos. Thanks for an amazing mom, and may you be with her as she drops Dad off at the airport for his trip to Australia to facilitate change. May he have a safe trip, and may he inspire others to change their lives and the lives of those around them. I know he's going to rock it out, just like he always does. He's amazing, intuitive, and has the respect of so many, me included. What a life he leads and what a servant's heart he has. The song and video she sent was Mandisa—"He Is with You." Yes, he is!

Thank you God, for being with me, through thick and thin. I can feel your presence…and I feel more connected to you now than ever before in my life. You are constantly on my mind.

In your name I pray,

Authentic, Humble, Surrendered, and Spiritual

S. Michael Edwards

Friday, February 4, 2011

I Have Found | Prayer #157
God,

I love this song, and it speaks from my heart to you. You are all I need, and your grace guides me. It's a beautiful day outside, with five feet of snow, and the beauty is amazing.

I pray that you will be with the families that lost their loved ones in the ice and the family that died due to carbon monoxide poisoning. It's hard to understand, but I know you have a plan. Thank you for the song "I Have Found," by Kim Walker. Truly inspiring.

In your name I pray,

Authentic, Humble, Surrendered, and Spiritual

S. Michael Edwards

Friday, February 4, 2011

Me and Jesus | Prayer #158
God,

Stellar Kart—"Me and Jesus." This song speaks to where I was for twenty-one-and-a-half years…an atheist, turning my back on you. And you were with me. I pray that my friends and family who may be questioning your existence hear these words… may they see you through my actions.

I pray these things in your name,

Authentic, Humble, Surrendered, and Spiritual

S. Michael Edwards

Friday, February 4, 2011

Fixed Bible Roulette | Prayer #159
God,

So instead of just opening the Bible to see what passage spoke to me, today I looked in the back on violence, to pray about the violence in Egypt. I saw Matthew 5:28–42, and I think it's ironic that while I was looking for a passage on violence, I find one on loving your enemies and how it mentions "taking someone to court."

Hmmm, interesting considering I have been praying about the court settlement between Ed and I.

Matthew 5:28–42

"Here's another old saying that deserves a second look: 'Eye for eye, tooth for tooth.' Is that going to get us anywhere? Here's what I propose: 'Don't hit back at all.' If someone strikes you, stand there and take it. If someone drags you into court and sues for the shirt off your back, gift wrap your best coat and make a present of it. And if someone takes unfair advantage of you, use the occasion to practice the servant life. No more tit-for-tat stuff. Live generously."

Well, with that being said, I guess I will practice the servant life. No more attorney fees, no more striking back for being taken advantage of. Just practice a servant life.

I guess that settles that. As unsettling as it is.

In your name I pray,

Authentic, Humble, *Surrendered*, and Spiritual

S. Michael Edwards

Friday, February 4, 2011

Seventy Times Seven—Forgiveness | Prayer #160
God,

It was a boulder I carried for a long time, unwilling to forgive. Now I read in Matthew 18:21–22

"At that point Peter got up the nerve to ask, "Master, how many times do I forgive a brother or sister who hurts me? Seven?"

Jesus replied, "Seven! Hardly. Try seventy times seven."

Ah, a lesson I could have used awhile ago. Thanks for reminding me of forgiveness.

In your name I pray,

Authentic, Humble, Surrendered, and Spiritual

S. Michael Edwards

Friday, February 4, 2011

Where You Go I Go | Prayer #161
God,

I love that you are introducing me to God-Rock! I'm so inspired by the musicians who believe and the messages they sing about. Contemporary God Music! Kim Walker/Jesus Culture—Where You Go I Go. It's uplifting, and speaks to my heart. It's message to song...it's just what I need.

Thank you for inspiring these artists to sing your messages and filling my cup, God.

In your name I pray,

Authentic, Humble, Surrendered, and Spiritual

S. Michael Edwards

Friday, February 4, 2011

Holding Nothing Back | Prayer #162
God,

You definitely picked me up and turned me around...and I'm yours forever now. We've sure come a long way, haven't we, God? Thanks for sticking with me...I'm feeling better every day, stronger in our relationship, and bolder in my declaration that I believe. There are just too many serendipitous moments, or God Winks, to not believe. Too many amazing things happening that are bigger than I could imagine or do on my own.

It's through you, that all things are possible. I am open to the possibilities God, however that may look. Now I listen to Jesus Culture—"Holding Nothing Back."

In your name I pray,

Authentic, Humble, Surrendered, and Spiritual

S. Michael Edwards

Friday, February 4, 2011

Lead Me to the Cross | Prayer #163

God,

I pray that you will quiet my soul and let your love pour out. That you will use me as a vessel of hope and honor and that I would be an example of what glorifying you is all about. The lyrics to Hillsong, "Lead Me to the Cross," couldn't have been more perfect for me today.

I pray that you will be with all the students of Sam Camp and allow them to find the strength in themselves so they can grow and make a difference in the world. I pray for the past graduates of Sam Camp, and all Klemmer classes, that they remember the traits of a compassionate samurai and live a life of contribution and service and that their hearts be filled with joy and love.

I pray these things in your name,

Authentic, Humble, Surrendered, and Spiritual

S. Michael Edwards

Friday, February 4, 2011

TGIF | Prayer #164

Thank you, God, for an amazing week. I am so blessed and thankful and it's Friday! Now the fun begins, with embroidery and who knows what else you have in store for me.

I pray that the weather warms up enough that I can actually get out of the house and go do something this weekend. It's been fun working from home this week, but I think I'm in need of some human interaction in person. :)

May my dad have a comfortable snooze on his long flight to Australia today and be rejuvenated and ready to rock some worlds when he gets to his destination.

In your name I pray,

Authentic, Humble, Surrendered, and Spiritual

S. Michael Edwards

Saturday, February 5, 2011

Glorious Day | Prayer #165
God,

What a glorious day you've created. The beauty I see all around me is inspiring me. All the amazing snow that will melt today will change the beauty but not take it away.

I am so thankful for another day of joy and fun. I am committed to a day with you, using my talents you have given me.

I'm also committed to taking a shower. I know it's been a few days, and after being "in this cabin," I'm sure that will help my figurative fever go away…I've been so wrapped up in working from home…and since my bathroom is frozen, I just went all Grizzly Adams. It's not like I couldn't take my gear to another bathroom in the house, I have just chosen to go all granola. I think today is a great day to clean up, start the day fresh, and then embroider something special, in the your honor, for the beauty you have created.

In your name I pray,

Authentic, Humble, Surrendered, and Spiritual

S. Michael Edwards

Saturday, February 5, 2011

Bible Roulette—No Way! | Prayer #166
God,

You know in my heart that I just prayed about taking a bath…and then I did my Bible roulette. What do I open it up to? Ruth 3:3–4.

"Take a bath. Put on some perfume. Get all dressed up and go to the threshing floor. But don't let him know you're there until the party is well under way and he's had plenty of food and drink. When you see him slipping off to sleep, watch where he lies down and then go there. Lie at his feet to let him know that you are available to him for marriage. Then wait and see what he says. He'll tell you what to do."

You sure do have a great sense of humor, God. This made my day, another God Wink. I guess you can tell that I could use a bath today. Maybe a little Ralph Lauren Black and a quick shave. My body, your temple could use some housecleaning today.

Since you're having fun with me today, here's a little before shot. I'm totally stepping out of my "Looking Good" programs and into vulnerability. What do I have to lose? Nothing…maybe this will make you laugh.

Looking Good?

Thanks for the laugh today, God,

In your name I pray,

Authentic, Humble, Surrendered, and Spiritual

S. Michael Edwards

Saturday, February 5, 2011

I am Here | Prayer #167

God,

Ah, fresh as a daisy, and what shirt do I find to put on, but the Google Maps shirt that says "I am here." LOL. You are on a roll today, God, yes, you are here. You are with me…and thanks for the reminder.

God is RIGHT HERE!

Now I'm off to prepare the machine, to create something beautiful to glorify you, God. Maybe I will get some more coffee, too. :)

In your name I pray,

Authentic, Humble, Surrendered, and Spiritual

S. Michael Edwards

Saturday, February 5, 2011

Redeemer Lives | Prayer #168

Hey God,

Got a great song and message from Mom this morning. We're having virtual coffee while Dad is probably snoozing on his flight to Australia. This song is so beautiful. I think I have an amazing playlist of songs, with all the inspiration you are giving Mom and me...Let the praise music lift me up today!

> "This is one of my very favorite songs by one of my very favorite artists. I know that my Redeemer lives...I spoke to Him this morning...and I know, that I know, that I know...He lives! I know that you know it, too, and that brings such a big smile to my face. I also know that he's with your dad as he's in the air right now traveling to Australia. He's with us, too. We love and serve a great big God. Make it a great day. I love you so much. Mom"

So I listened to a beautiful Song by Nicole C. Mullen titled "Redeemer," and was moved.

Thank you for the sacrifice you gave, for the love you have, and for surrounding me in your glory.

In your name I pray,

Authentic, Humble, Surrendered, and Spiritual

S. Michael Edwards

Saturday, February 5, 2011

I Can't Talk to You, You're Not a Christian? | Prayer #169
God,

I spoke with a dear friend last night and she said that one of your followers told her that she couldn't talk to her anymore because she was not a Christian. Say what?! I don't think that is in the Bible. In fact, I'm pretty sure that if that were the case Jesus wouldn't have been hanging with the "out" crowd. Who better to talk to than non-believers?

I pray that you will fill the heart of this "Christian" so that she may come to realize how valuable her beliefs can be, and yet wash her with humility. If she only wants to surround herself with perfect people, she'll be lacking for friends.

It baffles my mind, but I know that you can help her see the light.

It's the opposite of what I was doing all those years. I didn't want to hang with Christians, because I couldn't relate to them. As soon as I let them into my life...whoa!

Things shifted into the speed of light…with blessings all around me. I wouldn't be walking the walk of Christ if I decided that now that I believe again, I should just hang with the believers. I mean, talk about singing to the choir?!

Can't we all just get along and do your work to help those in need? Can't we be an example for others to follow?

May you fill this lady's heart who was rejected by a "Christian" and allow her to see that not all Christians are alike.

I'm so thankful that I ran into a man who was open and willing to be my friend, even though I wasn't a believer. If it wasn't for Brett Stokes, walking the walk and not judging me for my beliefs, I wouldn't be here today, talking to you.

What an opportunity lost, but definitely not forever. I spent a good one-and-a-half hours talking to my friend about my journey and how I could relate to what she was saying. The hypocrisy of it all is unnerving.

I suggested she read the book *Jim and Casper Go to Church*. In fact, I might just recommend that book to the lady who rejected my friend.

In your name I pray,

Authentic, Humble, Surrendered, and Spiritual

S. Michael Edwards

1 comments:

Linda Edwards said…

My dear friends, if you know people who have wandered off from God's truth, don't write them off. Go after them. Get them back, and you will have rescued precious lives from destruction and prevented an epidemic of wandering away from God.

Saturday, February 5, 2011

The Ultimate Gift Part 2 | Prayer #170
God,

Thank you for an unexpected gift last night. Ed said he was going to watch a movie, and since Mom had given me a copy of *The Ultimate Gift*, I thought what a great movie for Ed to watch. He said, "It's not one of those Christian movies is it?" I said, "No, it's actually quite good and I think you'll like it." He asked me if I were going to watch it again, and I said I would.

So we watched the movie together, and he actually liked it. Go figure. May the message of the movie inspire Ed to be more compassionate and make more of a contribution.

Thanks for allowing us to share that movie together. It was perfect. Can't wait to see what Ed creates as a result of being inspired by the movie. I'm sure I'm not jumping to conclusions...how can you watch that movie and not be inspired to action?

In your name I pray,

Authentic, Humble, Surrendered, and Spiritual

S. Michael Edwards

1 comments:

Linda Edwards said...
   Wow! Like, check!

Saturday, February 5, 2011

Leaky Pipes | Prayer #171
Oh God,

I guess I should have anticipated broken water pipes when I prayed about the thaw. It rained over the porte-cochere...glad it wasn't the living room or anything other than the driveway. Plumber on the way. I pray that it won't be terribly expensive to fix.

Lesson learned, let the water drip before it freezes or get some VESIcare (they say it's for leaky pipes).

All in all, I'm like, "whatever"—it is what it is. Nothing I can do about it now. No reason to get all upset.

Palms together, palms apart…deep breath in, deep breath out.

In your name I pray,

Authentic, Humble, Surrendered, and Spiritual

S. Michael Edwards

P.S.—can you get the plumber here quickly? I am so glad I took a shower, now that the water is off…it would have made for another day stuck in the house. Like I would go out tonight looking like Grizzly Adams! Ha! So at least the prayer this morning about showering and the story of Naomi in Ruth 3:3–4 made some sense. The timing couldn't have been more perfect:)

Saturday, February 5, 2011

The Rose | Prayer #172
God,

Here's the shirt I made today, in honor of the beauty you have created all around us. "Beneath the bitter snow, lies the seed, that with the sun's love, in the spring, becomes the Rose."

I love how my friends have said the snow melt that caused the busted pipes could be a carwash. LOL. I am just glad that the plumber is here, and can't wait to see how little he charges us to fix the damage.

Praying to you for a win/win on this deal, God. He gets paid a fair price, and we get our water lines fixed without getting gouged.

Funny, how I was making a shirt with a rose, then this song, *The Rose* by Bette Midler, played in the background, and the water pipe bursting…it's all good, and just another God Wink.

Saturday, February 5, 2011

Plumbing | Prayer #173
Is it okay to sigh, God? Big sigh. Just got the plumber's estimate. We had five pipes bust, turns out the builder put the pipes next to the bottom and insulated on top

of them toward the top…not very bright. The estimate was $1,600 for plumbing fix alone…we still have to get the estimate to make it look like it never happened.

They will be back tomorrow to fix the pipes, then we will have to find someone to fix the ceiling. My day of joy ended with a slightly lower bank account.

If I spoke French, I would say, *"C'est la vie,"* but I don't so I won't.

I am thankful that this isn't going to bankrupt me, and that we are able to pay to make things right. I pray for those families who can't afford heat, let alone a plumber and remodeler to fix their minor disaster. I guess that's what this is, just minor.

I am thankful I'm not in the middle of a hurricane, a flood, or in Egypt right now. I guess everything is relative.

So with gratitude, I thank you for things not being as bad as they could be. Although it could have been fun to have a carwash to drive through every day, the water bill would have been mighty high. Certainly need to fix this so we can sell the house. Any word on when that might happen?

Keep me posted, it's been a month, and no offers. Now I am praying for, "What next?" I'm sure you'll let me know…You haven't let me down thus far.

It's funny, we started the day with some fun, and ended with some sobering reality.

I'm not done, though. Going out to dinner with a friend and determined to end the night with some fun.

I did enjoy the embroidery today. I can't wait to do some more tomorrow!

In your name I pray,

Authentic, Humble, Surrendered, and Spiritual

S. Michael Edwards

Sunday, February 6, 2011

Touch the Hem of His Garment | Prayer #174
God,

What a beautiful way to start the day, a heartfelt email from Mom and the most amazing song, and lyrics. As I embroider today, I will remember you and this song… and the story behind it. You make me whole.

> "Whether you're just putting on your garments today or you're creating new garments…think about touching the hem of his garment. His love heals your soul, and you'll know you've been made whole. Thank you, Jesus! Praying you'll be blessed today and always. Love, Mom"

God, I am so thankful for my mom and her inspiration. She loves me unconditionally, and I appreciate how she starts her day thinking about me and my sister and how much she cares for us. She sent me "One Touch," a beautiful song by Nicole C. Mullen. Amazing lyrics.

In your name I pray,

Authentic, Humble, Surrendered, and Spiritual

S. Michael Edwards

Sunday, February 6, 2011

PSALM 30:2-3 | Prayer #175

My God,

I can so relate to this passage in the Bible, on my journey, and in my life, it is perfect.

> Psalm 30:2–3
>
> God, my God, I yelled for help and you put me together.
>
> God, you pulled me out of the grave, gave me another chance at life
>
> when I was down-and-out.

Indeed you did, and I'm forever thankful in your patience with me all these years. I'm grateful you have given me another chance at life, and the life you have given me is bigger and better than I could have even imagined in my wildest dreams.

Thank you, God,

In your name I pray,

Authentic, Humble, Surrendered, and Spiritual

S. Michael Edwards

Sunday, February 6, 2011

Safety First—Plot Second | Prayer #176

God,

I remember when I was in the Air Force that we'd give a safety briefing before each weekend to the airmen. It was always "Safety First." I don't know why that came to me today, but I just got off the phone with Mom. She was on her way to church and said that Dad had landed safely in Sydney and is on his way to Brisbane. I pray his last leg of this part of his journey is safe.

What a great song to celebrate safety, by Lecresia Campbell, "Safety."

I also pray that those affected by the flooding in Australia are comforted and know that nothing is too big for them to handle, through you. I pray that the disaster is an opportunity to receive something even greater than they had before.

I don't know what's in store for me, after the flooding yesterday from broken pipes...but I'm sure I'll find out in due time. I love how you reveal your plan for my life, in a well-scripted, precise way. It's like the book of my life has been written, and I get to live the chapters out, and then find out what it was all about.

Those are the best types of books, where you don't know what's coming, and then bam! the plot thickens.

Here's to the next chapter of my life!

In your name I pray,

Authentic, Humble, Surrendered, and Spiritual

S. Michael Edwards

Sunday, February 6, 2011

Chicken Soup for the Soul | Prayer #177
God,

I pray that you bless this chicken soup to my body, and nourish my soul. I thank you for the farmers who grew the rice and carrots and raised the chickens. I pray that you will watch over the farmers and provide them with abundant crops this year. It's a tough life being a farmer, and yet, they help sustain us.

I pray these things in your name,

Authentic, Humble, Surrendered, and Spiritual

S. Michael Edwards

Sunday, February 6, 2011

Seventy Sevens | Prayer #178
God,

I opened the Bible to Daniel 9:20–21 this afternoon: "While I was pouring out my heart, baring my sins and the sins of my people Israel, praying my life out before my God, interceding for the holy mountain of my God—while I was absorbed in this praying, the humanlike Gabriel, the one I had seen in an earlier vision, approached me, flying in like a bird about the time of evening worship."

I totally get the being absorbed in praying and praying my life out before you. As I have documented prayer #178 today, I reflect back on when I started this journey. It seems that I am in constant contact (not the email software) with you and that you are in my thoughts and with me in all that I do. What was a journey to reconnect with you has become much bigger than I expected. Reminds me of the song, "You Were Always on My Mind," or at least the title. You are always on my mind.

I think it's safe to say that this journey to 365 prayers is really a journey to the most unexpected gift.

Thank you,

In your name I pray,

Authentic, Humble, Surrendered, and Spiritual

S. Michael Edwards

Sunday, February 6, 2011

I feel Like Mexican Tonight | Prayer #179

God,

If I were stranded on a desert island, I'd want Mexican food! That's what I'm having for dinner tonight. I pray you will bless the food to my body, and all the nourishment you can get from tortillas and beef and some spicy hot sauce. They say "you are what you eat," and if that's the case, I'm a Mexican! I could eat it seven days a week, four or five times a day!

As I prepare to have a good burrito (definition by my dad, "If the grease don't run down your arm, it ain't a good burrito"), I am thankful to you for the abundance you have provided for me.

Now as I prepare to watch the Super Bowl (okay, really the commercials, the game is just filler for what I truly enjoy), I pray that you will be with those that are watching as well. I saw a commercial tonight about people getting drunk and then driving home after the game. Please God, watch over those who are watching the game and give them the wisdom to hand over their keys to a sober driver.

I don't care if the Steelers or Packers win, but I am rooting for the Packers…I like the underdog! (I mean if I'm going to watch the commercials, as an advertising guru, I guess I should pick a team to root for, huh?)

In your name I pray,

Authentic, Humble, Surrendered, and Spiritual

S. Michael Edwards

Passing | Prayer #180
God,

I just got a note from Janet Henze, an amazing woman who has championed me, changed my life and inspired me. She mentioned that her dad will most likely be "passing tonight." I don't know how she knows, but I know that you know. I pray that you will be with her and her family and her dad in this difficult transition. I pray that you will make it a peaceful transition and fill their hearts with love, compassion, and strength as they deal with the loss of their husband, father, and friend.

I can't imagine what it would be like to lose my father. I just can't. I am thankful that Janet has had the opportunity to create memories that will last a lifetime. I just pray that you will lift her up in this most difficult time. I also pray that you will comfort her mother, as I know this must be a struggle for her to lose her husband.

I pray these things, in your name,

Authentic, Humble, Surrendered, and Spiritual

S. Michael Edwards

1 comments:

Linda Edwards said...
Thanks for the post, Michael. I pray in unity with you for peace and comfort for the family. I pray that her father is at peace with his maker. Thank you, Lord, for your provisions for us to enter into your presence. May the precious memories be a healing balm for the family. Amen.

Sunday, February 6, 2011

Mom Loves Rap? | Prayer #181
Seriously God?

Mom loves rap music? What a blessing she sent to me today. I love these lyrics in particular God. The song by TobyMac, "Lose My Soul," touched me deeply.

"This is my favorite almost rap! I'll bet you never expected your mama to send a rap song! I have to keep you guessing. I love the message in this song. I don't want to gain the whole world and lose my soul. Hold me close, Father God, and thanks for having your grip of grace on my family, too. Love, Momma"

Go Packers!

In your name I pray,

Authentic, Humble, Surrendered, and Spiritual

S. Michael Edwards

Sunday, February 6, 2011

You're All I Want | Prayer #182

God,

Mom's on a roll tonight, she sent me this video which is titled "Draw Me Close," by Kutless, and the message is perfect…touching, and it's like a prayer I haven't spoken yet.

"Thank you, Father, for drawing us all close to you. My heart is full and over-flowing with love for you, Lord, and for joy that my family will be together in eternity.

P.S. We sang this song at First Friends Church today during our time of worship. Mom"

I couldn't have said it better, God, You're all I want, you're all I've ever needed, help me know you are near…You are my desire, help me find a way to bring me back to you. I know you have done that, and so much more, and I'm so grateful.

In your name I pray,

Authentic, Humble, Surrendered, and Spiritual

S. Michael Edwards

Monday, February 7, 2011

Clear My Mind | Prayer #183

God,

I had such an amazing rest last night, but my mind is still cluttered. I pray that you will clear my mind to allow creativity and joy into my mind and heart today. It's the first day back to the office after working from home four-and-a-half days last week.

I pray that this is an amazing week and that my call with our small group for Sam Camp be an opportunity for all of us to bond, and build relationships. I pray that the students open up to possibilities and vulnerability.

In your name I pray,

Authentic, Humble, Surrendered

Monday, February 7, 2011

Suicide Prevention | Prayer #184
God,

I just heard from a dear friend that her son tried to kill himself. I pray that you will help the professionals who are treating her son for his mental state and that you also surround the family in love and comfort in this most difficult time.

I can only imagine how difficult this must be for them, and I pray that you will embrace them and lift them up as they deal with this. They are very much aware that you were there and helped prevent the suicide.

I pray that you will be with all the people today and always and help them see their true value and purpose in life and that they are loved and important.

In your name I pray,

Authentic, Humble, Surrendered, and Spiritual

S. Michael Edwards

Monday, February 7, 2011

Clarity Answered | Prayer #185
God,

Thanks for the clarity today as I had my Sam Camp call. I learned a lot about our small group and their passion and desire for growth. I appreciate you being with me and having Craig and Cody on the call to support me. It was a great team effort and an amazing call.

In your name I pray,

Authentic, Humble, Surrendered, and Spiritual

S. Michael Edwards

Monday, February 7, 2011

Shout To the Lord | Prayer #186
God,

Another great praise song forwarded by Mom, with Darlene Zschech and Hill-song—"Shout to the Lord!"

She wrote, "Here's another great song we sang in worship today. Thank you, Father, that you're our comfort, shelter, tower of refuge, and strength. Let every breath, all that I am, never cease to worship you. Praise to the King of kings and Lord of lords."

You are my comfort and shelter and my strength. Praise be to you, and I sing for joy today and always. Thanks for being there my friend!

In your name I pray,

Authentic, Humble, Surrendered, and Spiritual

S. Michael Edwards

Monday, February 7, 2011

#184 Tied to Prayer #187
God,

Mom sent a great video that tied into the prayer #184 about suicide. She wrote, "This morning we're having goose bumps and tears with our virtual coffee time together. Will you tell me how can it be any better than this? You're all I want; you're all I need. Thank you, Father God, for never giving up on us and giving us the desire and courage to find our way into your arms. I love you! " The song she sent was "Lifehouse Everything."

Little did she know about my friend's son...and then to watch this video of the troubles this character goes through and how she threatens suicide.

You are my strength, God. I want to feel you, I need to hear you. You are my light... and you lead me in such an amazing and powerful way.

I am grateful for your presence in my life and the lives of my friends. I am also hopeful for your presence to be known to those who do not know you or choose to not know you.

Thank you for this beautiful message, lyrics, and play. Powerful.

In your name, I pray,

Authentic, Humble, Surrendered, and Spiritual

S. Michael Edwards

Monday, February 7, 2011

Does "Low Ball" Have a Hyphen? | Prayer #188
God,

We got our first offer on the house today, which was 11 percent below our asking price. Doesn't seem like a big difference, but I'd like to see it more in the 3–4 percent range. We'll counter their offer, and I pray that you'll help us get the best price possible. I'm not in such a big hurry to get out of the house that I want some fire sale pricing. The good news is, we'd make money, and in this market, that's a good thing.

Lord, I'm praying for some movement in the price upwards.

Thanks for your support,

In your name I pray,

Authentic, Humble, Surrendered, and Spiritual

S. Michael Edwards

Monday, February 7, 2011

Tough Decisions—Sick to My Stomach | Prayer #189
God,

Ed just offered to buy me out of the house. I'm sick to my stomach. I don't know what to do. Do I take the buyout and move and stay here at the ad agency? Do I take the buyout and sell my shares in the company and move to Florida, my dream state? Now that I know he wants to keep the house, I'm wondering what you want me to do. I'm just sick about all these decisions and ramifications and possibilities, and I could really use some guidance.

We had a great conversation, open, honest communication about what we each want. He wants me to stay at the agency (of course he does, I bring in the majority of the revenue), yet he pays me less than someone who just "breaks even" on revenue and salary and makes a ton more than I do. I want to be fairly compensated, and it really comes down to a crossroads for me.

It's scary to up and move to a new state and start all over. There's the fear of the unknown. I have opportunities all around me, and staying in my comfort zone but making less than I could be is a competing commitment.

Do you have any guidance for me, God?

In your name I pray,

Authentic, Humble, Surrendered, and Spiritual

S. Michael Edwards

Tuesday, February 8, 2011

Praise You in the Storm | Prayer #190
God,

I woke up with a sense of serenity and peace, and can feel your presence this morning. Mom sent the most beautiful prayer and the perfect song. She's amazing. I've got my prayer army working overtime to lift me up. Mom sent me, "Praise You in the Storm," by Casting Crowns. Great lyrics and great music as always.

She wrote: "Okay, it's time for the big guns…I'll praise you in this storm…though your heart is torn, I'll praise you in this storm. God hasn't left your side, and he'll see you through. His promises are true, and He will never leave you nor forsake you.

"I'm praying that you'll find peace in the midst of this storm and decision making. May God give you wisdom, courage, and clarity of purpose as you choose and move (don't make that mean anything other than what you know I meant). We are here for you…we love you, we support you, we will do anything we can to help you through this process. Right now, the best I've got is to lift you up to our heavenly Father…He loves you even more than I do…and that's a lot. Blessings.

"Would love to chat but time for my Master Mind call and then I have a meeting at church. Hugs, Mom"

God, though my heart is torn, I praise you in this storm and know that you will help guide me in making the best decision.

I praise you, God, and know that you are with me today and always.

In your name I pray,

Authentic, Humble, Surrendered, and Spiritual

S. Michael Edwards

Tuesday, February 8, 2011

He Will Carry Me | Prayer #191
God,

The prayers are flooding in and I am feeling the love. I know that the footsteps in the sand are yours, and that you are carrying me. I am thankful for the song mom sent, by Lynda Randle, "He Will Carry You."

Mom wrote me last night and said, "Michael, I know you have some decisions to make that are heavy on your heart and on your mind. I pray this song with be an encouragement to you to trust in Jesus and know that if he carried the weight of the world on his shoulders…I know that he will carry you. May you get so close to him that you have no doubt what God wants you to do. I bind the enemy from confusing you and pray for focus and God's will. I love you so much. Mom"

Tears of joy are welling up as I read my mom's prayer. Praise God!

Thank you, God, for calming the storm. I pray that you'll give me clarity of mind as I make these decisions on how to separate assets and whether I should stay in the business or move.

In your name I pray,

Authentic, Humble, Surrendered, and Spiritual

S. Michael Edwards

Tuesday, February 8, 2011

God of the Mountain | Prayer #192

Oh my amazing God,

I am lifted up in your arms today, and my mom is by my side supporting me. I do appreciate her support, and these songs and lyrics are so helpful in giving me peace. Lynda Randle, "God of the Mountain," is a great song. "Fear not for I am with thee" (Isaiah 41:10). God, I know this and it's the unknown that I fear, but why do I fear, knowing that you are with me? Why don't I trust that all will work out? Ah, surrender, I end every prayer with that word…deep breath, I surrender to you, God, and pray that this peace I woke up with will remain as you carry me up the mountain.

From Mom:

> "Praying for peace and joy for the journey. May you know, trust, believe that the God of the mountain is also the God of the valley. Isaiah 41:10 says, 'Fear not for I am with thee.' (P.S. Grandma is smiling down cuz I sent a song from the Gaither Homecoming Series. Love and hugs mom"

In your name I pray,

Authentic, Humble, Surrendered, and Spiritual

S. Michael Edwards

Tuesday, February 8, 2011

Bless Janet Henze | Prayer #193
God,

I pray that you will continue to hold Janet Henze, her mother, and family in your arms after the passing of her father yesterday. I pray that she be filled with memories and love as they prepare for the funeral. I am so grateful for Janet in my life, and pray that you will lift her up as she celebrates her father's life and grieves his passing.

In your name I pray,

Authentic, Humble, Surrendered, and Spiritual

S. Michael Edwards

Tuesday, February 8, 2011

Sizelove Prayers | Prayer #194
God,

Karen has asked the following:

Personal: With the love, support, and integrity of my Master Mind team and knowledge that where ever I am…God is, I graciously make the following requests: I am so happy and grateful that my income is now at least $5,000 or more a month on or before February 28, 2011, by noon EST.

Professional: With the love, support, and integrity of my Master Mind team and knowledge that where ever I am…God is, I graciously make the following requests: I am so happy and grateful now that I have personally sponsored two or more active Chocolatiers on my team on or before February 28, 2011, by noon EST.

Esoteric: With the love, support, and integrity of my Master Mind team and knowledge that where ever I am…God is, I graciously make the following requests: I am so happy and grateful now our house is completely remodeled and furnished comfortably on or before March 31, 2011.

I pray that you are with Karen as she grows her business and generates $5,000 or more a month by the end of the month, and I pray that in doing so she is able to sponsor two or more active members on her team by the end of the month and that she has completed the remodel of the house by March 31.

I pray these things in your name God,

Authentic, Humble, Surrendered, and Spiritual

S. Michael Edwards

Tuesday, February 8, 2011

Psalm 107:28-31 | Prayer #195

God,

Thank you for my prayer army! Lisa Darden sent me this passage, which is perfectly timed, of course!

Psalm 107:28–31

Then they cry out to the Lord in their trouble, and He brings them out of their distresses. He calms the storm, so that its waves are still. Then they are glad because they are quiet; so He guides them to their desired haven. Oh, that men would give thanks to the Lord for His goodness, and for His wonderful works to the children of men!

God, I have cried out to you for help and you have calmed my storm. I am glad and give thanks to you for your goodness, grace, and love.

In your name I pray,

Authentic, Humble, Surrendered, and Spiritual

S. Michael Edwards

Tuesday, February 8, 2011

Agros—Contribution and Service | Prayer #196
God,

As my friend and new client meets with Agros today, I pray that they will allow us to submit them to Google for a grant and allow us to run their account, out of contribution and service. It's a win for them and a win for us. I love their mission and would love to help them generate more funds.

I pray the meeting goes well and that they are thrilled to have an agency run their account for free.

In your name I pray,

Authentic, Humble, Surrendered, and Spiritual

S. Michael Edwards

1 comments:

S. Michael Edwards said...

> Great news! Agros committee was thrilled that I was willing to run their Google Grant program for them. Thank you, God! I'm so excited, as this is a huge opportunity for me to be of service and contribution. It also allows me to get my name out to their largest contributors, and their CEO and founder. Thank you, God! Prayer answered this week!

March 11, 2011 11:43 AM

Tuesday, February 8, 2011

Bonus | Prayer #197
God,

An amazing thing happened today, but you already know that. I'm confident you planted the seeds to enable Ed to be compassionate and give me an extra $2,500 distribution. That means he gets $7,500, which I could be mad about, but I'm grateful for the extra cash.

We decided to not respond to the offer on the house. He still has to figure out if he can get his dad to pony up the dough to buy me out of the house, and if he can refinance without me on it.

I'm still up in the air on what I want to do. Do I stay with the ad agency, or start my own and move to Florida? Or do I wait for a few months, then move? I just don't know what you want me to do.

I felt a sense of calm, instead of panic today, and I thank you for calming my mind, heart, and soul.

I know that all the answers are there, it's just a matter of tapping into them. I'm in a much better space, even though nothing is really resolved.

A good friend of mine suggested I make a list of pros and cons and financial implications of each option I have in front of me. I think it's a great idea, and after my meeting in Austin with one of the opportunities (okay, he's not an opportunity, but has one for me), I will have a better idea of what this new opportunity could look like for me.

So I'm surrendering to you and your grace and wisdom, and putting it out to my prayer army to support me in making the right decision to honor you, myself, and my fellow man.

Thank you, God, for a great day.

In your name I pray,

Authentic, Humble, Surrendered, and Spiritual

S. Michael Edwards

Wednesday, February 9, 2011

Bright Shiny Day? | Prayer #198
God,

As the cold winter hits us again, I am thankful that we found a remodeler to fix the damage done by the last storm, and he was able to get the pipes insulated, as the snow falls and the cold air blows. I am also thankful that Ed has been generous enough to give me more money. We still have a lot to work through, and I pray you will continue to fill each of our hearts with compassion and allow us to create a win/win solution that we are both thrilled about. Now for some visualization of what that day will look like!

From Mom:

> I can't wait to send this to you tomorrow morning so I'll just send it now! I can see clearly now the rain is gone…gonna be a bright, bright sun-shiny day. I think I can make it now the pain is gone…here is the rainbow I've been praying for…LYMI, Mom (Author's Note: LYMI is shorthand for Love Ya Mean It)

> P.S. Thanks for calling, Michael. It was a pleasure spending the evening with you. You actually rode to Portland and back with me!

I encourage you to look around you and listen to the words of Jimmy Cliff, "I Can See Clearly Now," so many layers in the lyrics.

Oh what a day that will be.

God, I pray that today is an amazing day filled with joy!

In your name I pray,

Authentic, Humble, Surrendered, and Spiritual

S. Michael Edwards

Wednesday, February 9, 2011

Leaning on the Everlasting Arms | Prayer #199
God,

Mom sent me this song by Iris Dement, "Leaning on the Everlasting Arms," and it reminds me of Dolly Parton, whom I adore. The message is clear and powerful.

Mom wrote: "This song has lifted me up and given me comfort in times of struggle and doubt. I pray it will be an encouragement to you too. I can't think of a better place to be than 'Leaning on the Everlasting Arms.' Here's a virtual hug from me to you, too. May today bring you continued peace and calm as you seek God's perfect will for your life. With love, Mom"

God, I couldn't agree with Mom more, as I surrender to you and lean on your everlasting arms. Thank you for bringing me peace to my heart, and for clearing my mind. The love all around me is a blessing, and I am grateful for all you have done to lift me up.

In your name I pray,

Authentic, Humble, Surrendered, and Spiritual

S. Michael Edwards

Wednesday, February 9, 2011

What If His People Prayed? | Prayer #200
God,

It's documented prayer #200—and what better song to glorify you, than this one by the Casting Crowns, "What If His People Prayed?" This song lifts me up.

Mom wrote: "This video really resonates with me because of your example of your goal to reconnect with God with 365 prayers in seven weeks. Do you have the picture of you praying at Grandma's house? It would so fit right into this video and song. (It was in the video you made for Grandma's funeral. February 12, it will be five years since she went to heaven.) Thank you for your awesome example of praying without ceasing. You touch my heart! With love, Mom"

It is definitely an example of my goal to reconnect with you, and you do answer prayers. I sent the passage below from Mom to the friend who said she couldn't relate or talk to my other friend who was not a Christian.

> *My dear friends, if you know people who have wandered off from God's truth, don't write them off. Go after them. Get them back and you will have rescued precious lives from destruction and prevented an epidemic of wandering away from God.*

> *James 5: 19 and 20 The Message*

Which was a comment on Prayer #169. I found out this morning that said "Christian" realized she was "judgmental"—eyes open, God. Thank you for hearing my prayer and for helping open her eyes.

I can't find the picture of me on my knees praying, I'll have to look for it and see if I can find it. I'll be praying for Grandma on the twelfth, the anniversary of her rising up to Heaven. So much to be thankful for with Grandma—she was a true believer and an amazing example of God's love.

It's prayer #200, God, and I feel closer to you than ever before in my life. I truly feel you with me, lifting me up, holding me tight, and carrying me through life with all your might.

Joyful tears,

In your name I pray,

Authentic, Humble, Surrendered, and Spiritual

S. Michael Edwards

Wednesday, February 9, 2011

Refinance | Prayer #201
God,

I just talked to Ed about him refinancing the house so it's only in his name. Then we talked about me refinancing the boat so it's only in my name. We talked about what things would look like, and there are still many unanswered questions. With his trip home this weekend, I pray that he'll get clarity and answers on how we can untangle our assets, and pray that I get the same clarity.

I'll be reaching out today to see what a refinance on the boat will look like. With me being off the house, I am praying that I can refinance and get a good deal.

In your name I pray,

Authentic, Humble, Surrendered, and Spiritual

S. Michael Edwards

Wednesday, February 9, 2011

Settlement | Prayer #202
God,

I just had an epiphany, as I was gathering the documents to refinance the boat, I realized that I could just settle with Ed on the legal dispute and that would give me more money. Rather than just let it die on the vine, why not recoup my attorney fees that have already been paid? This would help me pay off the debt I have on my 401(k) loan or the interest free loan and make it easier to refinance.

I'm getting ready to talk to Ed about what it would take to make that happen. I'm just surrendering…and I feel good about it.

Thanks, God.

In your name I pray,

Authentic, Humble, Surrendered, and Spiritual

S. Michael Edwards

Wednesday, February 9, 2011

Settlement Part Deux | Prayer #203
God,

Thanks for helping me stay grounded and centered and seeing this settlement as a win-win. After reviewing the documents, I am comfortable signing them and getting the payout. It will go along way and my fear of "being let go" once I signed, are actually a blessing—I get the money and if I get terminated, then I can go do what I want to do outside of the agency.

So Ed is working out the details so we can put this settlement to bed—it was a very calm discussion and seems like we're back on track.

In gratitude, God,

Authentic, Humble, Surrendered, and Spiritual

S. Michael Edwards

Wednesday, February 9, 2011

Devotional Roulette Is Back | Prayer #204

God,

I finally got my devotional back and opened it up to see what you wanted me to read today.

Philippians 2:2–4

> "Agree with each other, love each other, be deep-spirited friends. Don't push your way to the front; don't sweet-talk your way to the top. Put yourself aside, and help others get ahead. Don't be obsessed with getting your own advantage. Forget yourselves long enough to lend a helping hand."

You have perfect timing, God. I feel like that's what Ed and I are doing. I know that helping others is my mission. I'm definitely helping Ed get ahead by not fighting him anymore on the settlement, allowing him control of the 25 percent of the company that I should have had first right of refusal on. It's not worth the fight, and as soon as I gave up resistance to it, everything seems to be falling into place.

That which we resist persists. Thanks, Brian Klemmer!

Thank you, God, for a great passage today.

In your name I pray,

Authentic, HUMBLE, Surrendered, and Spiritual

S. Michael Edwards

Wednesday, February 9, 2011

Prayers for Lesha | Prayer #205

God,

Lesha has the following requests that I pray you will honor.

With the love, support, and integrity of this Master Mind team and the knowledge that where ever I am…God is, I graciously make the following requests.

That on or before March 31, 2011, we have four new restaurant contracts for Grow Green.

That Mi Querencia has two jarred products on store shelves on or before September 1, 2011.

That on or before September 1, 2011, Mi Querencia and Grow Green are adding an additional $1,000 a month to my income.

God, I pray that you help Lesha get four or more new restaurant contracts for her Grow Green endeavor by March 31, and I pray that her amazing food is on store shelves on or before September 1, 2011 (I hope one of the two is her fabulous pesto!), and I pray that by September 1, 2011, that her Mi Querencia and Grow Green have added $1,000 or more in additional income.

As a servant and Godly woman, she deserves these things and more. I pray that you bless Lesha with abundance and fill her servant's heart with love. I pray that she remain vulnerable to the possibilities and step into her true authentic self.

In your name I pray,

Authentic, Humble, Surrendered, and Spiritual

S. Michael Edwards

Wednesday, February 9, 2011

Prayers for Nelson | Prayer #206
God,

I'm so grateful to be on a Master Mind team with other Godly people. I pray that you will honor Nelson's requests.

With faith in God and a great sense of gratitude I ask the following:

Professional: That on or before 10 February 2011, I created ten or more hours of weekly study time dedicated to the H-65 helicopter first pilot syllabus.

Personal: That on or before 10 February 2011, I have a heart connection with three or more vivacious, genuine, caring, powerful, and captivating women.

Esoteric: That on or before 14 February 2011, law and order has been restored to Egypt under the oversight of a coalition government that promotes an open, prosperous, and free society.

I pray that he has studied ten or more hours for his syllabus and has found a heart connection with three or more vivacious, genuine, caring, powerful, and captivating women by February 10. He's such a caring and giving man and deserves a relationship and friendships. I also pray that by 14 February, law and order has been restored to Egypt under the oversight of a coalition government that promotes an open, prosperous, and free society.

I know Nelson's heart is the in the right place God. He wants peace and order in Egypt, and through you anything is possible. He also wants to attract more female companions into his life, as he searches for a new relationship. I pray these things in your name,

Authentic, Humble, Surrendered, and Spiritual

S. Michael Edwards

Wednesday, February 9, 2011

Ozzie | Prayer #207
God,

Please be with my dad and Scott as they facilitate change and transformation in Australia for some deserving and amazing students. I pray that their students open their hearts and minds and release what's holding them back. I pray that they find the inner strength to move forward and truly believe in the power they have and the difference they can make in the world.

I pray these things in your name,

Authentic, Humble, Surrendered, and Spiritual

S. Michael Edwards

Wednesday, February 9, 2011

Burned out on Religion | Prayer #208
God,

I was burned out on religion, still am a bit. I'm not burned out on you, though. I'm energized by you and your messages and grace.

Matthew 11:28–30

"Are you tired? Worn out? Burned out on religion? Come to me. Get away with me and you'll recover your life. I'll show you how to take a real rest. Walk with me and work with me—watch how I do it. Learn the unforced rhythms of grace. I won't lay anything heavy or ill-fitting on you. Keep company with me and you'll learn to live freely and lightly."

I get it! I feel your grace and you lift me up. You give me strength when I am down. It's like a shot of Red Bull!

Thank you for the company, and for allowing me to live freely and lightly when I am with you.

In gratitude and in your name I pray,

Authentic, Humble, Surrendered, and Spiritual

S. Michael Edwards

Wednesday, February 9, 2011

Fireplace Guy | Prayer #209

God,

Thanks for sending the fireplace guy over. He couldn't fix the fireplace, but he saw all my embroidery equipment and asked for a bid on seventy-five shirts. LOL. He said, "Great day for me, sucks for you"—actually, the fireplace is the least of my worries. Love that I have the opportunity to bid on his embroidery request.

Thanks, God!

In your name I pray,

Authentic, Humble, Surrendered, and Spiritual

S. Michael Edwards

Wednesday, February 9, 2011

A Gift From Heaven | Prayer #210
God,

The timing for a coaching call with Centa Terry couldn't have been more perfect. She had some amazing questions around my situation and I felt this overwhelming sense of calm, serene, and "Yes, I can" attitude. It's such a pleasure to speak with Centa, and her gift is so awesome. To have her share that gift with me and so many others in this world is truly a gift to the world.

I had a grin bigger than life after the call. I had clarity of purpose, future, and confidence in where I want to be in six months.

Thank you, God.

The timing was perfect, the coaching was priceless and I am grateful.

In your name, I pray,

Authentic, Humble, Surrendered, and Spiritual

S. Michael Edwards

Thursday, February 10, 2011

To God Be the Glory | Prayer #211
Good Morning God,

I lift my hands up to you today and glorify you for all that you have done for me in my life. Today will be a beautiful day!

Mom sent me this song, and the lyrics, as usual, ring true: Sissel and Oslo Gospel Choir, "My Tribute (To God Be the Glory)."

She wrote:

> "After talking to you this is the song that God put in my heart. To God be the glory...for surrounding you with like minded Godly people (more than I could have imagined); for sending a team of prayer warriors into

your life; for never giving up on you but pursuing you relentlessly; for loving you and giving you a passion for His Kingdom; for answers to so many of your heart cries and desires for joyfully creating a world of equality for all; for so many amazing opportunities both personally and professionally; To God be the glory for giving me such an amazing, compassionate and loving son and daughter! (Grandma Storlie was born in Oslo! I'm sensing a theme here this week as we listen to Sissel and the Oslo Gospel Choir.) LYMI, Mom"

Thank you, God, for all you have given me and all that you do for me.

Off to change the world today!

In your name I pray,

Authentic, Humble, Surrendered, and Spiritual

S. Michael Edwards

Thursday, February 10, 2011

I Will Not Be Moved | Prayer #212
Hey God,

I think you've created an amazing DJ, who has in turn blessed me with a great playlist, based on where I am in my life. Mom's choice of music is thoughtful, timely, and a gift much appreciated (not like the tough skins jeans she used to buy me!). The latest song to add to the playlist is by Natalie Grant, "Will Not Be Moved.

Great lyrics and message, God. It's almost like it was written for me as my life's anthem. I wake this morning, and after coffee, you're the first thing that comes to my mind. It's like I awake, think about you, and then get coffee, have a cigarette, check Facebook to see what treasure Mom has sent me, then to my computer to pray to you, God.

I'll eventually cut the smokes out of my routine. June 30, God, that's my deadline. There, it's out there.

In your name I pray,

Authentic, Humble, Surrendered, and Spiritual

S. Michael Edwards

Thursday, February 10, 2011

To Be Or Not To Be | Prayer #213
Hey God,

So I opened up the devotional today to 1 Timothy 6–8.

> "A devout life does bring wealth, but it's the rich simplicity of being yourself before God. Since we entered the world penniless and will leave it penniless, if we have bread on the table and shoes on our feet, that's enough."

I started this journey, thinking I would make my prayers funny and entertaining… and that never really happened, God. What I found was I stepped into being authentic, and I truly believe that is why my earlier vision of "trying to be funny" never came to fruition.

On that note, I did have a great morning that started with laughter and fun. Had a great call with my buddy Craig and his amazing team. I learned a lot from Viviane and enjoyed the growth today.

I am wealthy in riches, maybe not money, but in the richness of your love and grace, and I am grateful.

In your name I pray,

Authentic, Humble, Surrendered, and Spiritual

S. Michael Edwards

Thursday, February 10, 2011

Trading My Sorrows | Prayer #214
Oh God,

I love this song. Darrell Evans, "Trading My Sorrows." Mom sent it to me, and of course, it's the perfect song for the place I am right now. Its' a great upbeat song about trading my sorrows and laying them down for the joy of my Lord.

Mom wrote:

> "I'm trading my sorrows, I'm trading my shame, I'm laying them down for the
> joy of the Lord! Yes, Lord; Yes, Lord; Yes, yes, Lord…amen! Woo hoo!"

That's exactly how I feel today God. Exuberant and joyful. Not abandoned, but
blessed…and your joy is overflowing and fills my heart.

Thank you, God, great message, perfect timing, as usual!

In your name I pray,

Authentic, Humble, Surrendered, and Spiritual,

S. Michael Edwards

Thursday, February 10, 2011

The Heart of Worship | Prayer #215
God,

It's all about you, Jesus. You look into my heart, and I'm coming back to you…that's
what this journey is all about. What an amazing journey it's been thus far. The extra
gifts have been the connection with you that is bigger and better than I could have
ever imagined, and the connection with my mom, who is on this journey with me.
What a joy. Mom sent me this song, the DJ that she is, and it's nice. Great message.
Thanks for inspiring her to inspire me. The gifts keep on coming. She is definitely
bringing me, as are you, more than songs. But the songs are a great way for us to
connect. The latest song, Hillsong, "Heart of Worship." Powerful!

Mom wrote:

> "I'm coming back to the heart of worship and it's all about you, it's all about
> you, Jesus. I'm sorry Lord for the thing I've made it when it's all about you,
> Jesus.
>
> May you be blessed by this incredible worship song. Make it the best day! I love
> you so much. Mama-cita"

I think Mom's gone all bilingual on me—Mama-cita. :) LOL

It's all about you.

Yep, God, it's all about you!

In your name I pray,

Authentic, Humble, Surrendered, and Spiritual

S. Michael Edwards

Thursday, February 10, 2011

I Surrender | Prayer #216
Hello God,

I sign surrender at the end of each prayer and have prayed about surrender, and Mom sends me a great song about surrendering. I know I was not yours, at least not in my mind. But I have surrendered and am yours now, in both my mind and heart. Every part of my life, I surrender and you have rewarded me handsomely with peace, love, joy and happiness. She sent me this song by Planetshakers, "Surrender."

Mom wrote:

> "Surrender!! You chose this word and God gave me this song!! You are an inspiration to me!!! May I surrender all. "

God bless the Planetshakers, for an amazing song and for my mom for continuing to send me inspirational songs and words of encouragement. I pray you will be with my dad as he dives deep into Advanced Leadership Seminar in Australia. May you be with him as he and Scott touch the lives of so many people.

I am humbled by you God,

In your name I pray,

Authentic, Humble, *Surrendered*, and Spiritual

S. Michael Edwards

Thursday, February 10, 2011

Where No One Has Gone Before | Prayer #217

God,

Just looking for some more inspiration and found this passage which ties into the prayers I have been praying.

Ephesians 3:20

God can do anything, you know—far more than you could ever imagine or guess or request in your wildest dreams! He does it not by pushing us around but by working within us, his Spirit deeply and gently within us.

Perfect, I think I'll share this with some of my friends. Clearly you are moving me forward at lightning speed (hence the Star Trek reference)—and I know your love and power can help move my friends to achieve their greatness.

Thanks for the reminder, and I pray these things in your name,

Authentic, Humble, Surrendered, and Spiritual

S. Michael Edwards

Friday, February 11, 2011

Easy Like Sunday Morning | Prayer #218

Good Morning God!

I woke up today with a sense of vigor and excitement and it's Friday! Whoo-hoo! I am so thankful for the amazing week and revelations you have given me this week. It's been an amazing week of growth and learning.

I can't wait to see what you have in store for me this weekend. A little fun, some embroidery, some glorifying you!

It can't get any better!

Let the day begin!

In your name I pray,

Authentic, Humble, Surrendered, and Spiritual

S. Michael Edwards

Friday, February 11, 2011

Italian Prayer | Prayer #219

God,

My computer was in its case last night, and I chose not to pull it out to document my prayer over my amazing meal. So, I am praying for that meal this morning. I did enjoy the spaghetti, but more importantly, it was a hearty meal and an evening of rest and relaxation. Much needed rest.

I thank you for the abundance you keep showering me with. We signed a deal with a huge client yesterday. Seems we have moved to a different sized pond where advertising spends are in the six figures instead of four. I do enjoy that growth and how it releases us from being totally dependent on one big client. We now have at least four big clients to diversify. A far cry from where we were a year ago!

Thank you for the food, and for the rest and for renewed energy you have given me. I'm on fire.

In your name I pray,

Authentic, Humble, Surrendered, and Spiritual

S. Michael Edwards

Friday, February 11, 2011

Devotional Roulette | Prayer #220

My God,

I start this prayer with a passage from my devotional roulette this morning.

Acts 26:17–18

"I'm sending you off to open the eyes of the outsiders so they can see the difference between dark and light, and choose light, see the difference between Satan and God, and choose God. I'm sending you off to present my offer of sins forgiven, and a place in the family, inviting them into the company of those who begin real living by believing in me."

Nice! I'm there for you, God. May I serve as an example of how an outsider can change. How amazing the shift can be in one's life, when they believe, accept, and follow, and surrender.

Thanks for this passage this morning. As I go about my daily life today, it will be on my mind. In my heart. In my actions.

In your name I pray,

Authentic, Humble, Surrendered, and Spiritual

S. Michael Edwards

Friday, February 11, 2011

Liar, Liar, Pants on Fire | Prayer #221
God,

Just had an amazing conversation with a friend about how people can twist the passages in the Bible to suit their own agenda. I then opened up my devotional and read this passage:

> 1 John 6:8–10
>
> If we claim that we're free of sin, we're only fooling ourselves. A claim like that is errant nonsense. On the other hand, if we admit our sins—make a clean breast of them—he won't let us down; he'll be true to himself. He'll forgive our sins and purge us of all wrongdoing. If we claim that we've never sinned, we out-and-out contradict God—make a liar out of him. A claim like that only shows off our ignorance of God.

Ah, this reminds me of the Christian who couldn't relate or talk to a non-Christian. We're all sinners, so why wouldn't we all just work together to do good in the world?

I choose to love unconditionally (okay, with the exception of Rick Warren…maybe one day I'll get over his support of Prop 8), hmmm, maybe that's something I could be working on?

Oh, how a prayer turns into a lesson that I wasn't planning!

Thanks, God!

In your name I pray,

Authentic, Humble, Surrendered, and Spiritual

S. Michael Edwards

Friday, February 11, 2011

I Refuse | Prayer #222
God,

No empty prayers for me, and I refuse to stand by and act like everyone's all right. Great song from Mom…it's a call to arms! Josh Wilson, "I Refuse." Thanks for the message, and the inspiration to choose and move!

Mom wrote;

> "I don't want to live like I don't care. It talks about making a difference when you see a need and not turning away as if you didn't see. Do what you were made to do and show them who Jesus is…by being his hands and feet. There's a lot to this song. Father God, thank you for the compassionate heart you've given Michael. Open my eyes to see the needs all around me. Amen."

I love that my Mom is open to seeing the needs around her. She is a supporter and a compassionate samurai and does so much. So I'm curious why she thinks her eyes aren't open to the needs around her. That's certainly not my experience of her…but you and she know better than I do.

I think this song is a great call to arms for everyone—to make a difference in this world God. Bring it on!

In your name I pray,

Authentic, Humble, Surrendered, and Spiritual

S. Michael Edwards

Friday, February 11, 2011

Oooh, This Is Good! | Prayer #223
God,

What an amazing prayer Mom just sent me, and song Hillsong United, "Search My Heart" (of course, praise through music is rocking my world…pun intended).

> "Father God, thank you for the intimate relationship you have with Michael. Thank you for hearing the cries of his heart and drawing him so close to you. Thank you for allowing me to see this transformation and the joy in Michael's life as well as the joy he brings to others. I know you have great plans for him. I pray that as your plan unfolds doors will continue to open wide and that ultimately you will be glorified and the lost will be found. Amen."

God, I am so glad that my journey is touching lives beyond my own. I pray that as my journey continues and these prayers and this journey become a book, that even more lives and hearts will be touched.

God, you took the cross, you took my shame, you restored my life, and now I live to glorify and worship you in all that I do. Thank you for hearing my prayers, God.

In your name I pray,

Authentic, Humble, Surrendered, and Spiritual

S. Michael Edwards

Saturday, February 12, 2011

God Bless Grandma | Prayer #224
God,

I pray that today you will be with my grandma's family and friends as we honor the fifth anniversary of her going to meet you. She was an amazing woman, and she was a great example for her children and grandchildren and great-grandchildren.

She was Godly. She was funny. I remember holding her hands in church as I was mesmerized by her hands and her ring. She let me hold her hand as she sang the hymns and praised you.

I miss her, but I know she is with you and what an amazing day she must be having. Today I will celebrate her life on earth and make a garment in her honor. She loved purple. So it shall be.

In your name, I pray,

Authentic, Humble, Surrendered, and Spiritual

S. Michael Edwards

1 comments:

Linda Edwards said...
Michael, I think it is so fitting that you're saying a prayer for your grandma because I don't think there was a day go by that she didn't pray for you. I visualize Grandma, Grandpa, and Jesus in a circle with their arms wrapped around each other, and then they put their hands in the center and lift them high with a joyful "Yes!"

Have the best day as we celebrate her life! Love, Mom

Saturday, February 12, 2011

It Is Well with My Soul | Prayer #225
God,

Mom wrote the most beautiful note, and I wanted to share it because it made me cry this morning reading it. I know what my mom means by "Your prayers have been answered"—and I know that she is talking about her family seeing her in heaven one day, that we would all believe.

My grandma didn't care that I am gay. In fact, she told my mom, while in her seventies, something to the effect of if I don't come around because I'm gay, she didn't care, she just wanted to see me. Pretty amazing love, but I would expect nothing less from such an amazing woman. Every time I saw her, I would leave and cry because I feared it would be the last time I would see her. Now I know that I will see her again. Now my tears are joyful.

Mom wrote:

> "February 12, the fifth anniversary of my mom's passing. I chose a song that
> would bless her heart. Mom, it is well with my soul (and Michael and Kim have
> something they want to tell you, too). Thank you for being such a loving mom
> with a big heart and so much compassion. Thank you for being an example of a
> Godly woman. Thank you for being a praying mom and grandma. Your prayers
> have been answered. You were a great role model. I love you and I miss you.
> Until we meet again...Linda"

Here's a song Grandma would like, although I'm sure she would be swinging to the Gaithers. This is more contemporary. Hillsong, "It Is Well with My Soul."

God, bless my mom, and all the lives my grandma touched today as we remember what an amazing woman she was.

In your name I pray,

Authentic, Humble, Surrendered, and Spiritual

S. Michael Edwards

Saturday, February 12, 2011

We Shall Behold Him | Prayer #226
God,

My mom has blessed me with song this morning, in celebration and tribute to Grandma King. I love these words...more tears of joy. Sandi Patty, "We Shall Behold Him."

> "Here's another tribute to your grandma King (my mommy). Sandi Patty sings
> this like an angel. I just got holy ghost goose bumps listening to it. Dottie Ram-
> bo is in the audience, and she wrote the song. The camera cuts to her often,
> and she's obviously pleased. The joy and excitement I get listening to this is
> nothing compared to the joy and excitement I'll have when I too shall behold
> Him...face to face, my Savior and Lord! Wow! Thinking of my mom today and
> happy to know I'll see her when I meet my Lord Jesus Christ. Amen."

God, my mom is an amazing mom, and I just pray that she won't be leaving this earth anytime soon. She has much more work to do here on earth!

In your name I pray,

Authentic, Humble, Surrendered and Spiritual

S. Michael Edwards

1 comments:

Linda Edwards said...

Just listened to this, again, while I exercised. Great inspiration and joy! I don't normally smile while I exercise but I did today.

I noticed that the man with a hat on sitting next to Dottie Rambo was Danny Gaither. He was also very ill and has since passed away. The joy on his face while Sandi sang was so genuine. Thank you, Father God, for giving us joy for this journey and hope for eternal life with you. Amen.

Saturday, February 12, 2011

I've Just Seen Jesus | Prayer #227
God,

I know so many people think they have seen Jesus in toast, or on a tree, or who knows where. I'm sure that's not what this song is about. I know my mom is remembering her mother today and I pray you lift her up and fill her heart with all the joyful memories of her life. I cannot imagine what it is like to lose a parent, and so I just pray you will lift my mom and her brother and sisters up today as well as all the grandkids as we remember an amazing woman who had a servant's heart.

From Mom:

"Grandma deserves another song. I think when I get to heaven I'll be able to sing like Sandi Patty! This is about as perfect as you can sing! The thrill, joy and anticipation of seeing Jesus is unspeakable! Hold me close, Jesus, and never let me go. I love you, Lord. I'm blessed. Amen."

What a great prayer, Mom—and you can sing like Sandi Patty. Tribute Song by Sandi Patty/Larnelle Harris, "I've Just Seen Jesus."

Oh God, all that I've done before won't matter anymore, now that I have embraced you in my life. What a blessing you are in my life! What a blessing my grandma was in my life, and what amazing children she raised to be your followers.

In your name I pray,

Authentic, Humble, Surrendered, and Spiritual

S. Michael Edwards

1 comments:

Linda Edwards said...
I love your heart. I love that I won't have to look so hard for you when we see Jesus face to face. I love that we both see him as he walks with us, moment by moment. I love that you think I can sing like Sandi Patty. Bring on the karaoke and maybe…

Great being on this journey as your cheerleader. You indeed bring so much joy into my life. Love, Mom

Saturday, February 12, 2011

Devotional Roulette | Prayer #228
God,

As I open my daily devotional, to Romans 15:1–6.

Those of us who are strong and able in the faith need to step in and lend a hand to those who falter, and not just do what is most convenient for us. Strength is for service, not status. Each one of us needs to look after the good of the people around us, asking ourselves, "How can I help?"

That's exactly what Jesus did. He didn't make it easy for himself by avoiding people's troubles, but waded right in and helped out. "I took on the troubles of the troubled," is the way Scripture puts it. Even if it was written in Scripture long ago, you can be sure it's written for *us*. God wants the combination of his steady, constant calling and warm, personal counsel in Scripture to come to characterize *us*, keeping us alert for whatever he will do next. May our dependably steady and warmly personal God develop maturity in you so that you get along with each other as well as Jesus gets along with us all. Then we'll be a choir—not our voices only, but our very lives singing in harmony in a stunning anthem to the God and Father of our Master Jesus.

Nice! May I continue to step in and help out as opposed to stepping aside and walking around. May my fellow man do the same. If we were to all do this, what an amazing world we'd live in God. The choices we make on a daily basis can touch a heart or hurt a soul; may we make the right choices and be in harmony, as one.

God, I am so grateful for the progress in Egypt this week. I pray for a transition that is peaceful and celebrate with the Egyptians as they move toward democracy.

In your name I pray,

Authentic, Humble, Surrendered, and Spiritual

S. Michael Edwards

1 comments:

Linda Edwards said...

Another amazing, miraculous answer to prayer with Egypt! Nothing is too hard for God!

Saturday, February 12, 2011

I Won't Let Go | Prayer #229
God,

I was driving down the road the other day, praying to you, and this song came on the radio by Rascal Flatts, "I Won't Let Go." I felt like you were singing to me, sending me a message that I needed to hear. It was a difficult day, and when I heard this song, I heard you say I was not alone, and that you would dry my eyes, fight my fight, and hold me tight, and not let go. God, I will stand by you, too, and together we will make a difference in this world.

Amazing song, thanks for blessing me with this message, God! (I just looked up the release date of this song, and the album was released on my birthday, November 16, 2010—which was the best birthday I have ever had!) Sweet!

In your name I pray.

Authentic, Humble, Surrendered, and Spiritual

S. Michael Edwards

1 comments:

Linda Edwards said...
Whew! What a great relationship song! My DJ son is adding to my music library, too. The ultimate relationship is with Jesus Christ, and his promises are true. I will never leave you nor forsake you. Amen and amen.

Saturday, February 12, 2011

Glorious | Prayer #230
God,

Today I celebrate your glory as the ruler of my heart. I praise you today and always. I am grateful for all you have given me, and all you have taught me on my journey to reconnect. I know there are many more lessons to come, but a strong theme has emerged…that you are glorious! You are with me. I am grateful. Now I listen and embrace this song, "Glorious," by Paul Baloche.

I praise you, God. In your name I pray,

Authentic, Humble, Surrendered, and Spiritual

S. Michael Edwards

Saturday, February 12, 2011

Dropped In Our Lap | Prayer #231
God,

Wow. What an amazing meeting Brett had last night. It's so awesome how you are providing opportunities for us left and right, and we are open to receiving your gifts so we can give back to the world. We are very excited about taking FrozenX-Plosion to the next level and working with an amazing man who has taught us so much in such a short time about social business.

I can see huge growth opportunities both financially and personally for Brett and me, and I'm so excited that we get to work together to create a legacy and to glorify you.

More details to come, but right now I just wanted to thank you for this gift. It's going to change lives, and we will make you proud!

I'll be meeting with this amazing man on the twenty-sixth, and we'll be getting things running as soon as possible!

God, you are great!

In your name I pray,

Authentic, Humble, Surrendered, and Spiritual

S. Michael Edwards

Saturday, February 12, 2011

Prayer #206 Happens Early | Prayer #232
God,

I'm so blessed that the prayers of millions, and especially those of Nelson Brandt, that the unrest in Egypt has subsided and that the regime has been toppled. Nelson's request and my prayer for his request that it happen on or before 14 February, actually happened on February 11, 2011, a day that will go down in history.

Thank you for hearing our prayers and for restoring order in Egypt.

May you bless the rest of the Middle East as it seems to be at a tipping point after what happened in Egypt.

I pray these things in your name,

Authentic, Humble, Surrendered, and Spiritual

S. Michael Edwards

Saturday, February 12, 2011

My Niece | Prayer #234
God,

My niece is so wonderful, smart, talented, and gifted. I pray that you will fill her heart with confidence, joy, and wisdom to know the greatness that is within her. She can make a difference in the world, if she chooses to embrace the past and move forward in life.

I pray that you will surround her with love and Godly people so that she can experience the joy that you have given me, under the same circumstances.

I pray this in your name,

Authentic, Humble, Surrendered, and Spiritual

S. Michael Edwards

Sunday, February 13, 2011

Good Morning God | Prayer #233
Good morning, God!

What a glorious day you have created for me. I woke up and got the house ready for a second showing, then headed off for an hour and just drove around looking at the beauty around me. I pray that the people who looked at the house make an offer that is within 4 percent of our asking price. Of course, Ed could come home and have a plan for buying me out and him keeping the house, which would be awesome, too.

Next week I pray that Ed and I can come to terms on the settlement, the house, and our assets. It all hinges on his conversation with his dad this weekend.

I don't have to know what your plan is, but I am sure it will revealed in due time. Is that this week? I sure hope and pray it is!

Going to read some emails from Mom, and I'm sure she's sent me some great praise songs.

I am grateful for the sense of peace you have giving me today God. Thank you!

In your name I pray,

Authentic, Humble, Surrendered, and Spiritual

S. Michael Edwards

Sunday, February 13, 2011

There Will Be a Day | Prayer #235
God,

I got goose bumps listening to this song by Jeremy Camp, "There Will Be a Day." Thinking about the day of no more pain, no fears, and the part that got to me: "But until that day, we'll hold onto you always, I know the journey seems so long, you feel you're walking on your own, but there has never been a step, where you've walked out all alone."

I know this now, God. You have carried me, you have guided me, and you are with me. Until the day I see you face to face, I will honor and glorify you and your name. I will proudly proclaim that I believe. I am not ashamed, and I give my life to you. I will make a difference in this world, when I walk the walk you have laid out before me.

I see this happening now, and it's exciting!

In your name I pray,

Authentic, Humble, Surrendered, and Spiritual

S. Michael Edwards

Sunday, February 13, 2011

Devotional Roulette | Prayer #236
God,

I love the devotion for today and of course it's about love uncontaminated by self-interest and counterfeit faith.

> 1 Timothy 1:5–7
>
> The whole point of what we're urging is simply love—love uncontaminated by self-interest and counterfeit faith, a life open to God. Those who fail to keep to this point soon wander off into cul-de-sacs of gossip. They set themselves up as experts on religious issues, but haven't the remotest idea of what they're holding forth with such imposing eloquence.

Ah, if I had a billboard, what a great message this would make for all the world to see. I love the part about experts not having the remotest idea of what they're holding forth with imposing eloquence. I mean "let's get real"—that's what this is about, real honest love. Loving you unconditionally and loving each other unconditionally, right, God? No judgment—that's your job. Got it!

In your name I pray,

Authentic, Humble, Surrendered, and Spiritual

S. Michael Edwards

Sunday, February 13, 2011

Come out Wherever You Are | Prayer #237
God,

Funny that I just prayed about not being ashamed, and then I read this email from Mom, which had a link to this amazing song with Joy Williams titled, "Hide." I pray that all the children of the world are able to come to know you and your love for them. I pray that those who hold their pain inside or feel unworthy will be comforted by your love. I lift them up to you, God, so that your grace and glory will fill them and heal them.

In your name I pray,

Authentic, Humble, Surrendered, and Spiritual

S. Michael Edwards

Sunday, February 13, 2011

God Only Cries | Prayer #238
Hey God,

Great message in this song by Diamond Rio, "God Only Cries," and I buy it! You only cry for the living because we're the ones that are far from home. I miss my grandpa and grandma, but I know they are in a better place, so I am joyful that they are looking down and watching over their families. They touched so many lives, and now those lives are touching so many lives. They have a legacy that I don't think they could have imagined being as grand as it is.

God, I am grateful for such an amazing set of grandparents. For the example they set.

In your name I pray,

Authentic, Humble, Surrendered, and Spiritual

S. Michael Edwards

Sunday, February 13, 2011

Consume My Thoughts | Prayer #239
God,

This song by Hillsong United, "Second Chance," could be my prayer to you! The words are perfect, and the song is beautiful. I am really digging this group Hillsong, which I had not heard of before I started this journey to reconnect with you. Your amazing grace, your redemption the moment you re-entered my life is priceless.

I am noticing that my thoughts are consumed with you. That was the unexpected gift, and so is the deeper connection with Mom—another unexpected gift of this journey.

The gifts keep coming, and the prayers keep flowing.

I see a theme today of love. Thanks God! Will you be my Valentine?

In your name I pray,

Authentic, Humble, Surrendered, and Spiritual

S. Michael Edwards

Sunday, February 13, 2011

I'm Reaching for You God | Prayer #240
My God,

I'm praising you today. I'm honoring myself today. I thank you for a great song to remind me about how on this journey, I have been reaching for you and giving my heart to know you. "Reaching for You," by Lincoln Brewster, touched my soul at a deep level.

 I am thankful for this time together (hey, that sounds like Carol Burnett, doesn't it?). Through you, all things are possible. I know I've said it before, but it's like my contract statement at the end of each of my prayers, the more I say it, the more I own it!

Yes! I am living my life to serve you, God. However that may look.

In your name I pray,

Authentic, Humble, Surrendered, and Spiritual

S. Michael Edwards

Sunday, February 13, 2011

Today Is the Day | Prayer #241
God,

I remember singing the song "This is the day the Lord has made, I will rejoice and be glad in it" in Sunday school as a kid. This song is much better! "Today Is the Day," by

Lincoln Brewster. I love how the message is kicked up a notch, and the beat is great! It's a great way to rock out with you! "I'm reaching my hand to yours, believing there's so much more, knowing that all you have in store for me is good." So maybe today is the day for many more things to come? I know it's the day you made, and I'm glad.

Who knows what tomorrow may bring, so I rejoice and celebrate and live in the moment with you today. *Carpe Diem!*

In your name I pray,

Authentic, Humble, Surrendered, and Spiritual

S. Michael Edwards

Monday, February 14, 2011

Big Glorious Day | Prayer #242
Good Morning God,

It's another gorgeous day, and a beautiful sunrise. I pray that today you will grant me the serenity and wisdom to close the deal with Ed on the settlement. We chatted briefly last night, and the only thing he was concerned about was the part about me giving two week's notice. He wants me to guarantee that I stay through the end of June.

I'm not sure why that bothers me. I guess it shouldn't. Any guidance would be appreciated. I told him last night if he wanted me to stay through the end of June, he'll need to pony up some more cash.

I pray you'll give us both the wisdom to come to terms and put this settlement to bed.

In your name I pray,

Authentic, Humble, Surrendered, and Spiritual

S. Michael Edwards

Monday, February 14, 2011

Devotional Roulette | Prayer #243

God,

Great devotional I opened up this morning: Philippians 3:15–16.

> So let's keep focused on that goal, those of us who want everything God has for us. If any of you have something else in mind, something less than total commitment, God will clear your blurred vision—you'll see it yet! Now that we're on the right track, let's stay on it!

Well, I guess that about sums it up…My goal, 365 prayers on or before March 2, 2011. I'm on 243, and I'm on track! I had some questions early on, and you cleared my blurred vision on the twenty-ninth, and that's when I got back on track, so I'm on it God.

As for the other goals—the settlement (hopefully today), the house (we're going to be speaking to bankers this week), and the goals I don't even know about yet, well—I'm sure they will all be revealed and I am grateful for your guidance.

In your name I pray,

Authentic, Humble, Surrendered, and Spiritual

S. Michael Edwards

Monday, February 14, 2011

Stress! | Prayer #244

God,

My blood pressure is through the roof right now, and my serenity has been lost in the sofa. I pray that you will grant me the serenity that has served me so well over the last several months. I just had a most challenging meeting that pushed me to the edge, and while I feel a little better, I could still use a big wave of comfort and serenity.

Anything you can do to help bring me back from the edge would be appreciated!

In your name I pray,

Authentic, Humble, Surrendered, and Spiritual

S. Michael Edwards

Monday, February 14, 2011

Safe Travels from Down Under | Prayer #245
God,

I pray you will be with my dad as he makes his way back from Australia to San Francisco. I pray you will give him much needed rest and rejuvenation as he prepares for another class. I can't wait to connect with him when he is done teaching this class in San Francisco…he's been gone so long, I miss him!

In your name I pray,

Authentic, Humble, Surrendered, and Spiritual

S. Michael Edwards

Monday, February 14, 2011

Dad's Back! | Prayer #246
God,

Just a quick note of gratitude for the safe travels my Dad had back to the States. Thank you for watching over him, and I can't wait to connect and hear how his trip was. I felt disconnected with him, as he was so busy and out of country.

I'm feeling better about the serenity I requested. I don't feel like I'm going to throw a blood clot right now, after the intense meeting I had today. Great opportunity to practice being ground and center. May next week's meeting be even better. Choosing and moving is definitely a choice for people, and I pray you provide me the wisdom on how to help people see that, and provide a mirror on how they may be stuck.

In your name I pray,

Authentic, Humble, Surrendered, and Spiritual

S. Michael Edwards

Monday, February 14, 2011

A Day Without Music | Prayer #247

God,

With such a day filled with challenges, and no time to listen to praise music, I am so grateful that Ed and I were able to have an hour to talk about stuff. He treated me with respect and asked my opinion, and we talked about the settlement. I sent the revisions over to him for his signature. We are one step closer to finalizing the deal on his terms.

Thank you, God. The relationship that Ed and I have now is based on respect and mutual understanding. I couldn't ask for anything more.

In your name I pray,

Authentic, Humble, Surrendered, and Spiritual

S. Michael Edwards

Tuesday, February 15, 2011

Devotional Roulette | Prayer #248

God,

Today's devotional roulette is rather intense for me. I believe because of the sign of joy you stamped on my arm when I asked for more joy in my life. Then I read this passage:

> John 20:29
>
> Jesus said, "So, you believe because you've seen with your own eyes. Even better blessings are in store for those who believe without seeing."

This is something I'm going to have to noodle on. I'm not sure what you are telling me here. Or is it just a lesson about faith, because not everyone gets a sign?

My analytical brain is sparking on this one. I pray you'll provide clarity around this passage.

In your name I pray,

Authentic, Humble, Surrendered, and Spiritual

S. Michael Edwards

Tuesday, February 15, 2011

Wait and See | Prayer #249
God,

I could use some upbeat soul-filling music today. I was swamped yesterday and didn't have a chance to jam to music to praise you as much as I wanted. So today I am going to make up for it, by listening to all the songs Mom has sent me that I have waiting…

And I love this song with Brandon Heath, "Wait and See." Especially this part:

"But oh, he's up to something

And the farther on I go

I've seen enough to know

That I'm not here for nothing

He's up to something"

That makes me smile, to think that you are "up to something"—I mean in a good way of course. I can't wait to see what you are up to (or rather, what you have in store for me). I mean I guess I can wait, but I mean to say I'm excited to see what you have in store for me.

Thank you for a beautiful day, and I pray that you will keep those waves of serenity washing over me. I'm feeling a sense of calmness right now. Ahhhhhh

Here's what Mom wrote:

He's not finished with me (or you) yet! "And the farther on I go I've seen enough to know that I'm not here for nothing. He's up to something…He's not finished with me yet." Open our eyes to the infinite possibilities you have for us, Father God. I love you, Father God.

Praying especially for John right now as he's on his way from Australia to San Francisco. Give him extreme rest and safe travels. Thank you, Lord.

In your name I pray,

Authentic, Humble, Surrendered, and Spiritual

S. Michael Edwards

Tuesday, February 15, 2011

Testify To Love | Prayer #250

God,

It's funny how I love this song and have loved this song by Wynonna Judd, "Testify to Love," but never really read the words…had no idea it was a song about you and your creation. God, you are love. With every breath I take I will give thanks to you. Nice! Thanks for the uplifting song, Mom, and thanks to the talents of Wynonna for lifting my mood and allowing me to rock out to an amazing song. Sitting here bobbing my head, God, like I'm in a rock concert. I'm really taking in the words as she sings this song in praise of you and "be a witness in the silences when words are not enough"—it's in our deeds and actions that we can truly testify and be a witness. Living a life of example. Yeah, I like that.

Thanks to my mom for sending this song so I could actually look at the lyrics and learn that all these years I was loving a song and had my blinders on to what was being said in the lyrics.

In your name I pray,

Authentic, Humble, Surrendered, and Spiritual

S. Michael Edwards

Tuesday, February 15, 2011

Thank You, God, for Translations | Prayer #251

God,

I asked for support from my amazing group of friends and leaders on my journey last night to send me passages from the Bible.

Again, this morning I was stumped.

My friend sent me Proverbs 8:12 from the KJV.

> "I wisdom dwell with prudence, and find out knowledge of witty inventions."

With this explanation:

> Proverbs is a very practical book of the Bible that explains many spiritual principles that affect even things like finding out new inventions. This verse tells us that through wisdom and prudence people can discover witty inventions. The definition for prudent according to the Webster's New World Dictionary is: 1) capable of exercising sound judgment in practical matters, esp. as concerns one's own interests, 2) cautious or discreet in conduct; circumspect; not rash, 3) managing carefully and with economy.

So this threw me for a loop. What is the point here? I looked it up in different translations, and found one I could actually wrap my hands around. New Living Translation reads, "I, Wisdom, live together with good judgment. I know where to discover knowledge and discernment."

Okay, I can wrap my head around that. I know where to discover knowledge and discernment, and It's with you God.

If I'm living my purpose and glorifying you and using the talents you have given me, I find I am happier. When I seek knowledge, I turn to you.

Thanks to my friend for sending this, and thanks for translators, to help me understand the point.

In your name I pray,

Authentic, Humble, Surrendered, and Spiritual

S. Michael Edwards

Tuesday, February 15, 2011

Revelations 3:8 | Prayer #252
God,

My dear friend sent me this passage, and it puts a smile on my face as I listen to praise music.

> Revelations 3:8
>
> When God leads you to the edge of the cliff, trust Him fully and let go, only one of two things will happen, either He'll catch you when you fall, or He'll teach you how to fly.

I trust in you, God, on this journey and in life. I look to you for guidance and wisdom and know that nothing is impossible through you.

You have definitely caught me when I fell, and now you are teaching me to soar, like an eagle.

Thank you, God!

In your name I pray,

Authentic, Humble, Surrendered, and Spiritual

S. Michael Edwards

Tuesday, February 15, 2011

Joy and Music | Prayer #253
God,

So I see how many of my prayers are related to music. Then I thought I would find a passage in the Bible about joy—a word close to my heart. :)

1 Chronicles 15:16

David told the leaders of the Levites to appoint their fellow Levites as musicians to make a joyful sound with musical instruments: lyres, harps and cymbals.

Loving the joyful sound of the music I have been sent by my mom and friends. It introduces me to music that touches my heart and fills my cup.

Thanks to the talents of those that sing your praises as they are touching lives that they don't even know.

In your name I pray,

Authentic, Humble, Surrendered, and Spiritual

S. Michael Edwards

Tuesday, February 15, 2011

Here I Go Again | Prayer #254
God,

Here I go again. Great message, lyrics, and song by Casting Crowns, "Here I Go Again." It re-enforces that I not dance around the truth, that I share your love. Regardless of if my friends are dying or living. I pray you give me the fire in my eyes and that, just as Brett showed me it was possible to be real, cool, and a Christian, that I speak your love and live my life as an example.

In your name I pray,

Authentic, Humble, Surrendered, and Spiritual

S. Michael Edwards

Tuesday, February 15, 2011

He Knows My Name | Prayer #255
God,

I don't know what tomorrow may bring, but I do know that you know my name, and you have a plan and I surrender to you and your plan. I've prayed about this before, and this song is an amazing example of how I feel. You knew I would fail you, but you still took me back, and with loving arms, embraced me.

I'm grateful for that unconditional love. I am grateful for this song by McRaes, "He Knows My Name."

In your name I pray,

Authentic, Humble, Surrendered, and Spiritual

S. Michael Edwards

Tuesday, February 15, 2011

Google Rocks | Prayer #256
God,

I just had an amazing call with my team from Google. I so appreciate them and all they do to keep our team informed of the latest and greatest innovations. I absolutely love working with my dedicated team, and it's fun when I get to work with people who are genuinely nice, smart, caring, helpful, etc.

The call made my day! Funny how a little praise music and some prayers to you, God, can lift my spirits. I feel a sense of calmness and serenity, which is a far cry from where I was yesterday after that meeting when I thought I might throw a clot!

Thanks for your calming presence.

One more client meeting today, and the results look amazing. I just pray that they will be happy and in good spirits, too!

In your name I pray,

Authentic, Humble, Surrendered, and Spiritual

S. Michael Edwards

Tuesday, February 15, 2011

Revelation Song | Prayer #257
God,

My day of praise music continues. Singing a song, praising you, you are my every-thing, and I adore you! You continue to bless me and give me strength.

Thanks to Mom for a great song by Philips Craig and Dean, "Revelation Song." I love what she wrote:

> "Holy, holy, holy is the Lord God Almighty. Who was, and is, and is to come. With all creation I sing praise to the King of kings…You are my everything, and I will adore You. (Can't think of a better way to start the day than praising the God of the universe.) Make it a beautiful, serene day grounded in him. Love, Mom"

Praise to you and to God be the glory,

In your name I pray,

Authentic, Humble, Surrendered, and Spiritual

S. Michael Edwards

1 comments:

journeytoourlegacy said...
Love this song, used it in my last blog, too. Love you, and so great to read your deepening relationship with my best friend. Thank God for hope, huh?

Tuesday, February 15, 2011

Call on Jesus | Prayer #258
God,

Nicole has such a beautiful voice, and her song "Call on Jesus" reminds me of so many things. Call me, any time…rethink possible, "I'll be there"—so many songs that this reminds me of. All pointed to you. Such uplifting words and song. I much prefer a day of praise music to going without!

Thanks to Mom for sending this song. She wrote:

> "When you call on Jesus, all things are possible. Praying for God's Holy Spirit to surround you with an army of angels and prayer warriors to lift you up and give you peace, calm, serenity, and focus. May you not be distracted by the enemy

and distracted from your purpose. Do not be discouraged. God wins! Nothing is too hard for God. Loving you from a distance and praying for you…like, no kidding! Love, Mom"

What a blessing! I pray and praise, and my mom prays and praises. Thank you for a caring, supportive mom, God. I love how connected we've become (both my connection with Mom and my connection with you!).

Rocking to Jesus,

In your name I pray,

Authentic, Humble, Surrendered, and Spiritual

S. Michael Edwards

Tuesday, February 15, 2011

Beginners Mind | Prayer #259
God,

Thank you for giving me a beginner's mind today. The old me would have taken a decision as fact and not even tried to question it. The new me, with a beginner's mind, is able to ask questions, to dig deep and help people see the potential. I used to hate to say "You were right" or worse, "I was wrong"—and now those words mean nothing to me. The power of those words are gone. What's more important is being with, listening, understanding, and having open honest communication without defense.

I thank you for giving me clarity of mind, a beginner's mind, getting myself out of the way, so I can help others see the greatness in them that they don't see in themselves. I felt like you were with me, helping me to carefully choose my words and to help my friend move forward.

Thank you, God!

In your name I pray,

Authentic, Humble, Surrendered, and Spiritual

S. Michael Edwards

Tuesday, February 15, 2011

The Most Beautiful Card | Prayer #260
God,

I'm so grateful for my parents and got the most amazing Valentine's card (complete with chocolate-covered berries). It is truly touching.

"Sometimes I get all sentimental and wonder, if I had it to do over again, what would I do differently?

"I guess I'd be a little less serious and busy, and I'd make more time just to have fun with you.

"I'd tell you what to do less, and 'I love you' more, and let you learn your lessons in your own time and way, and I'd go easier on you on stuff that really doesn't matter…

"I'd do a lot of things differently, but the one thing I'd never change is having you for a son."

Note: "I've never loved you more…I'm amazed at how my love for you can grow any deeper because I loved you before you were even born! Love, Mom and Daddy-o"

What an amazing card and note. How precious are my parents? I'm so grateful that they have been there for me and never gave up hope. That they loved me unconditionally, even when things got messy.

I wouldn't change a thing—it's what makes today mean as much as it does. Without pain, how can you truly know joy?

I truly and blessed for such amazing parents God, and you have heard my parent's prayers.

In your name I pray,

Authentic, Humble, Surrendered, and Spiritual

S. Michael Edwards

1 comments:

Linda Edwards said...

Thank you for your kind words. You continue to bless and amaze me. I always knew you were compassionate but it was deep down inside you...and now you've put it out there for the world to see, feel, touch. I love being a part of your journey! Love, Mom

Wednesday, February 16, 2011

This Is the Day the Lord Has Made | Prayer #261

Good morning, God!

I woke up this morning with a Sunday School song in my head. It put a smile on my face. "This is the day, this is the day that the Lord has made, that the Lord has made. We will rejoice, we will rejoice, and be glad in it, and be glad in it. This is the day that the Lord has made, we will rejoice and be glad in it. This is the day, this is the day, that the Lord, has, made."

Amen to that! I will rejoice and be glad in another glorious day. Thank you, God, for today, and I pray it will be productive.

I also pray that you will be with Ed, who is sick. I really want to see a banker this week with Ed, sign the settlement, etc., but with him staying in bed all day yesterday and not feeling well, I pray that you will provide for a quick recovery. I hope that doesn't sound too one-sided. I really do want him to feel better. Of course I have some benefits if he does, but even if we don't get to see a banker this week, or sign the settlement, at least he'll be feeling better.

In your name I pray,

Authentic, Humble, Surrendered, and Spiritual

S. Michael Edwards

2 comments:

Linda Edwards said...

Refer back to prayer #241...I'm thinking that you've had that song in your heart for a while. I love that God knows what we need even before we think or ask.

Amen to that! As Ms. Amanda says, "Let God be God." I love you, and I too lift up "Ed" into the healing hands of Jesus. May God be glorified through all that we do and say. Amen.

February 16, 2011 8:44 AM

S. Michael Edwards said…

That is so funny. #241—and then days later, the Sunday school song in my head as I started my day. "Today Is the Day" is a great song! So is, "This is the day that the Lord has made"—just different generations!

Wednesday, February 16, 2011

Devotional Roulette | Prayer #262

God,

My devotional roulette this am, from Romans 12:1–2:

"So here's what I want you to do, God helping you: Take your everyday, ordinary life—your sleeping, eating, going-to-work, and walking around life—and place it before God as an offering. Embracing what God does for you is the best thing you can do for him. Don't become so well-adjusted to your culture that you fit into it without even thinking. Instead, fix your attention on God. You'll be changed from the inside out. Readily recognize what he wants from you, and quickly respond to it. Unlike the culture around you, always dragging you down to its level of immaturity, God brings the best out of you, develops well-formed maturity in you."

Well now! I guess that answers the prayer of what you want me to do! It's so true, too, that I not only place my life before you, God, but I embrace all that you have done for me. I have fixated my attention on you, and it has absolutely changed me from the inside out. Wow! Who knew when I started this journey how everything would fall into place?

Thank you, God, what an inspirational message to start the day!

In your name I pray,

Authentic, Humble, Surrendered, and Spiritual

S. Michael Edwards

Wednesday, February 16, 2011

Smile | Prayer #263
God,

I don't know what you put in my coffee this morning, but I have the biggest grin and can't stop smiling today. I appreciate the abundance of joy. What a great feeling to be so joyful and to exude it to all those around me. I just watched this video from the TED conference. The speaker talked about vulnerability and how if you repress it, you repress the good parts (and she said joy). So it's ironic that I had vulnerability in my contract statement a few months ago, and got joy out of it.

You make me smile, God. The video was perfect timing for me to realize that stepping into vulnerability (and I like to think of "Vulnerable to the Possible") brings joy.

In your name I pray,

Authentic, Humble, Surrendered, and Spiritual

S. Michael Edwards

Wednesday, February 16, 2011

Theme Is Joy | Prayer #264
Really God?

I just prayed about smiling and joy, and then I read this email from Mom where she sent me a song called "Joy," by the Newsboys (earlier this morning). It's a great song, and your sense of humor and timing are impeccable. I love the line, "I flipped a 'U' back to the first love I ever knew." I can get behind that. The fact that these lyrics talk about Tucson dirt—well, it was in Phoenix, Arizona, where this journey started. What a great song. I almost forced it to be prayer #265, a milestone, but the authentic me put it where it happened. Right after my prayer about smiling (#263). Thanks, Mom!

In your name I pray joyfully,

Authentic, Humble, Surrendered, and Spiritual

S. Michael Edwards

1 comments:

Linda Edwards said...

You're so welcome. I've sang along with this song many times but never knew it was called "Joy"! Get out! And why didn't I know that? What's up with that? Joy is your middle name. Just proves I'm not an analyst or I would have done the research. It also proves that God gave me the song when it would serve you. Perfect! It even has "amazing grace" in the song. Love, love, love it.

"You give me joy that's unspeakable

And I like it, and I like it yeah

Your love for me is irresistible

I can't fight it, I can't fight it yeah

You carried the cross and took my shame

I believe it, I believe it yeah

You shine your light of amazing grace

I receive it, I receive it yeah"

Thanks for your encouraging posts/prayers. I'm beyond blessed.

Wednesday, February 16, 2011

The Potter's Hands | Prayer #265

God,

What a perfect song for prayer #265: Darlene Zschech, "The Potter's Hand." The lyrics touch my heart. You gently called me into your presence, you set me apart, and you are drawing me to you! That's the whole goal behind the goal of my prayer journal. Use me, mold me, call me, guide me, I give you my life! Together we will make a difference, God. I pray that you continue to guide me down the path that will make the most difference to make the world a better place for so many.

For those who believe, but are not truly connected. For those who judge, but don't understand the sinful nature of that act. For those who are not sure about you. For those who have turned their backs. May they all see that miracles do occur and that we can all get along and love one another in peace and harmony.

In your name I pray,

Authentic, Humble, Surrendered, and Spiritual

S. Michael Edwards

Wednesday, February 16, 2011

Voice of Truth | Prayer #266

God,

> Into your hands I commit my spirit; redeem me, O Lord, the God of Truth. (Psalm 31:5)

As I learn more and more about the passages in the Bible, those passages that I have long ago studied and then discredited, I am lifted up and given strength.

Do not withhold your mercy from me, O Lord: may your love and your truth always protect me. (Psalm 40:11)

I am definitely not feeling that you are withholding your mercy and your love and truth has protected me on my journey!

> Teach me your way, O Lord, and I will walk in your truth. (Psalm 86:11)

I pray that your way is revealed, and that I walk in your truth and your desires for me God.

Thanks to my friend and employee who sent me this song by Casting Crowns, "Voice of Truth," which is amazing. I love the lyrics and they lift me up!

In your name I pray,

Authentic, Humble, Surrendered, and Spiritual

S. Michael Edwards

Wednesday, February 16, 2011

Love Thy Neighbor | Prayer #267
God,

I asked my support system to send me passages from the Bible, figuring that you would touch their hearts in the passages they sent me. I was not disappointed. I got this one from my friend Kathy.

> "Thou shalt not avenge, nor bear any grudge against the children of thy people, but thou shalt love thy neighbor as thyself. I am the Lord." (Eph. 4:31)

Funny I just wrote a prayer about love…the timing couldn't have been more perfect. And then the "Voice of Truth" video; if we just loved, and not grudged, what an amazing thing we could accomplish.

Let the flood of support wash over me! It's truly amazing having this connection with you, God. Having the support of my fellow believers, and the love and support of my family is awesome. Who could ask for anything more?

In your name I pray,

Authentic, Humble, Surrendered, and Spiritual

S. Michael Edwards

Wednesday, February 16, 2011

Wave Upon Wave | Prayer #268
God,

As the waves come washing over me, I pray you give me a surfboard so I can ride the waves and not get sucked out to sea. Metaphorically speaking, of course. Monday through Wednesday are always crazy busy days, and this week was no exception. As I prepare for my Master Mind call and my call with my Sam Camp 21 buddy, I pray that you will grant me peace of mind and clarity, and allow me to be with and ground and centered on these calls.

Let the hectic day be gone, and amazing things propel our group and my buddy and me forward.

I pray this in your name,

Authentic, Humble, Surrendered, and Spiritual

S. Michael Edwards

Wednesday, February 16, 2011

Sponge | Prayer #269

God,

As Brett Stokes meets with Jeff Ericson, I pray you will open his mind to be a sponge so that he can take in all the wisdom that this partner provides. The partner has so much wisdom and knowledge and feeds it with a garden hose, and I pray that you allow Brett the clarity of mind and a big ol' sponge so that he can absorb as much as possible, for this is the foundation of our new endeavor.

May they bond, connect, and make some forward progress. I am looking forward to connecting with Brett in the next day or two to catch up and find out what he learned.

In your name I pray,

Authentic, Humble, Surrendered, and Spiritual

S. Michael Edwards

Thursday, February 17, 2011

Brilliant Brett Strikes Again | Prayer #270

God,

I want to thank you for the amazing meeting Brilliant Brett Stokes had last night with our new business venture. We're in, he sealed the deal and had clarity of mind. They called me last night to discuss some details, and it's a go! I'm so excited for this opportunity (more details to follow), and thank you for blessing us both.

Ready, aim, fire!

In your name I pray,

Authentic, Humble, Surrendered, and Spiritual

S. Michael Edwards

Thursday, February 17, 2011

Praying for Lesha | Prayer #271
God,

My dear friend Lesha has the following Master Mind requests that I would like to pray for.

> With the love, support and integrity of my Master Mind team, and the knowledge that where ever I am…God is, I graciously make the following requests:

> That on or before 2/28/11, I have enjoyed time shared with my parents, connecting on an authentic heart level.

> That on or before 2/17/11, a meeting has been arranged with the Grove to discuss a contract with Grow Green for 2011 growing season.

> That on or before 3/31/11, Egypt's transition to a democratic state has been smooth and peaceful.

> And so it is!

> In Love and Light,

> Vulnerable, Authentic, Surrendered, and Passionate Lesha

God, Lesha has stepped into vulnerable in a big way with her parents, and I pray that she step deeper into vulnerable and surrender to share quality time with them while connecting on an authentic heart level by the end of the month.

I also pray that she rock the meeting with the Grove today, and get a contract for Grow Green's 2011 growing season!

God, I honor and support these requests as well as her request that on or before 3/31/11, Egypt transition to a democratic state is both smooth and peaceful.

We are all watching the events in Egypt unfold and are in awe at your power and grace and pray that you continue to watch over the process and allow the people their right to a democratic society, after all these years.

In your name I pray,

Authentic, Humble, Surrendered, and Spiritual

S. Michael Edwards

Thursday, February 17, 2011

Praying for Karen | Prayer #272
God,

Karen has the following requests that I am praying for with her.

With the love, support and integrity of my Master Mind team, and the knowledge that where ever I am…God is, I graciously make the following requests:

I am so happy and grateful now that:

I have abundant income that supports my interests, needs, and provides and maintains a beautiful home with all amenities on or before March 31, 2011, nine p.m. EST.

I am balanced in all areas of my life: spiritually, physically, mentally and financially on or before February 28, 2011 and thereafter.

I am in loving and supportive relationships on February 16, 2011 and thereafter.

I have obtained my teacher's certification on or before May 31, 2012, noon EST.

God, I pray that Karen has abundant income that supports her interests, needs, and provides and maintains a beautiful home with all the amenities on or before March 31, 2011, nine p.m. EST. I also pray that she is balanced in all areas of her life, spiritually, physically, mentally, and financially, on or before February 28, 2011, and thereafter. I pray that she continue in a loving and supportive relationship on February 16, 2011, and thereafter. I also pray that she obtain her teacher's certification on or before May 31, 2012, by noon EST.

I honor and support her requests and pray that you will as well, God.

In your name I pray,

Authentic, Humble, Surrendered, and Spiritual

S. Michael Edwards

Thursday, February 17, 2011

Praying for Nelson | Prayer #273
God,

I pray for Nelson's Master Mind requests this week.

With faith in God and a great sense of gratitude I ask the following:

> Professional: That on or before 18 February 2011, I provided the leadership and organizational skills needed to finalize the Coast Guard Air Station Atlantic City Aviation Engineering Department's action plan for the next three months.

> Personal: That on or before 23 February 2011, my family and I arrived safely in Florida for our vacation to Disney World.

> Esoteric: That on or before 23 February 2011, my children, Cooper and Bella, enjoyed the adventure of travel and have chosen to be at loving peace with one another.

Don't you love how we all believe in you, God? Every team member mentions you in our requests for the week. May you bless Nelson tomorrow as he finalizes the action plan for the next three months for the CGAS in Atlantic City, and may you watch over them as they travel safely to Florida on their vacation to Disney world, on or before 23 February 2011. Finally, God, I pray that on or before 23 February, his children enjoy the adventure of travel and are at loving peace with one another. (None of this, "Dad, he's on my side of the seat!") :)

I honor and support Nelson's requests and pray that you will honor and support them as well.

In your name I pray,

Authentic, Humble, Surrendered, and Spiritual

S. Michael Edwards

Thursday, February 17, 2011

Our Call Today | Prayer #274

God,

What a morning of laughing, snot, nearly spit out coffee—the humor this morning has been contagious. May that fun and joy spill over into our call today at eleven a.m.! I pray you bless my buddy with the wisdom to move people forward and to perhaps pull some levers to get people into their hearts and realize their big dreams.

The week has been awesome, and I am grateful for that gift, among the others you have blessed me with this week.

In your name I pray,

Authentic, Humble, Surrendered, and Spiritual

S. Michael Edwards

Thursday, February 17, 2011

Praying for Dad | Prayer #275

God,

A quick prayer for Dad today as he is facilitating Advanced Leadership Seminar in San Francisco. May he rock the students' worlds and create a space for personal growth and awakening. May the students be open to receiving that growth. I pray you will be with Scott, Kimberly, and my dad as they steer the ship and make a difference in their students lives today and the rest of the weekend.

In your name I pray,

Authentic, Humble, Surrendered, and Spiritual

S. Michael Edwards

Thursday, February 17, 2011

Fired Up! | Prayer #276
God,

Wow, so many clients wanting to spend more money! I love it. My heart is racing, and it's total excitement. The economy must be turning around, and for that I am grateful. I love it when clients see the value of what we're doing and want to spend more money, fast!

Thanks for the abundance. It's raining abundance right now, and I'm just singing in the rain!

In your name I pray,

Authentic, Humble, Surrendered, and Spiritual

S. Michael Edwards

Thursday, February 17, 2011

Stretch… | Prayer #277
God,

Nothing pleases me more than to hear Ed playing the piano tonight with his first piano lesson. He's talked about this for years, and it's because of Sam Camp that he finally stepped up to the plate and is taking this on as a goal. He's never played the piano before, and it's a big stretch for him. To tap into his creativity and out of his mind and into his heart is truly a blessing.

I pray that you will surround him with your love and that he will continue this journey. It's just amazing to see him step out of his comfort zone into something so totally unknown to him. It makes me happy to see him stretch himself.

Thank you for Sam Camp and for touching Ed's heart so that he can connect with his.

In your name I pray,

Authentic, Humble, Surrendered, and Spiritual

S. Michael Edwards

1 comments:

Linda Edwards said...

Amen! Wow, that's so cool. I wish I could have heard him, too. For him to slow down long enough to do that is amazing. SC rocks on!

Friday, February 18, 2011

7x70 | Prayer #278

God,

I prayed about this passage in the Bible and then my mom sent me this amazing song by Chris August, "7x70." "God picked up my heart and helped me through, and shined a light on the one thing left to do, and that's forgive you, I forgive you." What a message! It took me awhile to forgive Ed's parents, and yet you helped me through that process. It was a burden I chose to carry, and it was as easy as a decision to drop the rock and forgive.

Mom wrote:

"I'm so grateful that God healed our family. I thought the pain was here to stay but forgiveness made a way. Seven times seventy times, there's healing in the air tonight. The joy of where we're are with our relationship with Jesus Christ and each other is so healing. My heart is overjoyed, and that's a good thing. Love, Mom"

Thanks, Mom, for a great song, and thanks God for allowing me to see how forgiveness is as easy as a choice.

In your name I pray,

Authentic, Humble, Surrendered, and Spiritual

S. Michael Edwards

Friday, February 18, 2011

Waiting for Lightning | Prayer #279

God,

Mom wrote:

> "Thank you, God of the universe, for quietly calling Michael's name (and using the joy billboard on his arm, too)."

I couldn't agree more, I was waiting for a sign, and you gave them to me...and I ignored them. I was searching for answers, but you sent them and I didn't want to see them. I am so grateful for the amazing persistence that you had and the joy you stamped on my arm. I truly feel I'm living my purpose to bring joy and equality to the world. Thank you, God! Thank you for another praise song, by Steven Curtis Chapman, "Waiting for Lightning."

In your name I pray,

Authentic, Humble, Surrendered, and Spiritual

S. Michael Edwards

Friday, February 18, 2011

Devotional Roulette | Prayer #280
God,

Devotional Roulette time, and a great passage appeared, Luke 6:27-30:

> "To you who are ready for the truth, I say this: Love your enemies. Let them bring out the best in you, not the worst. When someone gives you a hard time, respond with the energies of prayer for that person. If someone slaps you in the face, stand there and take it. If someone grabs your shirt, gift wrap your best coat and make a present of it. If someone takes unfair advantage of you, use the occasion to practice the servant life. No more tit-for-tat stuff. Live generously."

I think I have read this before, maybe prayed about it. Maybe it is time for me to see it again. Maybe you are just repeating what I have been praying about—praying about Ed. I think I said, "Nothing fills my heart more." Well, that is not true, there are many things that fill my heart more than that. But I am truly pleased that he is stepping into something fun and productive with his idle time and stretching himself beyond his comfort zone. I pray for him because he deserves the prayers as much as anyone else.

May you bring him peace and surround him with love on his journey, that he get out of his head and into his heart. I pray you help him see your grace, as a nonbeliever, that he be surrounded by Godly people who can show him that not all Godly people are judgmental.

I pray this in your name,

Authentic, Humble, Surrendered, and Spiritual

S. Michael Edwards

Friday, February 18, 2011

Praying for My Client | Prayer #281
God,

I pray that you will be with my client who said today, "It's Hell around here." I don't know what she's going through, but she's a friend and an amazing woman, and I pray that you will give her strength and surround her with love and comfort.

I know her company just got an infusion of capital from some venture capital company, and she was worried about all their jobs. I pray that she is not going through some rounds of layoffs, either personally or with her team. I know that can be tough, and she has a strong team that she's built up.

May she be lifted up to you and surrounded by your glory today.

In your name I pray,

Authentic, Humble, Surrendered, and Spiritual

S. Michael Edwards

Friday, February 18, 2011

Mullet Makeover | Prayer #282
God,

Please be with the hairdresser who is giving my dear friend a makeover, and thank you for answering my prayer (kidding) that she ditch the mullet. LOL. Okay, just having fun with you, God. I'm so grateful to have her in my life, and what a blessing she has been. She truly walks the walk and makes me laugh out loud.

May you bless her life with abundance, joy, love, and happiness. She deserves more, but let's just give her a taste of what these four things can do for her! What do you say, God? You in?

In your name I pray,

Authentic, Humble, Surrendered, and Spiritual

S. Michael Edwards

Friday, February 18, 2011

Safe Travels, My Friend | Prayer #283
God,

As my Sam Camp 21 buddy travels to Dayton, Ohio, today, I pray that you will be with him and provide for safe travels. I got a request for a prayer for a family that lost their son in a tragic motorcycle accident, and I pray that you will be with the family. It just reminded me of how fragile life can be.

May you watch over Craig as he makes his journey safely to Ohio.

In your name I pray,

Authentic, Humble, Surrendered, and Spiritual

S. Michael Edwards

Friday, February 18, 2011

Bank Meeting | Prayer #284
God,

I pray that the meeting Ed and I have planned with our banker is fruitful today and that we are able to untangle our mortgage and yacht loan so that we are no longer on each of the loans together. I'm not sure what time we'll be going over, but he made the commitment to go with me to "figure it out."

I pray that you will help him keep his commitment to me to make that happen today! It's a huge step in making progress toward my previous request to divide our assets.

In your name I pray,

Authentic, Humble, Surrendered, and Spiritual

S. Michael Edwards

Friday, February 18, 2011

Layoffs | Prayer #285
God,

I hear that my client's firm laid off 60 percent of the office staff this week. I pray that you will help stabilize the company and provide for those families to find new jobs and that while this door to their career has been closed, they will find something bigger and better in the future.

I pray that you will be with those left behind at the company, as they are in the midst of turmoil and transition under new management. Be still their hearts.

In your name I pray,

Authentic, Humble, Surrendered, and Spiritual

S. Michael Edwards

Friday, February 18, 2011

Settlement Revised | Prayer #286
God,

Thank you for an answered pray. Ed said he would sign the settlement this weekend, which means I should get my money ten days after that. I'm so grateful! Glad to put it behind me and move on.

Thanks, God! Another answered prayer.

In your name I pray,

Authentic, Humble, Surrendered, and Spiritual

S. Michael Edwards

Friday, February 18, 2011

Banking Meeting Follow-up | Prayer #287
God,

Thanks for allowing Ed and me to speak with the banker about refinancing the house and yacht to get each other off the loans. This will go a long way to untangle us. Now it's up to the bankers to figure out the best way to do this. I pray they find an easy way and one that works for all involved.

I pray that it all works out and happens! I guess the refinancing for the house takes longer than for the yacht, and timing is crucial.

Money is sitting there waiting for me, and I can see it, taste it, and feel it. It will go a long way in getting me toward my goal of financial independence.

In gratitude for Ed keeping his word,

In your name I pray,

Authentic, Humble, Surrendered, and Spiritual

S. Michael Edwards

Saturday, February 19, 2011

Good Day! | Prayer #288
God,

I'm reminded of Paul Harvey, when he said, "Good day!" I remember listening to him on the AM radio, KTIL, Tillamook, Oregon, when Dad and I would go to the dump. Not sure why that memory is coming up for me now, but I am thinking about the day ahead and what's in store. I stayed home last night and just got some much needed rest.

Today, is another day, and I pray that you will provide me with a clear mind as I dive into a bunch of documentation and immerse myself in the contents to learn everything I need to learn about this new venture with Brett.

Lord, be with me today, as always, and allow me to absorb as much as I can, so that I can become an expert in all that I do.

I pray these things in your name,

Authentic, Humble, Surrendered, and Spiritual

S. Michael Edwards

Saturday, February 19, 2011

Devotional Roulette | Prayer #289
God,

Today's devotional roulette was Galatians 2:16

> We know very well that we are not set right with God by rule-keeping but only through personal faith in Jesus Christ. How do we know? We tried it—and we had the best system of rules the world has ever seen! Convinced that no human being can please God by self-improvement, we believed in Jesus as the Messiah so that we might be set right before God by trusting in the Messiah, not by trying to be good.

So I get the self-improvement (so maybe I should retract my last prayer? LOL) and trust in you, as opposed to being good. Funny this should come up after I just asked that I become an expert at what I am about to dive into. Of course I like to be good, do good, look good, and yet now I see it's through my personal faith and trust in you that I get to be good, look good.

In your name I pray,

Authentic, Humble, Surrendered, and Spiritual

S. Michael Edwards

1 comments:

Linda Edwards said...

Good morning, Michael. You've got me digging into my Bible this morning. Check out Colossians 3:15–17, "Let the peace of Christ keep you in tune with each other, in step with each other. None of this going off and doing your own thing. And cultivate thankfulness. Let the Word of Christ—The Message—have the run of the house. Give it plenty of room in your lives. Instruct and direct one another using good common sense. And sing, sing your hearts out to God! Let every detail in your lives—words, actions, whatever—be done in the name of the Master, Jesus, thanking God the Father every step of the way." I'm thinking God deserves the very best...excellence. You told me Brett's pastor said God doesn't like Folgers! So wanting to do good so you look good is far different than wanting to give God your very best because he is worthy. (Author's note, yes, the pastor did say God doesn't like Folgers. I think he was making a joke, but they definitely serve great coffee at Eastlake community Church. The point of the joke was to find another church if you don't like how they spend their money. Some of the members were complaining about the expense of the coffee...)

I'm getting ready to go to a discernment class at church today and I'm really excited about it. I prayed that I'd have beginner's mind and then laughed because that's why I'm going. I want to be able to hear God's voice and know it's him and not let the enemy distract and confuse me. So with that...have a great day and may everything you say and do be done in the name of the Lord. Amen (I love you so much).

Saturday, February 19, 2011

I'm on a Roll | Prayer #290

God,

Thanks for the clarity of purpose today. I was able to comb through all the documents, review the websites and provide feedback in a timely manner. I have done more in the last hour than I thought possible. I was thinking it would take me half the day to do what I have already accomplished, so thank you for clearing my mind and helping me out!

I'm very excited about what's ahead with this new venture with FrozenX-Plosion and I look forward to giving back in a big way.

In your name I pray,

Authentic, Humble, Surrendered, and Spiritual

S. Michael Edwards

Saturday, February 19, 2011

Yes or No Answer Please | Prayer #291
God,

Had the funniest call today from my friend Tammy. We talked about my prayers and how you need to be careful what you ask for. I think I found scripture on this before, but I mentioned how I wouldn't dare pray for patience, as you would probably let me learn it. She said she likes to pray for a yes or no answer, for clarity and to avoid any possible "learning." We got a chuckle out of that.

I'm not sure I want to go there with a question that requires a yes or no answer. I have no idea what that might look like. I mentioned that I don't mind "get back to me when you can" types of responses, because I know it's all on your time anyway.

I'm smiling as I pray to you and appreciate the beautiful day you have given us here in Dallas, Texas. From snow to the 70s in a couple of weeks. Crazy weather, but my mood is sure brighter and more upbeat when the sun is shining!

I pray for a day of serenity. So far, so good!

In your name I pray,

Authentic, Humble, Surrendered, and Spiritual

S. Michael Edwards

Saturday, February 19, 2011

Show Me the Money | Prayer #292
God,

This is the weekend that Ed is supposed to sign the settlement. I haven't asked him about it yet, but I pray that you will help him honor that commitment. It's been a long legal dispute and I would like to have it settled this weekend. I pray that is in your plan as well.

I also pray that you will open my mind to creativity today, so I can think outside the box and let my creative juices flow. I have so many ideas around business, and my best work is done when I can be creative. I am sitting in my sewing room stuck. I'd love some ideas to create something today.

I'm open to some creative ideas around embroidery today, God.

In your name I pray,

Authentic, Humble, Surrendered, and Spiritual

S. Michael Edwards

Saturday, February 19, 2011

Give Oprah a Break | Prayer #293
God,

I was reflecting on my past and how I used to think that if Oprah had me on her show and heard how many times I stayed with Ed after all the cheating, what would she say? I knew, of course, what she would say. "Why didn't you leave?" So then today I watched her show *Behind the Scenes* on her new network OWN, and it was about President Bush 41 and 43. The commercials on the show were about honesty, patience, and other values.

Then I think about the song that the Casting Crowns sing, where they sing, "Stop asking Oprah what to do." It made me wonder, why are people giving her such a hard time? I mean, she is making a difference in this world. Isn't that what we want? For people to make a difference in other people's lives?

She has a platform to change lives. On the show, she mentioned her meditation room. She clearly believes in a higher power. She said so. There was a Bible on her table. She didn't call out God, but who's to say she doesn't believe in you?

I say give Oprah a break. She is making a difference, much like I dream to make a difference.

It was good for me to see that show today. It shed new light on President Bush 43 and as much anger and hostility as I had at the time he was President, I could relate to him as a person.

Maybe I'm not as informed about why people would want to hate on Oprah. For me, she's doing amazing things with her wealth, she is making a difference.

Isn't that what it's all about? I'd ask for a yes or no answer, but as you can see from my earlier prayer, I am not ready to see what those look like yet. LOL

In your name I pray,

Authentic, Humble, Surrendered, and Spiritual

S. Michael Edwards

1 comments:

Linda Edwards said...

Hey, I agree with you; Oprah does a lot of good in this world. It makes me wonder if the Oprah haters are placing more importance on her and making her their God rather than going to the one and only God. Just another thought. There's always yes, no, and wait when we pray...God taking his time to answer is kind of like what 1 Cor. 1:10 says in The Message:

"I have a serious concern to bring up with you, my friends, using the authority of Jesus, our Master. I'll put it as urgently as I can: You must get along with each other. You must learn to be considerate of one another, cultivating a life in common."

I think it's hard to relate to Oprah's life but I also think getting along and being considerate can look different ways. How we talk about someone can be gossip, bitterness, anger, jealousy, envy, etc. We are called to a higher standard than that.

1 Kings 3:9 says, "Here's what I want: Give me a God-listening heart so I can lead your people well, discerning the difference between good and evil. For who on their own is capable of leading your glorious people?"

Lord, help me to be quick to listen, slow to speak and slow to become angry. I sometimes get it backward…quick to anger, quick to speak, and slow to listen. Thank you for not being finished with me yet. I love you, Lord. Amen.

Saturday, February 19, 2011

Heart Connection | Prayer #294
God,

I pray that you will allow my heart to show through and that I will be able to create a heart connection with an amazing person who has a passion waiting to explode. I know you know who I'm talking about, and I pray that you give me the wisdom and clarity to work with him to break through the walls and let his heart shine through.

In your name I pray,

Authentic, Humble, Surrendered, and Spiritual

S. Michael Edwards

Saturday, February 19, 2011

Brett Stokes Rocks | Prayer #295
God,

Have I thanked you lately for connecting me with such an amazing man? I absolutely love my buddy Brett Stokes and feel like he's my brother. We can talk and work really well together. We can share about when we get into our stuff, and we can celebrate the wins in life. Your bringing Brett and Carolyn into my life and all the abundance that has followed has been a true blessing to me.

I can't wait to see them again in March!

I pray you will bless them beyond their wildest dreams, as they have blessed me in the same way.

In your name I pray,

Authentic, Humble, Surrendered, and Spiritual

S. Michael Edwards

Sunday, February 20, 2011

If It's Sunday, It's Meet the Press | Prayer #296
God,

Good morning. Just got through watching *Meet the Press*, and what a mess. All this political posturing and I just don't get it. Our government has work to do, and yet they go off on vacation for a week, risking a government shutdown? I'd love to see some real leadership. Roll up your sleeves and get some work done this week in our government.

I've prayed for Egypt and now the protests are spreading to the rest of the Middle East. God, I pray you will watch over the Middle East and the violence there and allow for assembly without violence. I pray for equality in the Middle East. I pray that Israel and the Palestinians come to the table and negotiate a peace treaty.

When I look outside the window, beyond my front door and to the world at large, it's a mess. I pray that leaders stand up and do the right thing.

Now for my blood pressure medication!

In your name I pray,

Authentic, Humble, Surrendered, and Spiritual

S. Michael Edwards

Sunday, February 20, 2011

Devotional Roulette | Prayer #297
God,

In opening up my daily devotional to the page that calls my name (figuratively, of course), I turn to James 1:26–27.

Anyone who sets himself up as "religious" by talking a good game is self-deceived. This kind of religion is hot air and only hot air. Real religion, the kind that passes muster before God the Father, is this: Reach out to the homeless and loveless in their plight, and guard against corruption from the Godless world.

Funny that I would have a dream about going to church and not being welcomed. My dream was clear that there are churches that would not welcome me, and there are people who are pickers of the Bible. May they read this passage and realize that it's not about talking a good game, it's about reaching out to the people in need.

While they are in church today, I am with you. I pray your love for me will guide my actions today and always.

In your name I pray,

Authentic, Humble, Surrendered, and Spiritual

S. Michael Edwards

Sunday, February 20, 2011

Word of God Speak | Prayer #298
God,

What a beautiful song Mom sent last night, by Mercy, "Word of God Speak." She wrote: "Michael, may you rest in God's holiness and hear him speak to you. Enjoy being in his presence. Love, Mom."

I think it's the perfect song for where I am at in this journey to reconnect with you God. These lyrics, especially: "I'm finding myself in the midst of you, beyond the music, beyond the noise, all that I need is to be with you, and in the quiet hear your voice."

I do believe that I'm in the midst of you, God. This journey has become much bigger than I ever imagined, you consume my thoughts, and I am with you as you are with me.

In your name I pray,

Authentic, Humble, Surrendered, and Spiritual

S. Michael Edwards

Sunday, February 20, 2011

Prayers for Dad | Prayer #299
God,

I pray that you will be with my dad and Kimberly and Scott as they close out Advanced Leadership Seminar today. May they have touched hearts, changed lives, and moved people forward to knowing that they can achieve their wildest dreams, and many of those dreams they don't yet know. May their students be empowered, emboldened, and compassionate.

May you watch over Dad tomorrow as he travels safely back home. He's been gone a long time, and I pray you will help him recover quickly from his long journey.

In your name I pray,

Authentic, Humble, Surrendered, and Spiritual

S. Michael Edwards

Sunday, February 20, 2011

And God Said "Welcome Back" | Prayer #300
God,

I read a passage that was perfect for my 300th documented prayer.

Romans 11:20–36

There was a time not long ago when you were on the outs with God. But then the Jews slammed the door on him and things opened up for you. Now they are on the outs. But with the door held wide open for you, they have a way back in. In one way or another, God makes sure that we experience what it means to be outside so that he can personally open the door and welcome us back in.

Have you ever come on anything quite like this extravagant generosity of God, this deep, deep wisdom? It's way over our heads. We'll never figure it out.

Is there anyone around who can explain God?

Anyone smart enough to tell him what to do?

Anyone who has done him such a huge favor that God has to ask his advice?

Everything comes from him;

Everything happens through him;

Everything ends up in him.

Always glory! Always praise!

Yes. Yes. Yes.

Thank you, God, for opening the door. Thank you for allowing me back into your arms. Thank you for an amazing journey. Praise to you, and glory, too!

Yes, yes, yes!

In your name I pray,

Authentic, Humble, Surrendered, and Spiritual

S. Michael Edwards

Sunday, February 20, 2011

Your Love Is Extravagant | Prayer #301
God,

I simply love how you inspire me and touch my heart with music. You captured my heart again, and no love is greater that I have ever known. Your friendship, which I classified early on as my BFF. This journey, an intimate journey, not at all what I expected. Casting Crowns, "Your Love Is Extravagant," boy, is it ever!

I started this journey with expectations. I wanted my prayers to be humorous, like when I was at Best Buy and the lady was a test of patience for me, as she argued and gave the customer service personnel a hard time, I prayed, "Thank you, God, for giving me an opportunity to practice patience with this lady who is clearly here to test me!"

What I ended up with instead of throwing humor into my prayers was authentic me. Honest communication, not forced. I ended up with a connection with you greater than I have ever had or could have even dared imagine.

Thank you for an amazing gift—the gift of music to touch my heart and soul, and the gift of connecting with you and Mom on a deeper level. Thank you for occupying my thoughts and answering my prayers.

In your name I pray,

Authentic, Humble, Surrendered, and Spiritual

S. Michael Edwards

Sunday, February 20, 2011

God's a Big Boy | Prayer #302
God,

As I continue to open the Bible I am amazed at how you are speaking to me. It's not by chance, I know this.

Romans 14:1–4

Welcome with open arms fellow believers who don't see things the way you do. And don't jump all over them every time they do or say something you don't agree with—even when it seems that they are strong on opinions but weak in the faith department. Remember, they have their own history to deal with. Treat them gently.

For instance, a person who has been around for a while might well be convinced that he can eat anything on the table, while another, with a different background, might assume he should only be a vegetarian and eat accordingly. But since both are guests at Christ's table, wouldn't it be terribly rude if they fell to criticizing what the other ate or didn't eat? God, after all, invited them both to the table. Do you have any business crossing people off the guest list or interfering with God's welcome? If there are corrections to be made or manners to be learned, God can handle that without your help.

So I pray about not being welcome in many churches, and you show me this passage. I pray that you will show this passage to those church members. You are fully capable of handling corrections without the help of those who have "been around for a while."

I look at this as judgment…and it is perfect. Welcome with open arms, fellow believers who don't see things the way you do! Hello? Is anyone out there reading the same Bible I am reading?

Thanks, God, for the shot in the arm that I am hearing today.

In your name I pray,

Authentic, Humble, Surrendered, and Spiritual

S. Michael Edwards

Sunday, February 20, 2011

Come Quickly! | Prayer #303
God,

> Psalm 141:1–2

> God, come close. Come quickly! Open your ears—it's my voice you're hearing! Treat my prayer as sweet incense rising; my raised hands are my evening prayers.

God, what a great psalm. While it seems a little demanding to me, it's beauty is in the request to treat my prayer as sweet incense rising.

I pray that you will treat all prayers as sweet incense rising. May you be with those who are troubled today, and may they turn to you for comfort.

In your name I pray,

Authentic, Humble, Surrendered, and Spiritual

S. Michael Edwards

Monday, February 21, 2011

Praise the Lord | Prayer #304
God,

Good morning! It's a great day today, and I am thankful for another day to spread joy. I woke up this morning, checked my emails, and had some really encouraging progress from some of my friends.

One of my friends sent me this passage: "Dear brothers and sisters, whenever trouble comes your way, let it be an opportunity for joy. For when your faith is tested, your endurance has a chance to grow" (James 1:2, 3).

I love it! I have always said that trouble is an opportunity, and then to see that it's an opportunity for joy! Great word!

God, I pray that today is a day full of joy.

In your name I pray,

Authentic, Humble, Surrendered, and Spiritual

S. Michael Edwards

Monday, February 21, 2011

Devotional Roulette | Prayer #305
God,

I think this passage is perfect for reflecting on the past and focusing on the future. I particularly enjoy how it speaks of our parents and discipline, and how they did what seemed best to them. Then in the end, it pays off handsomely. I couldn't agree more!

Let the joy begin in abundance.

Hebrews 12:7–11

God is educating you; that's why you must never drop out. He's treating you as dear children. This trouble you're in isn't punishment; it's training, the normal experience of children. Only irresponsible parents leave children to fend for themselves. Would you prefer an irresponsible God? We respect our own parents for training and not spoiling us, so why not embrace God's training so we can truly live? While we were children, our parents did what seemed best to them. But God is doing what is best for us, training us to live God's holy best. At the time, discipline isn't much fun. It always feels like it's going against the grain. Later, of course, it pays off handsomely, for it's the well-trained who find themselves mature in their relationship with God.

God, I am rocking and rolling and enjoying this journey reconnecting with you. I feel like I'm floating on air and smiling like there is a million-dollar-prize patrol at my door!

Thank you!

In your name I pray,

Authentic, Humble, Surrendered, and Spiritual

S. Michael Edwards

Monday, February 21, 2011

Connection | Prayer #306
God,

The context for my meeting today is connection. I pray that we all connect at a heart level. I pray that you will work through me to make that happen for the amazing people I'll be talking to and listening to today.

May they connect and challenge and move each other forward to become bigger and better than they were before the call.

In your name I pray,

Authentic, Humble, Surrendered, and Spiritual

S. Michael Edwards

Monday, February 21, 2011

Deep Connection | Prayer #307

God,

Thanks for a great call today. It was laser focused with forward movement, while still getting some great heart connections from the team. Thank you for an amazing call with clarity.

I'm taking a deep breath and diving back into work to create value for our clients, and thank you for being with me on the call today so that I was grounded and focused and out of my stuff.

In your name I pray,

Authentic, Humble, Surrendered, and Spiritual

S. Michael Edwards

Monday, February 21, 2011

New Client! | Prayer #308

God,

We got another contract today for a new client and I am so grateful. Thank you! Our business is growing and expanding, and our employees are connecting and having fun. I pray that you will continue to guide me and the rest of the management team so that we can create a fun, creative environment for people to work and that they look forward to coming to work every day.

In your name I pray,

Authentic, Humble, Surrendered, and Spiritual

S. Michael Edwards

Monday, February 21, 2011

Settlement Update | Prayer #309

God,

Looks like we're making progress on the settlement. I pray that we are settled by the end of the month. I know this is in your hands, and the update I got today was that a few clarifying questions were asked of Ed's attorney. Then we should be good to go.

I'd love to have this settled before first weekend of Sam Camp, which I leave on March 2 to attend.

It's going to be an amazing weekend, with or without the settlement, but it would sure be nice to have this whole thing settled as we dive into personal growth with our students.

In gratitude for moving this forward, and in your name I pray,

Authentic, Humble, Surrendered, and Spiritual

S. Michael Edwards

Monday, February 21, 2011

To Know You | Prayer #310

Hi God,

This song is new to me, Casting Crowns, "To Know You," but since I bought all the Casting Crown albums, I am learning new songs and they are resonating with and my journey. This song is the perfect anthem for my journey to reconnect with you, and it totally speaks to what I am feeling. To know you is to want to know you more. Nice. It's a song that expresses what I have been feeling on this journey.

I couldn't agree more with the lyrics of this song, God. Thanks for putting it out there for me to find. These treasures are fuel to my journey.

In your name I pray,

Authentic, Humble, Surrendered, and Spiritual

S. Michael Edwards

Monday, February 21, 2011

If We Are the Body | Prayer #311
God,

This song by Casting Crowns, "If We Are the Body," really makes me wonder, for my fellow believers, where are we missing the mark? There is a way, but why aren't we doing it? "Jesus paid much too high a price. For us to pick and choose who should come, and we are the Body of Christ."

Lord, I pray that you will ring some bells and rattle some cages for your followers. Help them see that Jesus is the way, and that their actions are crucial, their love is instrumental in drawing people in, instead of turning people away.

In your name I pray,

Authentic, Humble, Surrendered, and Spiritual

S. Michael Edwards

Monday, February 21, 2011

Voice of Truth | Prayer #312
God,

I'm on a roll with songs that are speaking to my heart. "To step out of my comfort zone and into the realm of the unknown where Jesus is…The voice of truth tells me do not be afraid, this is for my glory!" Casting Crowns, "Voice of Truth."

I know that over the six months I have grabbed as many opportunities that have presented themselves to me for personal growth, professional growth, and spiritual growth. I have been rewarded handsomely. I am truly blessed, God. You are with me, you are carrying me, and together we're walking on clouds.

I will soar with the wings of eagles

when I stop and listen to the sound of Jesus

singing over me

God, you are singing over me, and I am rejoicing with you! Together we are creating a bond, and it's been an amazing journey watching and seeing and believing how you are with me, taking the stress away and comforting me. I surrender to you, and I am blessed as a result.

In your name I pray,

Authentic, Humble, Surrendered, and Spiritual

S. Michael Edwards

Monday, February 21, 2011

Connection | Prayer #313

God,

Tonight we have our team lead call for Sam Camp, and I pray that we have an amazing connection as a team; that we come together as one; that we learn from each other and connect at a heart level to propel ourselves forward. One of the sayings of Sam Camp is, "As go the leaders, so go the students." I want, more than anything, for our students to be connected as one and to achieve their goals—strike that, to exceed their goals, which are beyond their wildest dreams.

May you watch over our call tonight, filling our hearts with joy and surrender.

It's just a short time away from our first weekend of meeting all the students of Sam Camp, and I pray that we rock this call tonight. May it be bigger and better than last week's call, which was amazing.

In your name I pray,

Authentic, Humble, Surrendered, and Spiritual

S. Michael Edwards

Monday, February 21, 2011

He's Asking Me for Advice? | Prayer #314

God,

What a great day with Ed at work today. He came into my office and asked me for advice on his Sam Camp goals. It was a big turning point for me and for him. He is seeking my counsel on things that he thought he "had figured out." It was great to be able to connect with him as a leader, when he didn't consider me a leader before I started my Sam Camp journey.

I am so grateful that you have allowed me to step into my leadership and that Ed is noticing and asking questions and advice. What a gift, for him to see the value that I bring to our company and to him personally.

What a blessing. I am looking forward to his journey as he dreams big, plays big, and gets out of his head and into his heart.

I pray that you will open his heart so that he can connect at a heart level with his team and not just a "problem solver, intellectual level." He is a powerful leader, if he chooses to step into vulnerability. He doesn't particularly care for that word. Juanita, a dear friend, gave me a video on vulnerability from someone who hated the word, but found through her research that it's actually quite powerful…the good and the bad. I gave that video clip to Ed in the hopes that he would connect emotionally with what he wants in life and be able to communicate that to his team to get them enrolled in his goals.

Thank you, God, for allowing me to be a part of Ed's journey in Sam Camp. I certainly didn't expect it, but it's just another unexpected gift you have given me.

In your name I pray,

Authentic, Humble, Surrendered, and Spiritual

S. Michael Edwards

Monday, February 21, 2011

Bless My Inner Circle | Prayer #315
God,

I want to thank you for such an amazing group in my inner circle. They totally lift me up, fill me up, and inspire me to be all that I can be (okay, as an Air Force Vet, that's an Army Slogan, but it's a good one). Thank you for surrounding me with Godly people, who have my best interests at heart. Thank you for feeding my soul through them.

It's truly a blessing to be on this journey with them and with you and my parents.

In gratitude,

And in your name I pray,

Authentic, Humble, Surrendered, and Spiritual

S. Michael Edwards

Tuesday, February 22, 2011

Great Call | Prayer #316

God,

I prayed that our team call last night would allow us to be connected, and boy, were we! It was a fun, connected call. I am so grateful for the amazing people you have surrounded me with. I am learning a lot, and we're having a blast. I can't wait to give everyone a big hug when we meet next week!

Talked to my client today and am praying for her as her organization goes through major changes. I pray that you will be with her during this time and that she is comforted by your love.

In your name I pray,

Authentic, Humble, Surrendered, and Spiritual

S. Michael Edwards

Tuesday, February 22, 2011

You Are Good | Prayer #317

God,

Mom sent me this message: "God is good, all the time; all the time, God is good. This song captures the message of my heart. I'm so grateful for the goodness of God. I'm so blessed to be a part of your journey in seeing how much God loves you and without expecting anything in return, he continues to pour out his blessings on you. Everyone gets blessed. Love you, Mom."

What a beautiful note. I am grateful, God, for so much love and connection. Nichole Nordeman, "You Are Good," is a great song and is definitely a way to praise you. These lyrics capture that for me.

> I'll sing You a love song
>
> It's all that I have
>
> To tell You I'm grateful
>
> For holding my life in Your Hands

God, you are good, and I am grateful. Thank you for all the abundance and joy you have brought in my life.

In your name I pray,

Authentic, Humble, Surrendered, and Spiritual

S. Michael Edwards

Tuesday, February 22, 2011

The Heart of Worship | Prayer #318

God,

Thank you for blessing me with an amazing Mom, whose gift (one of many) is to inspire me to be a better man, a more Godly man…through song. This song, Matt Redman, "The Heart of Worship," is really about you. It's all about you, God!

Mom wrote:

> "When the music fades, all is stripped away and I simply come longing just to bring something that's of worth that will bless your heart. I'll bring you more than a song, for a song in itself is not what you have required. You search much deeper within, through the way things appear. You're looking into my heart. I'm coming back to the heart of worship, and it's all about you, it's all about you, Jesus. I'm sorry, Lord, for the things I've made it, when it's all about you! It's all about you, Jesus."

Mom is quite the gifted writer and has made this journey so enjoyable and so empowering for me. May you continue to inspire her to inspire me. It's like a snowball effect, and my heart swells with joy.

Yes, it is, God! It's all about you, and I thank you for looking into my heart and blessing me beyond my wildest dreams.

In your name I pray,

Authentic, Humble, Surrendered, and Spiritual

S. Michael Edwards

Tuesday, February 22, 2011

Devotional Roulette | Prayer #319

God,

In today's devotional roulette I opened up to Philippians 1:3–6:

> "Every time you cross my mind, I break out in exclamations of thanks to God. Each exclamation is a trigger to prayer. I find myself praying for you with a glad heart. I am so pleased that you have continued on in this with us, believing and proclaiming God's Message, from the day you heard it right up to the present. There has never been the slightest doubt in my mind that the God who started this great work in you would keep at it and bring it to a flourishing finish on the very day Christ Jesus appears."

Wow, that is exactly how I feel! How perfect is that? I am grateful, and believe and proclaim your message in my prayers, God. I pray with a glad heart. The thing about this journey is that you cross my mind so often, consuming my thoughts, and then I break out in prayer.

Thanks for this passage. I love the confirmation of my journey, and the results I am seeing are exactly what this passage in this Scripture is about!

In your name I pray,

Authentic, Humble, Surrendered, and Spiritual

S. Michael Edwards

Tuesday, February 22, 2011

Peace in the Middle East | Prayer #320
God,

When I wrote my vision statement out, I wrote that I wanted equality for all in the Middle East. Now we have this uprising of the people who want to overthrow their dictators. I pray that you will be with the people and provide for a peaceful transition to a democratic society, where everyone has a voice and everyone is treated equally.

How cool would it be if my twenty-year vision came true to fast? It's amazing to see what's happening over there, and I pray you will be with the people through the violence and give them the strength and conviction to make real change.

May you also be with the families of those who have been murdered or injured. I pray you will comfort them and surround them with your love so that they know they are loved.

In your name I pray,

Authentic, Humble, Surrendered, and Spiritual

S. Michael Edwards

Tuesday, February 22, 2011

Three Client Inquires Today | Prayer #321
God,

It's raining abundance, and I am grateful. We've had three new client inquiries today for our ad agency. Thank you so much. I pray that we're able to close the deal with all three, not to mention the new business we got yesterday. I am blessed that you are providing the wisdom for our team to continue to grow, and pray that you will keep our team connected and productive. A little laughter, a lot of fun, and happy clients—a great combination that we could use more of!

In gratitude,

I pray, in your name,

Authentic, Humble, Surrendered, and Spiritual

S. Michael Edwards

Tuesday, February 22, 2011

I Was Born This Way | Prayer #322

God,

I just listened to this song by Lady Gaga, "Born This Way," and I thought I'd put up a prayer. There are so many kids, and adults for that matter, who are confused, troubled, and not accepted for being gay, lesbian, transgendered, bisexual, etc. It just makes me sad. I mean, I know that we are your children and that you don't make mistakes. I honestly believe that I was "born this way."

I am at peace with it. I know there are many who are not—not with themselves and not with others. I'm sure it's controversial, and I don't really care. The fact is, we're all sinners. Right? I can't help who I'm attracted to. I tried to be straight, and I was married for six years. I was still gay, just married to a woman. It was me trying to fit into society.

God, I pray that you will be with those who are troubled on both sides of the issue and help them see that we are all children of God. I pray that the world sees we all deserve respect, and equal rights, and dignity.

In your name I pray,

Authentic, Humble, Surrendered, and Spiritual

S. Michael Edwards

1 comments:

Just a Girl said...

I saw Gaga in concert, and she was amazing. She made everyone feel so loved for who they were. She really tries to spread the message of acceptance and self-love. I love her new song for its message. If you ever get a chance to see her, you would love her. It is the best show/performance I have ever seen.

Wednesday, February 23, 2011

Gratitude | Prayer #323

Good morning, God,

I had a great conversation with my dad last night, it was nice to get to catch up after his long travels. I am looking forward to seeing him and Mom soon. I thank you for all that you have done to inspire my dad to be of service and contribution to the world. He is truly making a difference in people's lives, and it's inspired me to do the same.

I am thankful that we have a relationship where we can talk and he provides guidance to me and coaches me. I'm very lucky to have such a powerful, loving, and caring father.

In gratitude for you and my earthly father,

I pray in your name,

Authentic, Humble, Surrendered, and Spiritual

S. Michael Edwards

Wednesday, February 23, 2011

Devotional Roulette | Prayer #324

God,

My devotional roulette this morning is from Mark 12:28–31:

> One of the religion scholars came up. Hearing the lively exchanges of question and answer and seeing how sharp Jesus was in his answers, he put in his question: "Which is most important of all the commandments?"

> Jesus said, "The first in importance is, 'Listen, Israel: The Lord your God is one; so love the Lord God with all your passion and prayer and intelligence and energy.' And here is the second: 'Love others as well as you love yourself.' There is no other commandment that ranks with these."

Interesting, God. So I have prayed about there not being one sin greater than another…but this is clear that Jesus did rank the commandments. Love God with all your passion, prayer, intelligence, and energy. Then love others as well as you love yourself. I wonder why this second one gets missed by so many "Christians"? What a world we would live in if everyone followed these two most important commandments.

I pray that these words will energize people to see the importance of loving God and prayer and loving others as well as themselves.

In your name I pray,

Authentic, Humble, Surrendered, and Spiritual

S. Michael Edwards

Wednesday, February 23, 2011

Be Still My Heart | Prayer #325
God,

I am full of energy today, some of it nervous and some of it excitement for next week. I pray that you will calm my heart and fill me with serenity so I don't feel so anxious. I don't know what has me all riled up, but I could sure use some love and serenity. I don't think it's too much coffee!

I have a big client meeting today, and they are asking some tough questions. I pray that you will guide me through the meeting with the grace, compassion, and wisdom to satisfy their questions.

In your name I pray,

Authentic, Humble, Surrendered, and Spiritual

S. Michael Edwards

Wednesday, February 23, 2011

6.66 | Prayer #326
God,

I just realized after my last prayer that I have an average of 6.66 prayers before I've documented 365 prayers. Not really fond of that number, and so I am praying to you again to change that number! Forty prayers to go, and I will have 365 prayers documented by 28 February 2011, eleven p.m. Arizona time.

So I pray for continued wisdom, strength, guidance, and grace. I pray for the children of the world to find peace and love and positive role models. I pray for peace in the Middle East. I pray that you will fill me with joy today.

In your name I pray,

Authentic, Humble, Surrendered, and Spiritual

S. Michael Edwards

Wednesday, February 23, 2011

Texted PSALM | Prayer #327
God,

Bless my dear friend Debbie who texted me Psalm 100:1–5:

On your feet now—applaud God!

Bring a gift of laughter,

sing yourselves into his presence.

Know this: God is God, and God, God.

He made us; we didn't make him

We're his people, his well-tended sheep.

Enter with the password: "Thank you!"

Make yourselves at home, talking praise.

Thank him. Worship Him.

For God is sheer beauty,

All-generous in love,

loyal always and ever!

Praise to you, God! Glad to hear the password is "Thank you!" I have certainly used that password a few times. I do thank you and worship you. You are sheer beauty, generous in your love, and loyal. I love "the gift of laughter"! I love "sing yourselves into his presence." I have plenty of praise songs that have connected me with you at a deep level.

You gotta love technology where you can get a scripture at just the right moment.

In your name I pray,

Authentic, Humble, Surrendered, and Spiritual

S. Michael Edwards

Wednesday, February 23, 2011

Ahhhhhhh | Prayer #328
That was quick, God,

A sense of serenity has washed over me. Thank you for such a quick answer to my prayer! I am ground, centered, and ready to take on the rest of the day. I am blessed that you are with me, have calmed my heart, and blessed me with your presence.

As I prepare for the finish of the week, I'll be traveling to Austin to meet with my new business partner. I pray in advance that I will have a productive meeting, that we will connect and click, and that we will get a lot of things accomplished.

In your name I pray,

Authentic, Humble, Surrendered, and Spiritual

S. Michael Edwards

Wednesday, February 23, 2011

One Step Closer to Equality | Prayer #329

God,

Just read that the Obama administration will no longer defend the federal marriage act in court. This is a huge step forward for equality for a law that has been challenged as unconstitutional. I pray that the law will be overturned and that all God's children be allowed to be married, in love.

Thank you for giving the wisdom to our leaders, to love each other as they would love themselves. There is no room for discrimination in our great nation.

In your name I pray,

Authentic, Humble, Surrendered, and Spiritual

S. Michael Edwards

Wednesday, February 23, 2011

Master Mind | Prayer #330

God,

Tonight as I prepare for our Master Mind call, I pray you will be with each of our team as we share our requests with each other. I pray you will allow us each to have an open heart and a beginner's mind, and to think and play a big game. Our team is amazing and we're doing amazing things, creating amazing change. I pray you will be with us and continue to bless us with your abundance as we work to connect with each other and with you.

In your name I pray,

Authentic, Humble, Surrendered, and Spiritual

S. Michael Edwards

Wednesday, February 23, 2011

Waiting for the World to Change | Prayer #331

God,

I am so excited to see the positive changes happening in the world. While there is still too much violence, there seems to be momentum building for peace and democracy. I pray you will continue to empower the people as they risk their lives to bring about a better world. Equality for all! I pray that you will provide the wisdom, courage, and harmony around the world as the people rise up and demand equality. May their lives be blessed by the coming changes, and may the violence cease.

In your name I pray,

Authentic, Humble, Surrendered, and Spiritual

S. Michael Edwards

Thursday, February 24, 2011

Already Gone | Prayer #332
God,

My favorite client got laid off last night. The same one I had a great meeting with yesterday. She told me via email and said she'd call today. I am very sad for her and pray that you have an even bigger, more amazing opportunity around the corner for her. I pray that you will be with her and her family as she goes through this transition. She told me that the other people who got laid off were let go without any severance. So I am wondering if that's the case for her as well.

I don't know what this means for her, but I know you have a plan. I am keeping her in my prayers God and asking for your grace.

In your name I pray,

Authentic, Humble, Surrendered, and Spiritual

S. Michael Edwards

Thursday, February 24, 2011

What Faith Can Do | Prayer #333
God,

A friend sent me this song the other day, and it really resonates with me as I grieve the loss of my friend's job.

These lyrics are perfect for her as she goes through this career transition. Kutless, "What Faith Can Do":

I've seen dreams that move the mountains

Hope that doesn't ever end

Even when the sky is falling

I've seen miracles just happen

Silent prayers get answered

Broken hearts become brand new

That's what faith can do

God, I pray that she seeks your guidance and relies on her faith and comes out of this stronger.

In your name I pray,

Authentic, Humble, Surrendered, and Spiritual

S. Michael Edwards

Thursday, February 24, 2011

Nelson Brandt's Requests | Prayer #334
God,

Here are the requests from my friend Nelson this week.

With faith in God and a great sense of gratitude I ask the following:

Professional: That on or before 28 February 2011, I returned from vacation with sufficient awareness to resume my duties with poise and effectiveness.

Personal: That on or before 27 February 2011, my family and I returned to our respective homes safely following our vacation to Disney World.

Esoteric: That on or before 24 February 2011, my children, Cooper and Bella, enjoyed the adventure of their vacation and were great listeners.

God, I pray that you will provide the wisdom and awareness for Nelson to resume his duties with poise and effectiveness after the tragedy that occurred on his base. I pray that he have the sensitivity and strength to guide his organization through this difficult time. I also pray that you will allow him and his family a safe trip home this week and that you be with his children as they enjoy their vacation and listen to each other with open hearts and minds.

In your name I pray,

Authentic, Humble, Surrendered, and Spiritual

S. Michael Edwards

Thursday, February 24, 2011

Karen Sizelove's Requests | Prayer #335

God,

Karen sent the following requests, which I honor and support and pray that you will as well.

With the love, support, and integrity of my Master Mind team and knowledge that wherever I am…God is, I graciously make the following requests: I am so happy and grateful now that: I have signed up three Chocolatiers who are committed and income producing in Dove Chocolate Discoveries on or before February 28, 2011, by six p.m. EST.

With the love, support, and integrity of my Master Mind team and knowledge that wherever I am…God is, I graciously make the following requests: I am so happy and grateful now that: I am a TEAM Leader and already making $4,000 or more each month on or before March 31, 2011.

With the love, support, and integrity of my Master Mind team and knowledge that wherever I am…God is, I graciously make the following requests: I am so happy and grateful now that: All the children in Honduras prisons receive life-skills training to improve the quality of their life now and forever on or before March 31, 2011, noon EST.

God I pray that Karen attracts three or more business builders, who are energetic, committed, and as passionate about building their business under Karen by the end of February. I also pray that she finds the path to become a team leader and makes $4,000 or more a month on or before March 31, 2011. Finally, God, I pray that the children in Honduras prisons receive life-skills training to improve the quality of their life now and forever on or before March 31, 2011.

Karen has a big heart, and I pray that you will honor her requests.

In your name I pray,

Authentic, Humble, Surrendered, and Spiritual

S. Michael Edwards

Thursday, February 24, 2011

Lesha Kitts Requests | Prayer #336
God,

I pray that you will honor and support Lesha Kitts requests for this week.

> With the love, support, and integrity of my Master Mind team and knowledge that wherever I am...God is, I graciously make the following requests:

> That on or before October 1, 2011, I am enjoying my new car, a 2012 Veloster.

> That on or before March 15, 2011, I have completed Apple Butter Marinade recipe for Mi Querencia.

> That on or before March 1, 2011, Heather has found peace in her heart to do the right thing and is moving forward.

God, by October, I pray that Lesha has the means and opportunity to buy and enjoy her new Veloster car. I pray that you give her the wisdom, passion, and determination to complete her apple butter marinade recipe for Mi Querencia by March 15,

2011. I also pray that her friend Heather finds peace in her heart to do the right thing and moves forward in a manner that honors her and those around her by March 1.

I pray these things in your name,

Authentic, Humble, Surrendered, and Spiritual

S. Michael Edwards

Thursday, February 24, 2011

By Your Side | Prayer #337
God,

Mom sent me this song, Tenth Avenue North, "By Your Side," with the following message: "I'm so thankful that God's hands are holding us and he will never let us go. Thank you, Lord, that your promises are true. Thank you that the ground is level at the foot of the cross. For God so loved the world that he gave his one and only Son, that whoever believes in him shall not perish but have eternal life. Amen and Amen."

God, I love that you are by my side, and I do love and want to get to know you. The true purpose of my journey of 365 prayers. Thank you for holding me and loving me. I pray you give me the wisdom to help counsel my friend who lost her job.

In your name I pray,

Authentic, Humble, Surrendered, and Spiritual

S. Michael Edwards

Thursday, February 24, 2011

The Anthem | Prayer #338
God,

My fabulous friend Centa sent me this song, "The Anthem," by Jake Hamilton. I love the lyrics, of course. It's my turn to shine! God, I won't let you down. I will shake the world and make a difference, with your help and guidance. I pray for the wisdom to make choices that will honor and glorify you, God.

Yeah, I'm gonna change the world, God!

In your name I pray,

Authentic, Humble, Surrendered, and Spiritual

S. Michael Edwards

Thursday, February 24, 2011

Devotional Roulette | Prayer #339
God,

Great devotional today. Sort of feel like I've read it before, but regardless, it's where the devotional roulette landed today.

> 1 John 1:8–10
>
> If we claim that we're free of sin, we're only fooling ourselves. A claim like that is errant nonsense. On the other hand, if we admit our sins—make a clean breast of them—he won't let us down; he'll be true to himself. He'll forgive our sins and purge us of all wrongdoing. If we claim that we've never sinned, we out-and-out contradict God—make a liar out of him. A claim like that only shows off our ignorance of God.

Thank you, God, for this reminder, that we are all sinners and that by admitting our sins, you'll make a clean breast of them and not let us down.

I pray for all believers to recognize they are sinners and to turn to you to admit their sins.

I pray this in your name,

Authentic, Humble, Surrendered, and Spiritual

S. Michael Edwards

Thursday, February 24, 2011

Great Meeting | Prayer #340
God,

The grilling I was expecting with the tough questions from the client didn't happen. It was a great meeting, and the questions were easily answered with no resistance. We laughed and had a great connection. I pray that you will continue to be with this client as they go through major restructuring.

I forgot to publish this prayer, as it was prayer #330. Weird how the meeting went so well, and then the CMO got let go last night. I have changed the prayer sequence, as I don't know how to get it back to the time I actually prayed it, but I am saddened by my friend's departure and pray that she will find something bigger and better.

In your name I pray,

Authentic, Humble, Surrendered, and Spiritual

S. Michael Edwards

Thursday, February 24, 2011

Just Brakes | Prayer #341
God,

The brakes on the car went out—that sound of metal on metal was pretty intense. Luckily we have a client that is a luxury auto dealer and they gave us employee pricing! I am so grateful for the savings! I just wanted to thank you for that. They certainly didn't have to do it, but it is nice to know that we have a client who cares enough about us to provide a discount for their services.

I am constantly blessed by the abundance that you have showered me with.

Thank You God!

In your name I pray,

Authentic, Humble, Surrendered, and Spiritual

S. Michael Edwards

Thursday, February 24, 2011

Lift Off | Prayer #342
God,

Thank you for a successful lift off of the space shuttle. May you be with the astronauts on this historic mission, the last for *Discovery*. May they travel safely to the space station, and I pray they complete their mission without harm or tragedy.

May you also be with their families and comfort them as, I imagine, they may be stressed about the mission and their loved ones.

In your name I pray,

Authentic, Humble, Surrendered, and Spiritual

S. Michael Edwards

Friday, February 25, 2011

Power of Prayer | Prayer #343
God,

The daily devotional roulette was a refreshing notice on the power of prayer.

James 5:13–18

Are you hurting? Pray. Do you feel great? Sing. Are you sick? Call the church leaders together to pray and anoint you with oil in the name of the Master. Believing-prayer will heal you, and Jesus will put you on your feet. And if you've sinned, you'll be forgiven—healed inside and out.

Make this your common practice: Confess your sins to each other and pray for each other so that you can live together whole and healed. The prayer of a person living right with God is something powerful to be reckoned with. Elijah, for instance, human just like us, prayed hard that it wouldn't rain, and it didn't—not a drop for three and a half years. Then he prayed that it would rain, and it did. The showers came and everything started growing again.

What a perfect devotional to show me that the path I am on is the path you have in the Bible. The journey I have taken thus far, with prayer being a common practice, has helped me become whole and healed. I thank you for answering my prayers, God.

May today be a fruitful day of joy, abundance, serenity, and spiritual connection.

In your name I pray,

Authentic, Humble, Surrendered, and Spiritual

S. Michael Edwards

Friday, February 25, 2011

Wait and See | Prayer #344
God,

My dear friend Kristina sent me this amazing song by Brandon Heath, titled "Wait And See." I appreciate these lyrics, "The farther on I go, I've seen enough to know, that I'm not here for nothing, he's up to something." I know you are not finished with me yet. We're just getting started, and amazing things are happening.

I pray that you will continue to bless me and reveal your plan for me in your due time. I love the journey, and I am blessed beyond measure for all that you have given me. I thank you for my wonderful friends and family and all my support. I thank you for taking me under your wings on this journey, which seemed impossible. And yet, I'm seeing the light at the end of the tunnel. This time it's not a train I see, but you, my God.

In your name I pray,

Authentic, Humble, Surrendered, and Spiritual

S. Michael Edwards

Friday, February 25, 2011

Have I Told You Lately That I Love You | Prayer #345
God,

I'm stealing a line from a song and an email I got from a friend…Have I told you lately that I love you? My heart is filled with love and joy this morning, and I've got a big smile on my face. Tonight I head to Austin to entertain a client on the yacht—it's supposed to be 80 degrees F and sunny tomorrow. I haven't been down to the lake in months, and so I'm excited to go on a three-hour cruise. LOL, okay, not the *Gilligan's Island* kind of cruise, but a nice cruise along Lake Travis.

I pray that you will be with me as I travel down to Austin and provide for a safe trip. May the yacht engines start, and the client have a good time.

I love you, God!

In your name I pray,

Authentic, Humble, Surrendered, and Spiritual

S. Michael Edwards

Friday, February 25, 2011

My Friend | Prayer #346
God,

I spoke with my friend who was let go, and she seemed to be in a really good place. I told her I had prayed for her three times, and she was touched. She is such an amazing woman, and we had a good talk about what she wants to do next. She has seen the change in me over the last six months, as I have gone on the Klemmer Journey as well as this prayer journey, which she didn't know about until last night.

I pray that you will keep her spirits high and fill her heart with confidence, courage, and determination. That you help her find her passion as she transitions to a new phase in her life.

May you bless her as you've blessed me.

In your name I pray,

Authentic, Humble, Surrendered, and Spiritual

S. Michael Edwards

Friday, February 25, 2011

Venture Capital Vultures | Prayer #347
God,

I learned that the VC firm that purchased our client and let my friend go is not going to pay hundreds of thousands of dollars in debt. They just don't care, and now all these vendors are going to get ripped off. I'll refrain from posting the name of the VC firm for now, because they still have time to make things right. I pray that you will surround them with the wisdom to do the right thing. There are too many small businesses that they are willing to give the shaft. I don't understand how people can be so selfish. I pray that you will inspire them to pay the debt they owe.

Makes me sad to know that there are people like that.

In your name I pray,

Authentic, Humble, Surrendered, and Spiritual

S. Michael Edwards

Friday, February 25, 2011

Whatever It Takes | Prayer #348
God,

Mom sent me a new song today by Lifehouse, titled "Whatever It Takes." She wrote: "Father God, thank you for being on this journey with us; for guiding us, encouraging us, walking with us, and carrying us when you need to. May we do whatever it takes to stay close beside you. Thank you for your unconditional love. Amen."

God, what an amazing journey. I echo Mom's words. Thank you for your unconditional love. Thank you for helping me connect with you on a deeper level than I ever thought possible. Who knew the power of prayer could be so huge? I had no idea, even when I started this journey, but I did know one thing...I would do whatever it took to complete this goal of 365 prayers in seven weeks. The goal was just a mechanism for me to reconnect with you, and boy did that happen. Thank you, God!

In your name I pray,

Authentic, Humble, Surrendered, and Spiritual

S. Michael Edwards

Friday, February 25, 2011

Go Tucker! | Prayer #349
God,

I know I prayed about the irony of people praying for the Super Bowl teams, and how it was odd that they weren't praying for world peace, feeding the hunger, etc. Well, I have changed my mind, slightly.

I pray that you will be with my nephew as he wrestles for the Oregon State Championship in high school wrestling. He's already received letters of interest from Princeton and the Naval Academy for his wrestling and he's only a junior. (I think he's a junior, I should know that). Anyway, I pray that he wins, as this will bolster his opportunities to go to college and get a degree. He is a very smart kid, and this could be the launching pad for him to a bigger and better life.

Go, Tucker, Go! I pray you'll be with him and give him the strength, courage, wisdom, and passion to win the tournament.

In your name I pray,

Authentic, Humble, Surrendered, and Spiritual

S. Michael Edwards

Friday, February 25, 2011

Tripoli and Libya | Prayer #350
God,

Please be with the people of Libya and Tripoli as they are under siege from their dictator. There are so many lives being lost, I pray you will be with the families of those who are grieving and empower the people to overthrow the regime.

May you give them the courage, strength, wisdom, and guidance to take back control of their country. Equality for all!

In your name I pray,

Authentic, Humble, Surrendered

S. Michael Edwards

Saturday, February 26, 2011

The Great Adventure | Prayer #351
God,

My friend Sheri sent me this song by Steven Curtis Chapman, "The Great Adventure." She said it reminds her of me every time she hears it. As I read the lyrics, it's the perfect anthem for me. Thank you for inspiring Sheri to send this song. It rocks! Your grace set me free, and in those pages, I see a bigger frontier in front of me! I'm ready for the ride of my life. I'm going to leave long-faced religion in a cloud of dust, and discover all the new horizons just waiting to be explored.

In your name I pray,

Authentic, Humble, Surrendered, and Spiritual

S. Michael Edwards

Friday, February 25, 2011

No Tickets and Safe Travels | Prayer #352
God,

Thank you for watching over me and my radar detector. I made it safely to Austin without a ticket or accident. I'm sitting on the yacht charging the batteries with the engines. Apparently three months is too long to let the boat go without charging the batteries (well, it's been five or six months since I haven't been down here since September to run the boat).

I pray the boat starts up and I can take my client for a long cruise and not have to get towed! Hence, running engines to charge batteries (which should have been charged the whole time since the battery charger was turned on). I guess it's just one more thing to fix. The generator doesn't work, and either I need new batteries or a new battery charger.

Regardless, I am not complaining. I am grateful to have a yacht!

In your name I pray,

Authentic, Humble, Surrendered, and Spiritual

S. Michael Edwards

Saturday, February 26, 2011

Entertaining Client on Yacht | Prayer #353

God,

I pray that you will be with me today as I entertain a client and potential business partner, Jeff Ericson, on the yacht today. We're going to talk business and just get to know each other better. We'll be taking a tour of the lake, and all the beauty that you have created here at Lake Travis, and I pray that you will be with us and allow for a safe journey and fruitful discussions.

I pray these things in your name,

Authentic, Humble, Surrendered, and Spiritual

S. Michael Edwards

Saturday, February 26, 2011

Daily Devotional | Prayer #354

God,

Perfect devotional today, as I entertain my client, who is a Christian.

3 John 5–8

Dear friend, when you extend hospitality to Christian brothers and sisters, even when they are strangers, you make the faith visible. They've made a full report back to the church here, a message about your love. It's good work you're do-ing, helping these travelers on their way, hospitality worthy of God himself! They set out under the banner of the Name, and get no help from unbelievers. So they deserve any support we can give them. In providing meals and a bed, we become their companions in spreading the Truth.

Beautiful God. I am entertaining traveling Christians on my yacht today. One, a theology major, is an amazing, talented, and brilliant man. I have a copy of a book for him, *My Fight with God, How He Won and So Did I,* by Brian Klemmer. Maybe the topic of faith and religion will come up.

I'm excited to see what you have in store for us today. May you bless us on our journey as we bond.

In your name I pray,

Authentic, Humble, Surrendered, and Spiritual

S. Michael Edwards

Saturday, February 26, 2011

This Is It and I'm Satisfied | Prayer #355

God,

Thank you for an amazing day on the lake with my client/partner. We had a great conversation about the direction he wants to take the business, and how Brett and I fit into the picture. We had a nice tour of the lake and even better conversation about our roles and responsibilities.

I'm so excited for the future and this opportunity, and I believe that it is you who connected Brett and me with this brilliant man. I pray that we will be able to do your work, using this business as "fuel" for our philanthropy vision.

We have dinner planned tonight and then I am back to Dallas tomorrow. I pray that I have given him enough of my heart and that he knows how passionate and how capable I am to take his business to the next level.

It's just a matter of time before I tell Ed that I am leaving the ad agency and moving to Florida. I'm going to ship the yacht to Florida, live on it, and explode this business opportunity.

I am so grateful for this opportunity and am excited to see where we (you, Brett, and our partner) can take this business.

In gratitude and appreciation,

I pray,

Authentic, Humble, Surrendered, and Spiritual

S. Michael Edwards

Saturday, February 26, 2011

Brett Rocks! | Prayer #356
God,

Just got off the phone with Brett. We talked about business, and I'm all fired up! We are going to rock this world. I am so thankful that you put the two of us together, first and foremost, for introducing me to a loving God, secondly for showing me what a non-judgmental Christian looks like, and finally for introducing me to a guy who has a similar vision to change the world.

We talked at length today about our meeting with our new business partner…including strategy, strengths, weaknesses, and all the things in between. We make a strong team. I am so excited to be in business with Brett, that it truly makes my toes tingle.

Thank you, God! You have opened my eyes to remove judgment and opened them up to possibilities. Without that, I would not have been friends with my buddy Brett.

Let the games and abundance begin…bring it on, we're ready!

In your name I pray,

Authentic, Humble, Surrendered, and Spiritual

S. Michael Edwards

Sunday, February 27, 2011

Good Morning | Prayer #357
Good morning, God,

It's another beautiful day, and I'm grateful. Thank you for being with me at my dinner last night. It was an amazing dinner. Afterward, I went to see some friends that

I haven't seen in a long time. We talked about this new business, and they are very interested in brokering the products!

They will be coming over today at eleven a.m. to taste FrozenX-plosion, and I'm very excited about the possibilities. I don't want to give too much away, except to say that they are well connected with grocery stores, some big, big, big ones, and I pray that they will not only like the product, but be as excited about selling it as I am.

May the taste tests be blessed in your name,

I pray,

Authentic, Humble, Surrendered, and Spiritual

S. Michael Edwards

Sunday, February 27, 2011

Devotional Roulette | Prayer #358

God, as my journey to 365 prayers in seven weeks comes to a close, I open my daily devotional and I'm inspired.

1 Corinthians 1:26–31

Take a good look, friends, at who you were when you got called into this life. I don't see many of "the brightest and the best" among you, not many influential, not many from high-society families. Isn't it obvious that God deliberately chose men and women that the culture overlooks and exploits and abuses, chose these "nobodies" to expose the hollow presentations of the "somebodies"? That makes it quite clear that none of you can get by with blowing your own horn before God. Everything that we have—right thinking and right living, a clean slate and a fresh start—comes from God by way of Jesus Christ. That's why we have the saying, "If you're going to blow a horn, blow a trumpet for God."

I think this passage of scripture speaks volumes. As I reflect back on some of my previous questions and prayers, I realize that you have chosen me, a man my culture overlooks and exploits and abuses. You have chosen me with unconditional love.

I am grateful…and I played the trumpet in high school, too. Interesting.

In your name I pray,

Authentic, Humble, Surrendered, and Spiritual

S. Michael Edwards

Sunday, February 27, 2011

Follower of Jesus | Prayer #359
God, I asked my friend last night about my confusion around calling myself a "Christian"—I frankly don't like the word, or more importantly what it represents in this day and age. I asked him, a theology professor, what he called himself. He said, "When people ask me if I'm a Christian, I tell them no. I am a follower of Jesus."

That was pretty profound. He said not many Christians appreciate that answer, but I can totally relate. To walk the walk of Christ, and to believe in him. That the only way to Heaven is through Jesus. I don't know where "Christian" came from, but Jesus wasn't a Christian. He was a Jew.

So, I'm going to borrow from my friend, and say, "I am a follower of Jesus."

Hope you are okay with that. If not, I'm pretty sure you'll let me know.

In your name I pray,

Authentic, Humble, Surrendered, and Spiritual

S. Michael Edwards

Sunday, February 27, 2011

Safe Trip Back to Dallas | Prayer #360
God,

I want to thank you for the time we spent on the road together this weekend. As you are clearly aware, I made it home safe and sound, and without a ticket. I am grateful that the boat worked, enough for me to take my friends for a tour of the lake. They enjoyed it, too.

Thank you for the gift of abundance and for the joy that you have brought to my life. While my journey to 365 prayers is coming to an end, it's just the springboard to a new way to communicate with you.

The journey has taught me that I can talk to you about anything and that you talk back (not in a bad way). I have learned that on this journey, the more I think about you, the more I talk to you, the closer we become. You are in my thoughts constantly. I'm consumed with thinking about you, and that is not anything I expected on this journey.

I was nervous about this journey, and had some serious nerves about it. 365 prayers in seven weeks is a whole lot of prayin'. Just sayin'. But the gifts I've been given as a result have been priceless.

In your name I pray,

Authentic, Humble, Surrendered, and Spiritual

S. Michael Edwards

Sunday, February 27, 2011

A Far Better Life | Prayer #361

God,

I just read 2 Corinthians 5:14–15. "Our firm decision is to work from this focused center: One man died for everyone. That puts everyone in the same boat. He included everyone in his death so that everyone could also be included in his life, a resurrection life, a far better life than people ever lived on their own."

I couldn't agree more. My life is far better now than ever. I have you to thank for that, God. I love that Jesus included everyone in his death, so that we could all be included in his life, a resurrection life.

Hopefully, with your help, we can spread the Word. Everyone!

In your name I pray,

Authentic, Humble, Surrendered, and Spiritual

S. Michael Edwards

Sunday, February 27, 2011

Pour on the Blessings | Prayer #362

God,

I am closing in on 365, and using my Solo Devotional to find scriptures that speak to me, as guided by you, I'm sure. I found the following scripture:

2 Corinthians 9:8–11

"God can pour on the blessings in astonishing ways so that you're ready for anything and everything, more than just ready to do what needs to be done. As one psalmist puts it,

He throws caution to the winds,

Giving to the needy in reckless abandon.

His right-living, right-giving ways

Never run out, never wear out.

This most generous God who gives seed to the farmer that becomes bread for your meals is more than extravagant with you. He gives you something you can then give away, which grows into full-formed lives, robust in God, wealthy in every way, so that you can be generous in every way, producing with us great praise to God."

I couldn't agree more that you have poured on the blessings. As I was driving home today, I was thinking about my impending move, and how big of a change that will be for me. I realize now that it's been my vision, my goal to live in Florida, and here is the opportunity ahead of me. I asked for this, and I am ready. It allows me the freedom to be generous and move on to a full-formed life—a life that glorifies you and helps those in need.

Thank you, God, for pouring on the blessings. Keep 'em coming! My field is ready.

In your name I pray,

Authentic, Humble, Surrendered, and Spiritual

S. Michael Edwards

Sunday, February 27, 2011

Trust God | Prayer #363
God,

In Galations 3:5–6, "Answer this question: Does the God who lavishly provides you with his own presence, his Holy Spirit, working things in your lives you could never do for yourselves, does he do these things because of your strenuous moral striving or because you trust him to do them in you? Don't these things happen among you just as they happened with Abraham? He believed God, and that act of belief was turned into a life that was right with God."

Chill bumps, God. I absolutely agree that my life changed when I believed again. That all the things you are doing in my life are because I have surrendered to you and I trust in you. I am grateful that my act of belief has turned into a life that is now right with you, God.

What a beautiful reminder! Thank you!

In your name I pray,

Authentic, Humble, Surrendered, and Spiritual

S. Michael Edwards

Free From Pleasing Others | Prayer #364
God,

I admit I have a looking-good program. I want to look good, so that I am accepted. That doesn't always serve me. I see that in this passage I am free from pleasing others. It's not what I do, it is what you do. You have created a free life for me. Wow, does it feel good!

Galatians 6:14–16

"For my part, I am going to boast about nothing but the Cross of our Master, Jesus Christ. Because of that Cross, I have been crucified in relation to the world, set free from the stifling atmosphere of pleasing others and fitting into the little patterns that they dictate. Can't you see the central issue in all this? It is not what you and I do—submit to circumcision, reject circumcision. It is what God is doing, and he is creating something totally new, a free life! All who walk by this standard are the true Israel of God—his chosen people. Peace and mercy on them!"

In your name I pray,

Authentic, Humble, Surrendered, and Spiritual

S. Michael Edwards

Sunday, February 27, 2011

First Chapter | Prayer #365
God,

As I pray my last prayer on this journey, it's the first chapter of the new life you have given me. I want to thank you again for all you have bestowed on me. I want to thank my parents who have been with me on this journey. My sister and her family, whose love and support is never ending. I thank you for all that you have done to lift me up, and those around me. I thank you that you have given me new life. I thank you for Lisa Darden, an amazing Christian who challenged me in ways I was not expecting, and showed me your love through her. She was not afraid to proclaim her faith to me. I want to thank Klemmer and Associates, for without them, I wouldn't have met my buddy Brett, who showed me what a true Christian can look like. I want to thank his wife Carolyn, who took me to their church with Brett and who graciously hosted me in their home.

I want to thank Centa and Janet and all my fellow leaders and senior leaders in Sam Camp 21 for encouraging me on this journey. They have provided praise songs, inspirational scriptures, and words of encouragement.

Most of all, God, I want to thank you for opening my eyes and allowing me to see that this journey was destined to happen and for providing me an outlet that looks nothing like I thought it would in the end. I was going to record my prayers, then transcribe them, then look at where I ended up? Blogging my prayers to God.

I feel an enormous connection with you, God. A connection so deep that it's to my core. I feel your love and presence. I feel redeemed and blissful. I feel rejuvenated. I feel free.

Now it's on to my next journey, turning my prayer journal and journey into a book: An Atheist's Journey to the Most Unexpected Gift: A Lifelong Journey from Atheist to Believer.

My connection with you and the connection I have with my parents has never been stronger. This journey has provided me with so many wonderful gifts that I was not expecting. Most important is how connected I feel with you, in this moment, and in my daily life.

Who would have thought (well, besides you), that 365 prayers could bring about such a deep connection? It was not my expectation. I wanted to "reconnect" with you. I had no idea the impact it would have on my daily life.

I have prayed more in the last seven weeks to you, God, than I think I have prayed in my entire life combined.

I surrendered.

I'm grateful.

I'm humbled.

I am a follower of Jesus.

In your name I pray,

Authentic, Humble, Surrendered, and Spiritual

S. Michael Edwards

2 comments:

Linda Edwards said...

Father God, John and I just listened to Handel's *Messiah*, "Hallelujah Chorus," in celebration of Michael's 365th prayer. Michael was blessed beyond his wildest dreams by the outcome of this journey, thus far. I have to admit that I listened to more praise music and looked up more scripture and prayed more prayers, too. Truly we have all won…my walk is closer with my son and more important-ly with you, Lord. Thank you for allowing me the privilege of being involved in Michael's journey. We have laughed together; we have cried together; we have prayed together; and we have praised your name. I pray that my life will reflect the love that I have in my heart. May I have the courage and commitment that I see in Michael in sharing your love. May I be a light for those who are seeking their way into a relationship with you. Thank you for your love, mercy, forgive-ness and amazing grace. Thank you for allowing me the joy of seeing Michael find happiness, joy, and true peace. Thank you for hearing the cries of my heart and blowing me away with your goodness. I am so grateful. Amen with love from a very blessed mom.

February 27, 2011 6:57 PM

S. Michael Edwards said…
And all His people said, "Amen!" Love you, Mom!

Monday, February 28, 2011

Dad's Reaction to My Journey
Michael,

I love you son.

Dad

He wrote:

Lord, I am humbled by your presence, grace and love. Only you could write the perfect script for a life. Oh so many years ago I lost my way and took a path that, on the surface, seemed to be one separate from you. Little did I know that you were with me the entire time, gently nudging me, providing life-altering circumstances and unconditional acceptance. Although I thought I knew what was best for me, you never gave up. And then one day I felt your spirit within me. It was such an overwhelming love that I couldn't contain it all. I was compelled to share it with everyone I knew and met. Of the many, one was my son Michael. He promptly re-jected my advances and with just cause. Through my own ignorance, stupidity, and self-absorption, I had made his life hard, very hard. He didn't trust me or like me, and he completely turned his back on you. He has told you that for twenty-one-and-a-half years he was an atheist. Then through a series of events (you know what they were), Michael's life has been transformed. Your perfect script manifested in this, the year of our Lord 2011, what we in this day and age call a modern-day miracle. Thank you, Lord, for allowing me to live to see the day that once again Michael knows you and calls himself a follower of Christ. A powerful, confident, surrendered, and forgiving man, Michael will make a mark in the hearts of mankind that will bring glory and honor to you. Thank you, Lord, for hearing and receiving Michael's prayers and bringing about great change through him. He is prepared to do a great thing with you at the helm of his heart. Michael, you are an inspiration. Lord, I am a proud father who stands with his son just as you have stood with me. My heart is full and overflowing. Amen.

God, I am so grateful for my father, and as I told him, if I can be half the man he is, I will be blessed. What an amazing journey for us all.

In your name I pray,

Authentic, Humble, Surrendered, and Spiritual

S. Michael Edwards

Monday, February 28, 2011

Mom's Reaction to my Journey
Mom wrote:

Father God, I can only think of one song fitting for this momentous occasion of celebrating the 365th prayer from Michael. That is Handel's *Messiah*, "Hallelujah Chorus." This has been John's and my song since 1967 when we sang it in choir in high school. It's sung all over the world, and most everyone stands while this song is sung and your name is praised. Our whole family is praising you for this amazing journey that Michael is on. He was blessed beyond his wildest dreams by the outcome. I have to admit that I listened to more praise music and looked up more scripture and prayed more prayers, too. Truly we have all won…my walk is closer with my son and more importantly with you, Lord. Thank you for allowing me the privilege of being involved in Michael's journey. I pray that my life will reflect the love that I have in my heart. May I be a light for those who are seeking their way into your kingdom. Thank you for your love, mercy, forgiveness, and amazing grace. Amen with love from a very blessed mom.

She then included the link to Handel's *Messiah*, "Hallelujah Chorus."

God, I am so blessed that this journey of mine grew bigger and more grand than I could ever have imagined. I am blessed that my parents were on this journey with me and so grateful for your amazing grace. The unexpected gifts keep coming.

In your name I pray,

Authentic, Humble, Surrendered, and Spiritual

S. Michael Edwards

Epilogue

Tuesday, April 19th, 2011

God has blessed me beyond measure. I settled the lawsuit with Ed, sold my shares in the advertising agency, sold my equity in the house, sold most of the contents of the house to Ed, received a 1 year severance, and will move my yacht to Florida July 1st, 2011. Brett and I own FrozenX-Plosion, the fastest growing Frappe and Smoothie Company in the World with Jeff Ericson. Jeff Ericson is one truly amazing man. Jeff saw something in us and our passion to help build sustainable communities. He has entrusted us with his company to make a difference in the world. I am surrendering to God's will, and he is blessing me as I take this leap of faith, start my own advertising agency, and continue my passion of embroidery (www.smichaeledwards.com) and run www.frozenx-plosion.com. Agros International has allowed me to take over their online advertising, as my way to give back to an organization that supports my vision of sustainable communities in developing countries. (www.agros.org). I'm so grateful to God, and I'm looking forward to watching my vision and purpose play out as I make a difference in this world. Brian Klemmer passed away April 7th, and his 500 year legacy will live on. I am so blessed to have known Brian, and the impact he had on my family and my life is priceless. **Most of all, reconnecting with God was truly the most unexpected gift.**

Made in the USA
Charleston, SC
15 May 2011